SOFTWARE BY DESIGN

SOFTWARE
BY
DESIGN

Shaping Technology
and
The Workplace

Harold Salzman
Stephen R. Rosenthal

New York   Oxford
OXFORD UNIVERSITY PRESS
1994

Oxford University Press

Oxford   New York   Toronto
Delhi   Bombay   Calcutta   Madras   Karachi
Kuala Lumpur   Singapore   Hong Kong   Tokyo
Nairobi   Dar es Salaam   Cape Town
Melbourne   Auckland   Madrid

and associated companies in
Berlin   Ibadan

Published by Oxford University Press, Inc.,
200 Madison Avenue, New York, New York 10016

Oxford is a registered trademark of Oxford University Press

Library of Congress Cataloging-in-Publication Data
Software by Design / Harold Salzman and Stephen Rosenthal
p. cm. Includes bibliographical references and index.
ISBN 0-19-508340-7
1. Computer software–Development. 2. User interfaces.
I. Rosenthal, Stephen R. II. Title.
QA76.76.D47S25 1993   005.1'2–dc20   93-20812

9 8 7 6 5 4 3 2 1
Printed in the United States of America
on acid-free paper

To
Barbara & Linda

Acknowledgements

In the long journey from a National Science Foundation grant to the completion of this book, we have benefitted and incurred intellectual debts from the suggestions, ideas, and assistance of many people. The Ethics and Values in Science and Technology section of NSF provided funding for this project under Grant Number BBS-8619534, and we thank the section director, Rachelle Hollander, for her support and encouragement throughout this project. Support from the Bell and Howell Fellowship for Technology and Policy Studies was also provided to Harold Salzman. The initial planning and conceptualization for the NSF project benefitted from participation and contribution of key concepts by Philip Mirvis. The hospital study was conducted by Ross Koppel and he also contributed to other aspects of the study; Fred van Bennekom played a key role in conducting and documenting the field service cases of the study. We were greatly aided in our research by the encouragement and support provided by the Directors of the Center for Applied Social Science at Boston University, Michael Useem and Leonard Saxe.

Conducting field research depends upon the cooperation and participation of those in the field and without it we could not have even begun to engage in this research. Access to many of the companies studied, and for the survey, was provided by the Massachusetts Software Council—in particular, we are grateful to Joyce Plotkin, its Executive Director, and Michael Kinkead, its Chairman. Many in the software industry gave generously of their time for interviews and to provide information, suggestions, and other assistance vital to this study. We appreciate their time and assistance and, in particular, we thank Diana Klashman, Charles Wainwright, Michael Murphy, and Carl Ellison. We hope they and their colleagues will find this book of use and reward for their help.

In the academic community we are very grateful to those who took the time to read and comment on earlier drafts of the manuscript and provide suggestions during the research, improving the book immeasurably. With appreciation for their ideas, and leaving them blameless for the outcome, we thank: Paul Adler, Paul Attewell, Richard Badham, Egon Bittner, Nancy Eickelmann, Trond Knudsen, Jonathan Grudin, Rob Kling, Sarah Kuhn, Raanan Lipschitz, Jeff Livesay, Robert Lund, Agneta Olerup, Günther Ortmann, Daniel Smith, Menachem Student,

Robert Thomas and Friedrich Weltz. Improvements in the final manuscript are due in large measure to the fine editorial work of Daniel Gottlieb. Research assistance was provided by Katherine Ashford, Andrew Fromm, James A. James, Sally Moulton, and Katie Riley. Crucial to the completion of this book was Betty Ash's careful editing, Stephanie Morris' expert word processing, and Brenda Clark's superb graphics and typesetting. Donald Jackson, our editor at Oxford University Press, was most helpful and accommodating in shepherding the initial manuscript into its final form.

Most of all we thank our wives, Barbara and Linda, to whom we dedicate this book. Their many virtues and contributions to this book are appreciated, especially their tolerance for discussions about our research disrupting peaceful moments atop the hills of Vermont.

Table of Contents

I

STRUCTURING TECHNOLOGY AND THE WORKPLACE

I

Introduction

The concept of social values shaping technology design seems oddly out-of-place to many. Isn't the *design* of technology the province of engineers? Aren't values and technology and other social issues really outside the scope of engineering? Engineering decisions are not, after all, based on philosophy and sociology some would argue. Efficiency and economy are the objective criteria for making design decisions and these can be determined through a relatively precise calculus. Making these determinations is an objective engineering task not a matter of subjective preferences and interpretation. There is error, of course, and unintended consequences are inevitable, but these are matters to be corrected by better science and engineering.

Following in this vein, one might argue that the link between technology design and quality of worklife is even further removed from the concerns of engineering. Technology is delivered "as is" and the work organization must accommodate it. Perhaps technology can be fiddled with at the margins for better ergonomics for example, but again, the essence of design is independent of quality of worklife concerns. To take this argument a step further, it is commonly stated that, for most people, work is not an activity for pleasure but for sustenance. We may wish it were otherwise, but it just isn't so. Changing technology or other aspects of worklife is, therefore, of limited value in improving the human condition. (In fact, if changes made for worklife improvements decrease productivity, they could be detrimental by lowering prosperity and thus the quality of life outside of work.) One engineer (Florman, 1981, p. 103), writing that "blaming technology" is an "irrational search for scapegoats," states that "alienation cannot be cured by a fascinating job any more than it can be cured by a clean apartment." Engineers should thus concentrate on designing technology the best they

3

can and leave social issues or workplace concerns to others. It is only the application and implementation of technology that is relevant for social science. So runs the argument in many a discussion about how technology should be designed for the workplace.

In this book we begin with a different set of premises. We observe that workplaces are shaped by the design of the technology used. And there is a reciprocal relationship in which the structure of the workplace helps shape the design of technology. In this ongoing interaction, social values of some people or groups shape technology, the technology then embodies certain values, and it, in turn, becomes a significant factor shaping the workplace. Our analysis leads us to the conclusion that technology design is embedded in an interwoven net of people, organizations, and technology. Thus, we argue, social values and power are key components in the creation of technology.

Understanding the social dimension of technology design, and software in particular, can, we believe, help open the door to better design. There are certain types of designs that we find are better for both the worklife of users and the efficiency of their organizations. However, our intent is not to be prescriptive but analytical. It is the essential social nature of technology creation that we seek to understand.

This book is written to provide analysis of several different levels of that social process. At one level this book is a study of software design and its effects on workplace structure and users. It explores designs that provide powerful tools enabling users and organizations to increase their effectiveness and designs that were dysfunctional and that users felt degraded their worklives and performance, thus tightening the noose of an already suffocating job.

Design decisions can be seen to reflect certain choices and values by managers and designers which led to systems that users at the lower levels of the organization thought were poorly designed or found objectionable. However, these were not necessarily "bad" or careless design decisions. They often were thought out and reflected criteria software designers considered important. The problem, we find, is that software often reflects the contradictions of the workplace.

Software is not being produced for a neutral environment, one with a common goal and which operates entirely according to rationally determined policies and procedures. Rather, work organizations are a congress of often competing interests that are negotiated on the basis of tradeoffs, compromises, and power. Organizational rationality is also fraught with the irrationality of a negotiated order and political expediency. Software design, we suggest, may reflect many of the conflicts and contradictions characteristic of the "contested terrain" of the workplace. In the end, there may be no objectively optimal solution but rather choices among competing values and needs, choices that are influenced most by those who wield the most power in the organization.

The contradictions and conflicts in the workplace and software design may not be confronted to the same degree in other technologies or in different environments. Software may be different from other technologies in how it interacts with the organization. Organizations often have formally prescribed policies and procedures but operate according to an informal structure that allows for more autonomy by workers and flexibility in procedures. This may result in a more efficient and expedient way of doing business than operating in strict accordance with formal policies and procedures. Software may lead to a tighter coupling of the organization, narrowing the gap between the formal rules and procedures of an organization and the actual reality of what people do to get the job done, effectively and flexibly. This tighter coupling can lead either to significant leaps in quality, efficiency, and effectiveness for organizations moving beyond traditional forms of organization and management or it can lead to a crisis in organizations where efforts at improving work organization and quality are just rhetoric.

This book is also a study of how technology is socially constructed and the underlying values that come into play in that process. The construction of technology is a social process, not an individual one, even though individual (or groups of) designers are giving voice and form to the decisions. It is thus quite easy to mistake the source of the decisions as coming solely from those who express them, as some studies have done. By mapping out the technology design process, we intend to demonstrate that the latitude of action for individual designers is constrained. Expecting a change through simple injunction and exhortation to some identified guilty party (i.e., the designer) is not only futile but wrong in identifying causality.

The perspective taken in this book is that technology both shapes and reflects the social matrix of organizations and socio-economic systems, of which it is a part. This book provides a multifaceted view of software development and use. We argue that better design requires a greater understanding of how work organizations function and requires changes in work organizations to new forms of management and worker responsibility. It is only through corresponding changes in software design approaches and the organization of user firms that truly effective software can be designed and used in the workplace.

Much of the material in Part I (Chapters 1 through 3) presents arguments and frameworks that guided the descriptive case studies that we present in Part II of the book. Readers who are primarily concerned with our research findings and their implications, as distinguished from how our work fits within prior and contemporary academic contributions, may wish to move more quickly through some of this earlier material. With this possibility in mind, we offer the following road map.

Chapter 1 deals with the social shaping of technology and the contributions of social scientists who have explored this general phenomenon. The first half of the chapter concentrates on the field of engineering from the point of view of social influences on the design of technology. There we review literature that offers a total of five different views of this basic question: To what extent and through what mechanisms do values generally influence designs produced by engineers? We explain that our focus is on the social construction of the "design space" within which engineers work and identify prior contributors to this point of view. The second half of Chapter 1 traces the intellectual roots of the more specific position that technology destined for use in the workplace is inherently socially constructed. Here we make specific reference to earlier contributions dealing with organizations, power relationships, and the pursuit of innovation. These perspectives allow us to identify characteristics of the "action space" that indirectly shapes technology development through decisions about the organization of production activity and the procurement of new technology. Figure 1.2, at the end of Chapter 1, summarizes our dynamic organizational view of technology development and use.

Chapter 2 provides background perspectives on software used in the workplace as a central part of the organization's value-adding production activity. In the first section of this chapter, we explore the nature of software systems in connecting the work of people. We explain that these people need to be viewed simultaneously as workers in a system of production and as users of the software technology. The second section of this chapter presents a set of findings about how to design software from the user's point of view. We compare and contrast studies performed by social scientists in the U.S., England, and Scandinavia. The chapter concludes by identifying (in Figure 2.3) the framework that we have adopted for the study of software design.

Chapter 3, which concludes Part I, is based on our study of the segment of the software industry that develops systems for "mission critical" use in the workplace. We present findings on the process and structure of software design, with special attention to the role of software developers, marketing specialists, and conflicts that arise within software companies. We present our survey findings on forces within the user organization that lead to various assessments of the most important requirements that new software must meet. We conclude this chapter by presenting information on how these different views could affect the content of software specifications. By focusing on how organizational structure can lead to conflicting views on software design, Chapter 3 illustrates the more theoretical points, made in the first two chapters, about the different groups and interests that typically reside in the design space and the action space for new technology. This sets the stage for appreciating the particular issues and design choices contained in the set of cases described in Part II.

The concluding two chapters in Part III address issues for two different audiences. Chapter 8 brings together the managerial issues of our research for those with practical, day-to-day concerns about improving the procurement, implementation, and use of workplace software. This chapter analyzes our research findings in light of implications for technology management in the user firm. The pitfalls of procurement are discussed and suggestions are presented for managers or those who have influence over procurement decisions. Chapter 9 is written primarily for the research audience though it, too, addresses important issues of software adoption and use. This chapter examines the potential of mission critical software to bring to the fore conflicts between an organization's formal policies and procedures and the informal work practices through tighter coupling of the organization. We also address the prospects for change in software design and work organization. The first appendix contains a description of the research methods of this study. The second appendix consists of four teaching cases that are written for classroom use. They present in detail descriptions of the process of design and the social choices that were involved.

1

Social Shaping of Technology

Artists leave behind their names on their work and, with their face and story, provide some insight into the design of their creations. Not so with workplace technology. The design of technology often appears as received wisdom. A band of technicians descends upon an office or a factory floor leaving behind artifacts bearing the labels of companies whose names are familiar but whose identities are really anonymous. In some abstract way we all know that inanimate objects are *manu*factured, the product of human design. Yet, as we handle and look at these artifacts we use everyday, we seldom know the whys and wherefores of their design. We may judge the technology as easy or difficult to use, helpful or unhelpful in accomplishing the task at hand, and regard it as good or bad. But the calculus that went into the design decisions almost always remains a mystery.

If we inquire of the designers of a piece of technology, by which we mean those who engineered and made decisions about its features and functionality (decisions beyond its aesthetic appearance, which is a common connotation of design but too limited for our purposes), we are likely to be mesmerized by formulae, calculations, reports of the latest discoveries of science and state-of-the-art engineering. In short, we may be informed that "economy and efficiency" (with perhaps a bit of aesthetics thrown in) are the watchwords of engineering. Engineering is portrayed as an objective enterprise limited only by knowledge and creativity. Many would argue that, provided a task that is well defined and a mission to accomplish, the engineer can proceed to create the optimal technology.

To the social scientist these explanations generally form an impenetrable wall that precludes further inquiry. Although the social impact of technology has been widely studied, technology itself is usually treated as a "black box." Research instead tends

9

to focus on what to *do* with the black box, how to implement it, not how to create it. Thus social scientists have contributed little (and are seen as offering little) to the task of technology design, except in such realms as human factors for the user interface, a contribution viewed as rather peripheral to the "real" task of engineering. Ignoring the social influences in technology design, we believe, is a significant shortcoming because an understanding of this dimension can offer important insights on how to enhance its effectiveness, both from the standpoint of functionality and enhancement of jobs and worklife.

This book steps into relatively unmapped terrain. David Noble (1984, p. xii) observes that "although it has belatedly become fashionable among social analysts to acknowledge that technology is socially determined, there is very little concrete historical analysis that describes precisely how." Although Noble's observation is still largely true, since his pioneering work there has developed a growing interest in and body of research on the social shaping of workplace technology.[1] However, few studies examine the role of engineers in creating technology and specific technological designs.

This book focuses specifically on design of workplace technology. Through analysis of software design and use we show how essential tasks of engineering involve social values, though they may be hidden from view in the day-to-day decisions of design. These values reflect the economic and political dimensions of organizations and the values provide the background assumptions shaping people's perspectives of their world of work.[2] We also show how engineering design decisions, shaped by values and embodied in technology, have profound consequences for the worklives of those who use the technology and the efficiency of the organizations that implement it.*

---

* Throughout the book we use the terms design and engineering interchangeably to refer to the process of shaping technology. We also use these terms for both hardware and software design. There are, of course, differences between design and engineering and between designing and engineering software and hardware technologies. However, our focus is on a broader level of decisions made about the social shaping of technology that affect users in their worklives. At this level, there is a common core that cuts across technology type and specialty. At a more detailed level, which we address in the case studies, the unique characteristics of software are considered.

Perspectives on Engineering as a Social Process

The relationship between technology and society is a subject of longstanding debate. At a broad social level writers such as Jacques Ellul (1964) warn of technological dominance of human life with ensuing impoverishment of the human spirit. Others see technology liberating humans from toil and harsh conditions of the natural environment. In both perspectives technology is often viewed as autonomous from human control, following a logic distinct from (or dominating) the specific intentions of its creators.

Critics decry the lack of consideration for social consequences of technology by those who develop it, identifying engineers as the culprits. However, some argue that there is an inherent problem in the development of technology: Those building the technology operate in an environment *necessarily* devoid of concerns not relevant to its technical development. Sociologist Egon Bittner (1983, p. 258) writes that:

> The people who do best in a world like ours are the ones who keep their minds on what they are doing, while disregarding the environment of ethical implications surrounding their activities... *Whether* one should build a bridge across the river, and *how* one should build it belong to two different departments of the mind, so to speak, departments that are not even on speaking terms with one another (emphasis in the original).

This analysis leads to one of two conclusions about the relevance of social concerns in construction of technology. One approach is that social scientists should bring to builders of technology the body of knowledge about the social implications of their work. In this way these concerns can be integrated into an environment otherwise highly focused on goals of technological development. In this line of argument, engineers are prevailed upon to take more social responsibility for the consequences of their work. Alternatively, it is argued that "good" design requires engineers to be divorced from such concerns. Thus social scientists and others concerned with the effects of technology should independently conduct "social impact studies" and make policy decisions and some broad level design decisions about technological development, but not be involved directly in design issues.

These issues of the social responsibility of engineering have sparked fierce debate over the years, particularly as the high esteem of engineers became tarnished in the 1960s and 1970s. The criticisms evoked spirited, and sometimes shrill, defenses such as Florman's (1981) *Blaming Technology* and Petroski's (1982) *To Engineer is Human*. In both these works the authors argue that engineering is largely beneficial to society and that shortcomings are the inherent limitations of knowledge rather than profoundly moral, ethical, or value issues.

To argue that technology *design* is socially shaped runs counter to prevailing views. Reviewing studies of the impact of technology, we find five basic frameworks that appear to provide either explicit or implicit explanations for the logic of technology design relevant specifically to workplace technology.[3] Technology designs can be seen as following a logic of autonomous scientific development, of social development, of political-economic development, or as an outcome of individual choices. In all but the last of these perspectives, the development and influence of technology are viewed as a predominately technical process, having an inner logic that ranges from being partly to wholly autonomous from conscious choice. A fifth perspective, on which we build, views technology development as a social activity involving a network of actors, such as engineers and users, and structures, such as organizations and markets, that shape the way technology is constructed.

The scientific view is that advances in knowledge are largely independent of subjective influences and that technology reflects engineers' calculations of the most economic and efficient designs to utilize that knowledge. This is the dominant view of engineering as expressed, for example, in the Accreditation Board for Engineering and Technology definition of engineering as "the profession in which a knowledge of the mathematical and natural sciences gained by study, experience, and practice is applied with judgment to develop ways to utilize, economically, the materials and forces of nature for the benefit of mankind" (quoted in Thuesen and Fabrycky, 1989). Insofar as social values are considered, they are regarded as important for decisions about the use or development of a technology but not as an integral part of the design process.

The engineering community traditionally attributes responsibility for the effects of technology to those who order and implement the technologies rather than to themselves. Accordingly, engineers have claimed value neutrality in their work. Value choices are made by industrialists and politicians who make use of these tools which are inherently neutral. Another similar position is that technological development proceeds largely within the confines of science and, for a given objective, which is defined by "others," engineers merely determine the most economic and efficient manner to achieve those objectives, given the current state of knowledge. Although mistakes may occur, they are certainly not social or value issues. Failures in design are to be expected as inevitable, not as resulting from a lack of conscience or social awareness that engineers could be reasonably expected to consider as part of their activities. From this perspective, the solution is to perfect the technical expertise of engineering as an objectively defined asocial activity that solves any engineering shortcomings. Florman (1976, p. 33) argues that engineering mistakes are the result of "human error, lack of imagination, and blind ignorance," rather than social, political, economic, or moral decisions. Thus, from within the engineering community, the predominant view is that social and value issues are separate from essential, day-to-day design concerns.

The social perspective, such as that expressed by Jacques Ellul or Lewis Mumford, identifies a technological imperative permeating cultural values. In this view, industrial societies are morally and socially impoverished because the goal of advancing technology has become more important than other values. Technology becomes a reified social force that propels individuals to continue technology development without choice. Rather than specific technological designs, these social critics examine a technological view that dominates modern social values. It is the process of technological development that has prevented people from considering other values that might lead to a more humane society.

Political-economic perspectives of technology and organization are largely focused on workplace technologies with the technology viewed as one of the major, if not the sole determinant of social organization. In the nineteenth century, political economists such as Marx and Smith viewed technology as a driving force shaping the political-economic system.

More recently, social scientists and historians have turned this perspective on its head by examining the social factors shaping technology. Noble (1984, 1977), who contributed some of the first analyses of the social forces shaping engineering designs, challenges the idea of an inner logic driving technology development and leading to specific designs. He traces the rise of engineering as a profession within the confines of industry in contrast to other professions which developed as independent practices. As a result, he finds the values of engineers reflect those of their employers, only marginally distinct, if at all, from managerial objectives. Engineering work, Noble concludes, is oriented toward developing technology that reinforces the existing political and social order.

From the perspective of individual choices, some studies have been done on how technology reflects the values of its designers. The biases in technology design thus reflect individual or professional values. The values of the engineering profession, as examined through questionnaires of technology designers for example, are assumed to be the predominant influence in design decisions (Mumford, 1981). Other analyses of technology impacts assume that design choices directly reflect engineers' intentions. This perspective leads to the conclusion that changing the value orientations of designers, or constraining their actions by the involvement of others with different value orientations (e.g., social scientists, workers), will result in socially beneficial technology.[4]

The new social perspective developed over recent years builds on the research on social factors shaping design but represents a fifth view of technology. The guiding premise in this work is that technology is socially shaped or constructed and part of a larger network of things and people. Using this framework, sometimes referred to as a social construction of technology perspective, and building on the traditional studies of science, technology, and society, a number of studies have examined the ways that technology decisions are shaped by nontechnical factors. Such studies of the social shaping of technology vary quite dramatically in their field of view. Thomas Hughes (1987) proposes a broad view that society and technology form a "seamless web," thus blurring distinctions between technical and social determinants. At the microlevel, some researchers focus on how people who use the technology interpret or define the important characteristics of an object. In the extreme, some researchers view technology as having no inherent properties but as essentially open to interpretation by individual actors (e.g., it is in the eye of the beholder whether a personal computer is just a faster typewriter or a means for document composition in which typing is incidental to its use and the technical features of the computer are virtually irrelevant). Implied in this view is that technology will not constrain users in accordance with an embodied set of values because technology impact depends on how the users interpret it.[5] Although some research in this area tends toward a view that technology impacts are entirely the result of users' perceptions (and thus technology, *per se*, is not a relevant subject of study), these researchers do make an important point that we need to examine technology not just as an assemblage of artifacts but also in terms of the meanings people find in its use. A common thread uniting the spectrum of perspectives on the social construction of technology is the challenge to the technical view in engineering and the hard technological determinism view in the social sciences and humanities. Building on this perspective, we view the engineer and technology designer as actively shaping technology and reflecting the values and interests of their social environment.

The Role of the Engineer in Creation and Reflection

The engineer,* in his or her role as creator, works with external social as well as technical constraints. Just as every artist must play to an audience, so must every engineer. Although the engineer, like the artist, is the actor conceiving and shaping the artifact, it is not an immaculate conception. Individuals both mediate and reflect values shaped by organizations and by the society at large. Even when new forms of art develop, their creators are often viewed as giving expression to new ways of thinking or new developments in the world. They may be considered pioneers of a new form but it is usually related to changes in a broader context and rarely considered *sui generis*. Artists must often play to the art critic for success because the critics often wield the power to decide the fate of each artist's

---

* Engineer is used here as a generic category for those who are designing technology, including software designers, engineers, and programmers.

masterpiece. (If they go beyond the frontier of accepted expression, success may come too late for them to enjoy it.)

At the same time we know that the creation of artifacts is not just a response to the status quo but also reshapes existing structures and values. Again by way of analogy, language has similar properties of shaping and being shaped by the action of individuals.[6] We are educated and socialized to structure our expression according to very specific and highly proscribed rules of grammar. If this were a unidirectional process, language would never change. Language is considered "living" in the sense that it does change in response to changes in forms of expression by individuals who are, at the same time, expressing themselves largely in accordance with existing rules of grammar. The change does not usually reflect intentional decisions by individuals but the congealing of a number of factors that both give birth to a new form and sustain it to a point of acceptance (e.g., the need for a new word for a new technology or a new way of thinking about the world).

The design of technology is a process with similarities to the development of language and to the development of new art forms. It will reflect a prevailing set of values. Individual designers give expression to these values and they have limited latitude to introduce into the technology new values or values that are incompatible with their environment. Engineers must generally play to the preferences of those wielding power. Unlike artists who may achieve posthumous success for creations unappreciated in their lifetime, many creations of engineers do not see the light of day. Engineers in the modern world work in organizations that are subject to the vagaries of the marketplace. An engineer's superiors have the power to quash errant designs or the marketplace will provide the discipline, sometimes by eliminating organizations that are unable to develop effective internal controls.

At the same time, engineers do mediate the preferences of others when they interpret and translate them into a material technology. To some degree, designers can push the boundaries of existing structures by designing technology that becomes one factor reshaping those structures. Although the enlightened designer can push the boundaries a little faster and a little wider, significant change is not one of individual action but the consequence of a broader set of factors that must congeal to shape and support new design approaches. In summary, we argue that engineers neither unreflectively implement directives from above and outside nor do they spontaneously and independently shape technology.

We need to consider the environment in which engineers work and the environment in which technology is used. The environment or boundaries shaping and regulating the activity of designers and users may be defined as the "design space" of designers and the "action space" of users. Conceptually this notes two domains of action that are the amalgam of a number of different pressures. These are heuristic concepts, not entities with clearly demarcated boundaries (in contrast to, for example, a company which is an entity that is distinct from its environment). These are the "virtual spaces" in which organizational objectives, market pressures, professional training, technology, and the entire host of factors in the social and material world form the immediate environment individuals and groups experience (see Figure 1.1). Thus, the impact of a technology will be experienced as it interacts with other elements in the user's immediate environment. To some degree the action space might be seen as constructed by the user (e.g., to the extent that a person interprets organizational rules as a consideration in his or her actions), but it also has certain known, consistent, and externally imposed properties (e.g., certain actions rather predictably lead

Figure 1.1. Workplace Technology is Socially Constructed.

to discipline from supervisors or malfunctions in a machine and the power of some can be exercised to influence the action of others and the outcome of decisions).

Focusing specifically on workplace technology, we are interested in how the technology is socially shaped to mediate and regulate the work process. Features and functions of a specific technology or system are designed to operate in ways that shape the work process in a particular way, in accordance with a particular set of values. The technology is not deterministic in the sense that actual use can be deduced from design. However, the properties of the technology do provide constraints on, and impediments to, the scope of action of users; alternatively, their design can increase the scope of actions by users. At the same time, the organization of the workplace is a factor shaping the values guiding technology design. It is this interactive process that we examine in this book. For a deeper understanding of the theoretical foundations of the social construction view of technology design, it is useful to briefly consider the insights from organization and technology theory.

Notes on a Theory of Workplace Technology Design

Traditional perspectives on technology, while providing insights into one dimension of how technology is shaped or the impact of technology, are limited as a dynamic schema of the interaction between people and structures such as organizations and markets. In Marx's powerful analysis of macrolevel social organization and technology, for example, his perspective had shades of technological determinism. His view was that the fundamental type of technology used for production drives political and economic forms.[7] This perspective continued in the more recent and widely read analysis by Braverman (1974). Working within the Marxist framework, he touched on design of specific technologies as part of a larger study of changes in work under late twentieth century capitalism. His argument leads to a conclusion that political and economic social choices will drive technological development. The source of value choices in technological development is in the political-economic structure. Because specific technology designs are derivative of capitalist industrial relations, it is not clear in Braverman's analysis that

technology choices can be made independently of broader political-economic social choices.

Within this framework but from a different perspective, Noble
(1977, 1984) argues that technology choices will be driven by
political-economic imperatives when technology designers, or
those who can potentially influence the process (e.g., workers),
are unreflective about the value implications of technology designs. In this analysis there is a recognition of agency in design,
but those in a position to make design choices follow a logic of
design that is essentially determined by social structure. In his
analysis, the logic of engineering is largely derivative of the logic
and structure of the political economy. Design choices that do
not develop the logic of the existing political-economic structure
require conscious decisions that follow from politically guided
action. Again, the degree of latitude for changing technology
design independently of broader corporate and political change
is not clear. At the other extreme are the individual choice
perspectives. Neither of these perspectives is quite sufficient.
They need to be broadened in scope and need a more dynamic
concept of the process of technology creation. One of the crucial
links, we suggest, is a more developed perspective of the organization and the arena of action for both designers and users.

Design as Shaped by the Organization

The analytic framework in our perspective includes, in its field
of focus, the organizational level as well as larger macro structures. The extensive bodies of literature in the sociology of
organizations suggest that there are common and enduring
characteristics of organizations that exert systematic influence
on the activities of people in them. For our analysis we bring to
the fore the relationship between the structure of organizations
and the design and use of technology. We examine these
elements of the design process, drawing on insights provided by
structuration theory as developed by Anthony Giddens and
others.[8]

Just as technology embodies values in its design, decisions in
organizations are influenced by values and are not made solely
according to a neutral, rational logic to achieve a commonly
shared set of goals. Organizations operate as cauldrons of vested
interests, calcified patterns of operation, and in many ways as

"contested terrain" over which different groups vie for control. Central to organizational dynamics is how power is used in the organization. Decisions do not necessarily represent an optimal choice among alternatives or even one that is most effective for the organization or those it serves. The marketplace does serve to constrain the irrationality and ineffectiveness of organizations to a degree, but it is a very loosely coupled system as attested to by the survival of many inefficient organizations for long periods of time.[9]

Drawing on sociological perspectives of organizations, there are several social factors we find important in understanding the dynamics of technology design and use. Clearly, organizational decisionmaking is constrained by bounded rationality. In the search for the optimal solution, not all information about possible options and consequences is available to those making the decisions. But, the constraints are not just technical but also political. Organizations have multiple and conflicting goals. Even the overarching goal of an organization generally does not bring together all of its constituents and their interests. Different people and departments also have competing and conflicting goals. Understanding power and authority in the organization is central for analysis of how these conflicts are mediated and how preferences and objectives are reflected in decisions.

Power in Organizations

Decisions are influenced by the power different functional groups have vis-à-vis other functional groups and by the power vested in hierarchical differences of the groups and people involved. That is, power is held at a horizontal level, often by coalitions, and also in vertical, hierarchical form that tends to be stable and have characteristics common to many organizations. Power can also be differentiated as control over resources and as control over people in the organization. This is the difference between economic and political power and authority in the organization.

At the horizontal level we can examine power holders in an organization by dominant coalitions or groups, or particular to certain types of decisions, such as a marketing department having greater decisionmaking power over product design than an engineering group, or a computer department having more power than users in decisionmaking about computer equipment and software acquisition. This type of power can thus change with realignment of coalitions or from changes in control over resources; it can depend upon the type of decision at issue, and may vary from organization to organization.

From another perspective power is an attribute of hierarchical organization so that level in the organization indicates clear subordinate-superior relationships. This may also be considered a function of authority, that the superior relationship commands more expertise and is assigned greater responsibility over broader realms of decisions. However, our focus is on the uses of power in these arrangements, over the control of resources and the influence that is based on this control of resources and that leads to some preferences prevailing over others. In traditional work organizations there is generally a chain of command and a generally consistent realm of power and authority at each level. The power in the hierarchy tends to be relatively stable over time and inhere in the basic structure of the organization, whereas horizontal types of power may be products of specific coalitions or control of resources. Decisions about work process, for example, are traditionally regulated in a hierarchical manner. In recent years there has been a fair amount of attention to the need to change traditional hierarchies and decisionmaking, but this has resulted in changing only a small minority of work organizations.[10]

Organizations and Innovation

There is a long-established literature on how technology shapes organizations, but in recent years researchers have significantly qualified the degree of determinism in this relationship and some have severely criticized earlier research on technology and organizational structure.

Although a simplistic technological determinism is generally not an explicit foundation of current theory on technological innovation and organizational form, some researchers find it continues as an implicit factor. As Child, Ganter, and Kieser (1987, p. 99) note, "The failure to address this process [the interaction of technology and organizations] in effect abstracts technology and organization from their contexts and in so doing encourages the naive expectation of a mechanistic relationship that has infused a great deal of organizational research." Scott's

(1988) review of the literature on technology and structure concludes that the most promising theoretical perspectives are those that recognize the "dynamic properties of organizational structure." He suggests that the most fruitful technology-organization studies will be those viewing "structure as process" (building on Giddens' structuration theory, for example). Scott (1988, p. 29) points to research studies in this area that "emphasize the role played by organizational politics, by vested interests, by institutional arrangements in shaping and selecting technologies and in designing structures." Scott and others are critical of traditional technology and organization studies for often examining only one part of the technology-structure dynamic.

These larger issues of organizational form and technology are not our focus. Rather, we examine the dynamic of organizational structure and technology adoption, use, and design and the attributes of organizations that shape this process. Because organizations tend toward stasis as a way of perpetuating themselves and as a way for power holders within the organization to maintain their positions, one tendency is for organizations to resist technology that may lead to restructuring or disrupt the larger network and environment of which they are a part. As Hughes (1987, p. 57) observes, "Because radical inventions do not contribute to the growth of existing technological systems, which are presided over by, systematically linked to, and financially supported by larger entities, organizations rarely nurture a radical invention." Evidence from a study by the economist W. Paul Strassman (1959) lends support to this point in finding slow rates of technology diffusion. He found that for 10 to 15 years after a new technology came into use, the old obsolete technology continued to not only be used but to grow (e.g., in power generation and steel production). He concludes that many firms will not abandon current methods and technologies so long as old technologies and production methods are just profitable enough, even if not as profitable as new ones. A related phenomenon has been examined by others (e.g., David, 1985) as technological "lock-in." New technology may not replace existing ones that are locked-in through adoption and use by many organizations even if the new ones are much more profitable.[11]

Organizational factors impeding technology innovation and diffusion have been discussed by Child, et. al. (1987, p. 99) as organizational conservatism.[12] Understanding the innovation process, they argue, requires "a theory of the relation between technology and organization. This theory, however, remains underdeveloped, particularly with respect to the process by which technological investment, design of systems and organization, and implementation are decided, and the factors impinging on this."

These analyses of acceptance and rejection of technology in organizations address a dichotomous adopt-or-reject decision about a technology based on its properties as designed. They also generally focus on large-scale technology changes such as steam versus electric power. However, the dynamics of organizational conservatism also affect the process of technology adoption and its redesign during implementation and use. Adoption of a radical technology in an organization can be viewed as occurring through a process of assimilation and accommodation. Borrowing from Piaget's (1967) concepts of how children learn and his overview of structuralism (1970), we posit an analogous process of organizations assimilating or accommodating new technologies (this occurs at both the individual user level and at the organizational level as predominant practice).

A new technology may be assimilated into existing structures and work procedures so that it is used in a manner equivalent to previous technologies. In this way existing frames of reference may be imposed onto the technology and the impact of the technology will be minimal. Users and organizations will continue with only slight modification of previous patterns of technology use and organizational operations. Accommodating a new technology is a process of restructuring the organization with the adoption of new technology, sometimes to change the organization and work processes in ways that utilize new capabilities of the technology. Sometimes the technology provides the impetus for organizational restructuring that is related to many other factors as well.[13] However, there is a tendency toward assimilating technology rather than accommodating it.

In both cases the organization shapes the technology as it incorporates it into its structure. A personal computer, for example, may be assimilated into the organization and used as just a faster typewriter or there may be accommodation in which the activity of typing changes into document composition.[14] Assimilation and accommodation describe the process of organizations adopting technology as dynamic rather than

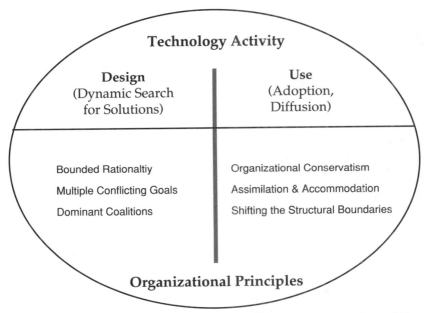

Figure 1.2. Organizational Principles Underlying Technology Design and Use.

deterministic. How the technology is used and how the organization is structured becomes an interactive process rather than one that is determined by the factors of the technology or intentions of those who acquire and implement it. Figure 1.2 summarizes our dynamic view of technology activity, both design and use, and its underlying organizational principles.

In Summary

The traditional engineering perspectives of technology see an inexorable march of progress that is independent of social influences in any significant way. Technology design, as distinct from its implementation, is thus viewed as an independent variable, outside the purview of social analysis. The main focus is on the impact of technology. Moreover, technology is viewed as an artifact isolated from a social or organizational context and as exerting a strong determinism in its impact. The design is generally accepted as preordained by science and engineering and organizational, individual, or social response is limited to various degrees of accommodation of the technology.

Our research addresses the theoretical issues of how technology and production organization interact. In this study, technology design, adoption, and use are interrelated in an ongoing process. "Structures" of both tangible technologies and intangible organizational norms and procedures shape action and are, in turn, shaped by actors. Moreover, the processes of design and use are embedded in organizations which, in turn, are embedded in the structures of their markets, which are shaped by broader characteristics of the society. It is a loosely coupled system so that the structures in each context exert influence on design and use of technology but these are also mediated by the actors and structures at each level. Thus, our analysis looks at how people design and use the technology while also realizing that they mediate and interpret a series of social influences. That is, decisions and actions taken by individuals are shaped by the social context in which they operate but individuals also push the boundaries of existing structures in ways that reshape those structures.

Having developed our conceptual frameworks of technology and the workplace, we turn, in Chapter 2, to a type of technology, applications software, that has already had dramatic impact on the modern workplace.

Endnotes

1. Beginning in the late 1980s a coherent body of work on the social shaping of technology began to appear. This is represented in collections such as Bijker, Hughes and Pinch (1987) and Dierkes and Hoffmann (1992). The former have brought together the sociology and history of technology into an area labeled Social Construction of Technology (SCOT), some building on perspectives in the sociology of science (e.g., Woolgar and Grint, 1991), and the Science, Technology, and Society (STS) field. Much of this research does not specifically address workplace technology. Some of the process technology innovation research, which does concern workplace technology, is more focused on the process of innovation, of the factors shaping the inception of the technology, initial design choices, and the diffusion trajectories rather than on the interaction of workplace structure and values and the design of specific technology. Recent research that does address the social side of workplace technology design includes Brödner (1990), Corbett, Rasmussen, and Rauner (1991), and Ehn (1989), among others.

2. We use the term values in a broad sense to refer to the explicit and implicit, the acknowledged and unacknowledged beliefs, assumptions, and judgments that inform and shape people's actions and provide the schemas with which

they interpret the environment. It shapes their views not only of how the world is, but also of how the world should be, providing a normative framework in addition to an interpretative one. At the same time, it is important to examine the structures of organization and the social environment that shape people's values. People's values will differ, in part, as a result of, for example, their position in the organization. The position of manager may tend to foster different values than position of engineer. It is also through "structure" that values are perpetuated. The role of values as shaping and as being shaped by structures can be viewed in the context of structuration theory (e.g., Giddens, 1984; Livesay, 1989; see also, Ortmann, Windeler, Becker, and Schulz, 1990, for a broader discussion of these issues in technology and organizations).

3. Related to social shaping of technology design is consideration of the responsibility and values of engineers. The usual list of engineering values, responsibility, and ethics may be broadly divided into three areas of concern. First, there is debate about the *type of work* engineers should or should not do, usually concerning the moral or ethical position of engineers vis-à-vis their participation in creating, for example, explicitly destructive technologies such as military armaments. In the second area of concern, the *ethical dilemmas* and professional standards of engineering practice are considered in decisions ranging from judgments about acceptable risk to explicitly criminal or negligent acts such as accepting bribes or being involved in designing knowingly dangerous products such as the Ford Pinto or Spaceshuttle Challenger.

In the third area, the *direction of development* of technology is considered. The discussion often centers on the extent to which technology development should be politically as well as technically guided. At another level, this area of concern focuses on the influence of technology in the development of society. This issue is addressed by social critics such as Jacques Ellul (1964) and Lewis Mumford (1934) as a problem of the "technological society" or "autonomous technology" (see Winner, 1977, for a review). These writings usually have been critical analyses of the inevitably detrimental social effects of technologies or of the more general problem of technology taking on a life of its own, independent of and dominating human will. Technology, once created, or use of a technique once it becomes the dominant paradigm, follows a logic distinct from (or dominating) the specific intentions of its creators.

Beyond these writers, we identified only a few contemporary empirical studies of engineers, their values, and/or factors important in decisionmaking in engineering (e.g., Perrucci and Gerstl, 1969; Mumford, 1981; Zussman, 1985; Whalley, 1986; Meiksins and Watson, 1989). Most of these studies focus on the professionalization of engineers and their class status and less on the implications of these factors for the technological decisions they make. Enid Mumford, the primary researcher examining engineering values, suggests that in software design, decisions directly reflect the value perspectives of software designers. Developing shared values and humanistic values in particular among designers, managers, and system users is Mumford's (e.g., 1981) suggested goal for effective system design. A glaring gap in the literature on technology, engineering, and social values is the lack of empirical studies of how certain values, either imputed or assessed, affect specific design choices.

4. Some representative studies and arguments are Mumford (1981), Kling (1984), Hedberg and Mumford (1975).

5. The work in the general area of social construction of technology has been an important counterbalance to the long tradition of studies that abstract technology from its social context of creation and use. This approach is important for focusing attention on how technologies are constructed and used through interpretation by users. That is, how the "meanings" of technology are constructed by users rather than inherent to a technology. These approaches provide important analyses of the shaping of technology within the user's action space.

Some argue that technology is just one type of node in actor networks and, in this network, technology holds no special status or attributes via-à-vis other parts of the network. That is, the people/technology distinctions are not particularly salient. Some of the writing in the extreme social constructivist school seemingly argues that there are no salient properties of technology because all depends on social context and interpretation (e.g., Woolgar and Grint, 1991; Grint and Woolgar, 1992; Kling, 1991, 1992, for a rejoinder). Certainly the variability and inconsistency of perceptions about technology and its impacts suggest that technology is not absolutely determinant in its impact. However, at times it does seem that the background "fuzziness" and contingency of propositions about technology and its impact become the dominant foreground for the social constructivist analyses. Instead, we argue that interpretations of technology by individuals are bounded and structured in some systematic ways that allow for analysis at the supraindividual level.

In a review of German perspectives on social shaping of technology, Rammert (1992, p. 83) writes:

> The works based on the social constructivist approach have had a mixed reception among German researchers of technology. On the one hand, they have been faulted for what is perceived to be their exaggerated theoretical pretensions. The interactional level is said to be treated as absolute at the cost of the sociostructural level....On the other hand, the empirical studies and the related procedures of the social constructivist approach have encouraged proponents to expand the field of inquiry and increase their consideration of sociocultural influences.

6. The process and the language analogy are based on a framework developed in structuration theory and interpretations of the role of language and the central role of power influencing design decisions and the "interpretations" by actors (e.g., Giddens, 1984; Livesay, 1989; Sewell, 1992; Becker, Windeler, and Ortmann, 1989; Orlikowski, 1992; Barley, 1986; Bourdieu, 1991). We draw on this body of theory (or theories) for our analysis but have not attempted to directly develop the theory further through our research.

7. In one respect, Marx viewed technological design as exogenous to social values; particular stages of technological development greatly influenced the values dominant in a particular social epoch and industrial organization. The extent to which Marx was a technological determinist has been debated as Winner (1977, p. 40), for example, points out that technology was also cast as the embodiment rather than the determinant of class domination. Rosenberg (1982, Chapter 2) argues that Marx was clearly not a technological determinist, instead viewing technological development as a social process.

8. Giddens has developed this theory through a number of books (e.g., 1984)

and others such as Sewell (1992) and Livesay (1989) have addressed specific dimensions of the theory. It has been discussed in terms of technology and organizations by Becker, Windeler, and Ortmann (1989), Orlikowski (1992), and Barley (1986).

9. See, for example, Leibenstein (1987) on inefficiency of organizations and Brunsson (1985) on *The Irrational Organization*. It is also apparent in the survival of many very large, and very inefficient, organizations, such as General Motors.

10. Most structural changes have led to some flattening of the hierarchy, removing middle levels in the chain of command and delegating decisionmaking to lower levels. This may widen the scope of decisionmaking by lower level workers, for example, but generally not change a structure of hierarchical power distribution. At some point the degree of power and decisionmaking by lower level workers could become quite large, eliminating many of the traditional hierarchical power issues (e.g., decisions about work process, work rules, etc.). However, evidence to date suggests that most firms have not significantly flattened their hierarchies, expanded the power of lower level workers or implemented in any significant manner work reorganization. In a survey by the National Center on Education and the Economy (1990, p. 16) it was found that "95 percent of United States companies still cling to old forms of work organization." Similar results were found in a study of worker involvement in technology design and production organization in manufacturing (Salzman, 1992; Lund, Bishop, Newman, and Salzman, 1993). *Fortune* magazine (Kiechel, 1992) observed that "In the course of the current economic unpleasantness progressive management has taken it on the chin...When business got bad, the top brass at too many companies sucked all the decision-making back to the top." Russell's (1988, p. 374) review of employee participation in the U.S. finds that, although there is widespread discussion of various forms of quality circles, work redesign, and other programs, "research on the impact of these programs, however, suggests that they tend to have either negligible or at best only short-lived effects. And American managers continue to shy away from the major commitments that appear needed to increase the likelihood that these efforts to increase employee participation will have both significant and lasting effects."

11. An interesting case has been made by David (1985) that, basically, historical accident in combination with other social factors can lead to a "lock-in" of less profitable, less productive technologies. In his essay on the standardization of the typewriter keyboard layout (known as the QWERTY keyboard), David argues that in the early days of the typewriter the QWERTY keyboard had a slight edge over other layouts. Although this keyboard was less productive than other designs, typists were beginning to be trained in its use and thus came the expectation that most typists would continue to be trained that way. With high turnover, employers decided that it was unprofitable for any individual employer to retrain his or her employees. It was this early lock-in that quickly led to widespread standardization of the QWERTY layout. David (1985, p. 336) writes, "despite the presence of the sort of externalities that standard static analysis tells us would interfere with the achievement of the socially optimal degree of system compatibility, competition in the absence of perfect futures markets drove the industry prematurely into standardization *on the wrong system*—where decentralized decision making subsequently has

sufficed to hold it" (emphasis in original). Relevant to our argument in this example and others is that design can be socially shaped even in the face of economic disincentives, or at least we must recognize that the economics of profitability may relate to a network of social choices.

12. They identify a number of factors about organizations that inhibit innovation such as the resistance to change from organizational actors who are invested in the existing structures of power, existing labor structures that may not accommodate new job arrangements, and few incentives that may be provided for change (Child, et al., 1987, p. 111).

13. As Piaget (1970, p. 63) describes the process, "assimilation is the process whereby an action is actively reproduced and comes to incorporate new objects into itself, and accommodation, the process whereby the schemes of assimilation themselves become modified in being applied to a diversity of objects." Piaget's analysis of cognition relies on a developmental/biological model, whereas our analysis is based on this process as a social process. It is the process of structuration that frames the interaction between technology and organization.

14. This can also be seen in the design of earlier word processors such as the Wang system. Dedicated word processing software for use on minicomputers tried to replicate manual typing procedures in order to ease the transition from typewriting to word processing and increase user acceptance. (One company used black type on a white background, advertising the similarity to using a typewriter and white paper.) These systems computerized typing tasks rather than computerizing document composition. They allowed the systems to be assimilated into existing work processes but they did not utilize the technical capabilities of computers to transform the procedures of document composition. However, in the case of the minicomputer-based word processors, preserving existing procedures did not always result in preserving working conditions; a variety of changes occurred, some of which preserved some aspects of working conditions while changing others. Minicomputer-dedicated word processors were sometimes viewed as too expensive to directly replace typewriters and were seen as an opportunity to rationalize secretarial work. In these instances, secretarial work was fragmented and word processing pools were created, exclusively devoted to typing.

In contrast, the use of microcomputers to replace typewriters preserved previous working arrangements while hosting word processing software that transformed the work procedures. The further diffusion of microcomputers into nonsecretarial positions transformed both procedures and conditions: More of the initial drafts of documents are done by their writers and additional tasks such as spreadsheet tasks and graphics preparation are being performed by secretaries (See Johnson and Rice, 1987, Chapter 4, for further discussion of different word processing adoption approaches).

2

Software in the Workplace

"The Workplace" conjures up images of cavernous factories where people stand shoulder-to-shoulder, dwarfed by huge machines. Though probably a popular image, it describes the conditions of work for less than 15 percent of the working population. Instead, a greater number of people find themselves face-to-face with a computer monitor, whose small displays they depend on for conducting their work. The computer has come to be an intermediary as we do our work. The keyboard, replacing various tools of the trade, has become the common instrument of work, not just in services but also in manufacturing. Work now involves sending instructions to various machines that perform the required tasks, whether retrieving data or turning lathes. Within organizations it has also distanced supervision. Instead of the boss breathing down the worker's neck, "objective" data on performance are collected and reviewed remotely, at a supervisor's pleasure and leisure. The mediation of work and regulation of the workplace through use of computer software raises anew central questions about how work should be organized and how the design of software dynamically shapes and reflects the structure of the workplace.

New software systems (which expanded, in part, because of new hardware technology) not only dramatically increase the use of information,[1] but also change the structure and working conditions of organizations. The "conversations and connections" that constitute an organization or business are "embodied in the structure of the computer system," according to Winograd and Flores (1986, p. 169), and thus software design is also the design of the user organization. Depending upon the choices made, computer systems can "reduce the space of possibilities open to workers in organizing their activities" or they can generate new possibilities. In this respect, software is increasingly significant in its effects as it has become an important "process technology" throughout the advanced industrial economies of the world.

Software as a Process Technology

Until recent years, software was an adjunct technology for most organizations. It was used for a limited set of organizational functions and one or two specific departments were its only direct users. It was commonly viewed as a technology subsidiary to hardware, providing support functions rather than crucial operations for achieving the organization's goals. In fact, there are few discussions of computerization that explicitly address the issues of software as a distinct technology.

Software, by its very nature, seems to allow a greater range of social choices in design than other types of technology, particularly when the software is used in the delivery of services. In such applications, software becomes part of the process technology for service work. The software performs or controls procedures and produces information, all of which are elements of the service being delivered to a customer. The software also controls or performs a significant portion of the users' service delivery job tasks and a single system may integrate the work of many different types of users. It is "mission critical" for the organization because essential ongoing service operations depend on the software system (see Figure 2.1).

In addition to its increased centrality to operations, software has expanded its reach in the organization, incorporating more functions and more people than other types of technology and than did previous generations of computer systems. These changes in the span and scope of systems have significant qualitative implications for the impact of software design on worklife.

Scope of Systems The functions of software have expanded from back office processing to supporting front office service delivery. This shift requires more online support systems for crucial service delivery operations as well as analytic tools for management decisions at all levels. Information analysis, access, and transmittal are increasingly important for the delivery of service of all types and thus computer systems have become the process technology necessary for a firm's operations. Computer systems, therefore, are becoming "mission critical," vital to achieving strategic and operational goals and to supporting executive decisions (Brown and Sons, 1986; Main, 1989; Rosenthal and Salzman, 1990). In fact, information technology is increasingly viewed as a competitive weapon affecting the composition of crucial products as well as the delivery of service.[2]

Span of Systems As a consequence of these changes in the scope of systems, people at nearly all levels of the organization are either primary or secondary computer users. Middle and senior level managers, who may put their fingers to the keyboard infrequently, or not at all, still rely on computers to obtain a greater proportion of their information from computer-based information systems. Managers are more directly affected by mission critical systems that conduct higher level operations relevant to their work. Software systems that encompass functions at all levels of the organization are integrative, tying together members at all levels and locations, spanning and integrating departments and functions horizontally and vertically. In banking, for example, computers support transaction

Fig. 2.1. Software as Process Technology

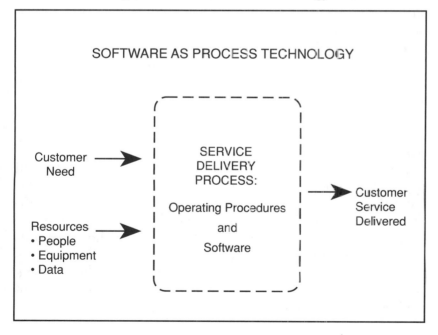

processing in branch and central offices, customer service operations, marketing analyses, loan origination and tracking, and other functions at nearly all levels and departments. An important change as systems broaden their span is that top management enters into the user community. Because a single, integrative system affects nearly all the crucial functions of an organization, higher level managers are therefore becoming involved in software procurement and design decisions. These decisions pose some problems that were not faced with other types of technology.

Designers of service sector software systems must consider a greater range of design options than those offered in manufacturing hardware design. In manufacturing, machines to cut or shape metal may be designed in a great number of different ways, for example with controls that are centrally programmed by technical staff or with controls that are programmed on the shopfloor by machinists. Although machine tool design differences such as these are significant, they still encompass a more limited scope of worker activity than many software systems. The range of design choices and nuances are broader for software that, for example, controls procedures for banking transactions and links people in different functions. As the case study in Chapter 5 illustrates, the designers of a banking system had to make decisions about how a banking transaction at a teller window should be conducted, the different goals of a transaction, and proper response to innumerable contingencies. As illustrated in the case study in Chapter 6, field services systems may link many departments. For example, information entered by field service engineers to allow one department to monitor product quality is used by managers to monitor work performance.

Software design is less constrained by the objective technical properties of the process, as with hardware specifications, and is more flexible and subject to more interpretation. Because software is more malleable and more likely to control people and procedures rather than physical material, design choices in software involve a greater range of social choices and value biases that are embodied in the technology. Design choices involve choices about how the user, as a worker in an organization, will perform his or her job.

The User as Worker

Unlike the home user of a personal computer, who is working toward self-defined goals, the user of large systems in the workplace is using the software in his or her role as "worker." Thus, generic discussions of users must, at least in these applications, be related to what we know about workers and work. It should also be noted that most people considered "users" by software designers would rarely identify themselves that way. Rather, they would define themselves in terms of their job as, for example, a bank teller, a manager, or an accountant.[3] This is particularly important because the software user literature fails to address issues that are widely discussed elsewhere about workers in organizations.

Particularly important in designing workplace software is understanding that, because it is designed for multiple users, across department lines and hierarchical levels, the system impacts are uneven. Computer systems generally mediate work activity to a greater degree for lower level workers than for managers and professionals. At higher levels, users depend on the software for crucial information but their actual work routines are not regulated by the computer. A bank manager or airline company accountant will use computer-generated information, but it is the bank teller or airline reservations clerk whose essential and ongoing activities depend on the system. A system crash may interrupt some work tasks of a manager or accountant, but there is a large portion of his or her work that can still be performed; for the bank teller or airline reservations clerk a system crash leaves them idle. Similarly, a poorly designed feature that is an inconvenience for the home PC user or the manager may be a significant impediment for effective work to the clerk. If it is a feature or function designed to control the flow of work or to regulate the worker, it, too, will be more acutely felt by those at the bottom.

Not only is the perception and impact of technology different at different levels of the organization, but interests and goals of workers will vary at different levels of the organization. One premise of management theory, from Taylor to contemporary human relations theorists, is that diverging interests and conflicts are not inherent to work organizations, they just arise from bad management or poorly socialized workers. Conflict is thus seen as a problem of managing a recalcitrant workforce not as the need to negotiate legitimate and rational differences. In a classic textbook on industrial sociology, Miller and Form (1980, pp. 124-126) compare the organization "to a machine that requires the individual to be mated to it," in which "every person in it must be molded to some degree into the image of the organization," in which there is a "fusion" between the individual and the organization which "tends toward equilibrium." This is considered the normal and desirable state of individuals in an organization.[4]

If conflict or lack of fusion between workers and organizational goals are seen as idiosyncratic, then they become peripheral to consideration of how a system should be designed. If the differences are viewed as persistent but irrational, or rational but illegitimate (e.g., "workers who just do not want to put in a 'fair day's work for a fair day's pay'"), then an objective of technology design may be seen as providing a means of increasing managerial control to maintain effective operations. This objective in software design is then viewed as not only legitimate but also as not being problematic. That is, software can be designed to help managers better accomplish what needs to be done and improve the rationality of operations without engendering significant resistance or inefficiencies.

We argue that this model of the workplace is not only inaccurate but does not lead to effective or desirable methods of software design. Rather than organizations operating on the basis of consensus around a common set of goals, we take the position of researchers who view organizations as operating to mediate diverging interests, as discussed in the previous chapter. This is not a view universally accepted in management theory or by technology designers.

Another important factor for software design is the divergence between the formal description and the reality of workplace operations (e.g., Weltz, 1991). Formal procedures, policies, and rules are not likely to represent the way the organization actually functions or how tasks are actually done. In fact, some researchers argue that organizations may need a loose coupling between the formal rules regulating procedures and actual practices.[5] This reflects the tension between the generation of bureaucratic rules to regulate procedures and the realities of the world that require flexible action (e.g., Brunsson, 1985). Informal work routines are not formalized in part because of their very nature (i.e., being ad hoc or at least not officially sanctioned) and in part because formal acknowledgment of nonstandard procedures might threaten the legitimacy of hierarchical and bureaucratic organization. Insofar as software mediates work tasks and procedures, the designer needs to confront these longstanding workplace issues as part of the design task.

Perspectives of work, therefore, play an important background role shaping the definition of requirements for design and, in the user organization, shaping the action space of workers. Studies of technology and regulation of the workplace suggest that historically one requirement has been to provide means of control to support managerial attempts to better regulate the work process.[6] To the extent that this occurs, the technology designer plays a role beyond the automation and regulation of tasks, moving, perhaps unwittingly, to the regulation of people. This perspective of work identifies issues far different than the typical consideration of the requirements of the line user in software design. Effective design must consider the role of work in people's lives and the role of the user as worker.

From a prescriptive perspective on work, we suggest that work should be an intrinsically meaningful activity. We recognize the longstanding debate about the intrinsic value of work and the extent to which promotion of fulfilling or unalienating work is both illusory and detrimental to productivity.[7] However, we argue that this debate has not framed the issue correctly: Work and technology design that promotes greater human development is not only desirable from a position of values but also for its effectiveness. In the current competitive environment there is a compatibility, if not synergy, between work that promotes improved worklife *and* organizational effectiveness. Current management philosophies, such as Total Quality Management, may recognize this link between improving efficiency of the production process and quality of products and services. It is to these issues of design for the user that we now turn.

Design in the Age of the User

User-centered criteria for the design of applications software, unlike those for hardware design, have been explicitly promoted in design methodologies.[8] In fact, it was even declared that, "The

1980s could go down as the decade of the user."[9] Design for the user was generally described in terms of user-friendly interfaces or, more generally, of providing features and functionality that make the system effective for the user. Nevertheless, systems continued to be designed that were ineffectual for users and/or that users would not use. A widely prescribed remedy became user involvement in development, a "user knows best" solution. Some argue that only by involving users in design can the designer ensure that the software is effective.

This nostrum for curing system deficiencies has widespread currency in both the research literature and textbooks and has a great deal of intuitive appeal. It is also very much in the spirit of current thinking about the customer's role in effective design of tangible products in general. However, with respect to software, the evidence that this approach is sufficient to improve end-user effectiveness is not compelling.[10] Examining the assumptions underlying user involvement and "better design" formulae provides some insight into their inherent limitations. To examine existing design criteria we first review discussions of user orientation in textbooks on software design. It is a narrow focus, we argue, that leads to an insufficient approach for evaluating user needs and, more generally, understanding the role of software in the user organization. Our concern here is with the underlying assumptions about users and work organizations, not with a specific design methodology.

Software Design by the Book

We reviewed 50 textbooks on applications software design to examine the nature of user considerations in design methodologies.[11] We first looked in the index for listings of "users." Twenty-eight of the 50 books had at least one such listing. We analyzed the sections in each of these books that referred to users for the types of user consideration in design that were being promoted. (These textbooks were all written by U.S. authors. Some of the European researchers have approached software design quite differently, as we discuss in a separate section below.)

Of the 28 books that had an index listing of user, only 17 had more than a passing reference to user consideration in design. These 17 books all note the importance of designing software that meets user requirements. Only six books mention specific reasons for difficulties in designing user-effective software. These problems are identified as users "don't know in detail what they want until they see it," lack of communication by designers with users and a "communication gap" because "verbal communication has its limits."[12]

These and the other textbooks propose four types of solutions: talking to all users, having an analyst or user liaison whose specific job responsibilities include determining user requirements (usually by formal user interviews), having frequent dialogue between designers and programmers and users, or even putting a user in charge of software development projects.[13] A few books on software development for practitioners have emphasized user involvement and it has been a prominent theme in research articles. Much of this literature focuses on the means for assessing user requirements in an attempt to illustrate the failure or success of a design methodology. Included in this literature are methods that software developers can use to determine user requirements: methods to obtain the data, such as interviews, surveys, and focus groups, and techniques to analyze the data and make optimal design decisions.[14]

Several limitations in these various solutions relate to the background assumptions in the design approach. One such assumption is that ineffective design is just a technical problem of inadequate methods for specifying or assessing user requirements. The unstated belief here is that there are optimal solutions to user needs and that efficiency and effectiveness can be objectively evaluated with the proper methods. Resulting failures or shortcomings in designing an effective system are, therefore, thought to stem either from poorly defined specifications (i.e., as a methodological issue involving better surveys, more representative and active participation by users, etc.), or technical limitations (e.g., tradeoffs or constraints imposed by hardware or software technology). In theory, there are no inherent limits to achieving an optimal design solution that meets user requirements.

Another limitation is the absence of design principles that address user needs in the workplace, apart from interface and ergonomic issues, and that make consideration of their needs an essential part of software design (comparable to technical principles for writing particular subroutines or certain algorithms).

Finally, textbook design methodologies contain few, if any, principles of design or generalized criteria about specific types of design as they affect job design and organizational issues.

The conclusion of these texts, sometimes explicit and other times implicit, is that designers also do not need to be concerned with learning about or considering the social or organizational dimensions of the workplace. There is no framework provided for systems designers to understand social and organizational implications of their work, such as that provided in some of the organizational literature. Rather, the prescription of involving users in the design process is assumed to be sufficient to ensure that systems are designed to be effective.

In general, the limitations of these standard approaches are an overly technical and narrow focus on the context of software use and role of the user. They divorce technology design from use and focus on the creation of software as just an abstract enterprise. Certainly much of software design is a strictly technical endeavor and in many ways improvements in technical methods will improve software design. However, particularly for software in the workplace, these methods do not address a larger set of issues. User involvement is certainly an important step toward designing user-centered software. However, thinking that the problem can just be handed over to "the user" is still an insufficient solution. To fully appreciate the design requirements for large-scale, workplace applications software (mission critical systems) requires a broader view of the role of the user and the role of technology in the organization. Our perspective adds another level of analysis to software design; namely, how software functions as part of the institutional web of technology and organizations that shapes the user's "action space" and how software, as a product of an institutional web, is itself shaped by the "design space" in that web.

The User in the Web of the Organization

There is a small but growing body of research that examines the broader organizational context of software use and views technology as one part of an interconnected web of the organization. Some of the initial theorizing about a new model of computers and organizations has been formulated by Rob Kling (1987; 1991), building on the insights from a number of different research directions.   We are not attempting a comprehensive review here, just outlining some of the key concepts that inform our research.[15]

As outlined by Kling (1987, p. 3; 1991), there are two underlying models in studies of computing: discrete entity models, which focus on "relatively formal-rational conceptions of the capabilities of information technology and the social settings in which they are developed and used" and web models, which are "a form of `resource dependence' models [that] make explicit connections between a focal technology and the social, historical, and political contexts in which it is developed and used."

The discrete entity studies, such as those previously discussed in our review, have a bias toward technological determinism. The underlying perspective assumes direct technological impacts with little consideration of the organizational structure, the web composed of the social relations, infrastructure, and history of the organization. Consensus among users within the organization is generally assumed in discrete entity studies. The locus of systems failure is limited to developer-user interaction. Although discrete entity consensus model studies may consider the social aspects of the developer-user interaction, remedies are cast as improvements in methods, techniques, and intentions of system designers and users. Power and values do not enter into such discussions because consensus models of social systems do not recognize inherent or structural value conflicts as legitimate, that is, intrinsic to existing organizations and social systems.

Another stream of literature, characterized as web or organizational model studies, takes a broader view of different user interests and organizational contexts.[16] These writers do not assume consensus or rationality in organizations. They emphasize analysis of technology in context and social aspects of technology development and use. These web models focus on three elements: the social relations between participants, the infrastructure available for their support, and the history of commitments made in developing and operating related computer-based technologies (Kling, 1991, p. 5). Building on this web model, we include a perspective on the environment of organizations, how they are shaped and how they shape the actions of their constituents, and links to the market and broader socioeconomic environment. Before outlining our elaboration of this model, we consider some of the representative research studies examining computers from an organizational or web perspective.

Existing research has addressed different aspects of this larger perspective of the web of computers and organizations. The various studies that fall within a web model can be viewed as analyses of different aspects of the web and as representing different perspectives on the role of the user. A number of researchers have examined issues of better design for the user and proposals abound for overcoming obstacles and devising solutions for greater user involvement and impact in design. As we and others have discussed, an unreflective reliance on the user as the solution is ineffective for a number of reasons.[17] Using the user as the solution to improving design will provide some benefit but, overall, it is an atomistic approach that is too narrow. Broadening the scope of analysis has led to a number of different perspectives on the web of computing by researchers in different countries.

Review of various approaches and issues in software design identifies striking differences among predominant approaches in various countries. Although there is variation, the different perspectives on users in the workplace have some consistency within each country. Examining some of the systematic differences, we focus on key elements of computer analyses conducted in the United States, the United Kingdom, and Scandinavian countries. More general characteristics of these countries seem to shape the researchers' analyses, the proposals for software design methods, and sometimes the actual technology developed in each country.

In the U.S. studies tend to address discrete dimensions of organizations, power, and the user.[18] For example, power in organizations has been addressed in a number of studies that examine the use of computer systems to strengthen the power of certain groups.[19] Studies addressing organizational aspects of software design also concentrate on the fit between the user organization and the specifications of the computerized system. The central focus of these studies is how computer systems may alter power relationships and control of information in the organization.[20]

These studies focus primarily on implementation and late life cycle design and the fit between the user organization and specifications of the computerized system. The adequacy or effectiveness of a design is explicitly or implicitly judged to be the extent to which it preserves the preexisting organizational structure and relationships. Systems that pose threats to existing power relationships are seen as likely to encounter resistance (e.g., Markus and Pfeffer, 1983) and addressing these potential problems calls for designers to accurately determine the power distribution and existing organizational relationships and then design systems that are compatible. Other studies have shown how organizational politics shape user requirements analysis.[21]

Some of the problems of power are identified as issues of expertise, of the monopoly of power through professionalism and technical mystique. For example, domination of technology design and use may be viewed as computer professionals exercising their body of knowledge and technical expertise to gain organizational power and fulfill their particular needs such as empire building. Thus, there is a focus on democratizing *knowledge* through user participation in software design as the countervailing force to power in the organization. The limitation of increasing user knowledge without increasing their power in the organization is generally not addressed.

This U.S. approach deals with specific and discrete aspects of organizational life and technology. This may be seen as consistent with a historical tradition of examining issues in technical and pragmatic terms, with issues of politics and power being subsidiary. Workplace theories and approaches to work reorganization, for example, tend to focus on techniques of management, not examining systemic issues of hierarchy and power (just as in the broader society, class is not an important concept in the U.S., particularly as compared to European perspectives and politics[22]). In terms of software this general perspective shapes both analysis and the subject studied. For example, issues of power tend to be seen mostly as the monopoly of power by groups or coalitions, not the type of power that represents different "classes" in the organization.

In summary, although some of the software literature discusses power as important, it is seen as residing in individuals and coalitions; thus, power is viewed as situational or temporal. In part this reflects a focus on the conflicts at the horizontal level of the organization (e.g., departments that are different functionally but hierarchically relatively equivalent, such as accounting, sales, and the Management Information Systems departments).

This perspective provides an important but incomplete part of the analysis. Power and conflicts are also an attribute of hierarchy and particular forms of management and thus inhere in the structure of organizations. They are less fluid than some of the analyses would suggest. Vertical relationships tend to be more stable and tend to have specific, core objectives around issues of management and work organization.

In the U.S. there is a very pragmatic approach in software design research and theory that reflects the reality of the workplace and markets in the country. The designer, or end-user, is not likely to have much effect in reshaping the workplace. Workers have rarely been able to exercise significant influence in structural organizational change and other types of workplace reforms. To suggest that, somehow, in the context of traditional organizational structure, a more democratic or participative approach to technology design will occur seems not to reflect the broader context of technology design and use in the U.S. Among the different studies of computing in the U.S., we can find all the elements of the broader scope of organizational and worklife issues we discuss, but they do not coalesce into a coherent body of theory about computerization and organizations.

A different approach comes from the English researchers based on longstanding traditions in studies of work in the sociotechnical school (Trist and Murray, 1990). A key premise of sociotechnical theory is that work and technology should be designed to improve worker satisfaction, which will, in turn, lead to higher levels of productivity. Most of this work focuses on job redesign to increase the meaningfulness of the job and provide workers with broader areas of responsibility and autonomy.[23] Developing this line of analysis specifically for software, Mumford (1981) suggests that software design decisions reflect the value perspective of software designers and she evaluates the extent to which several systems incorporate human, technical, and business values (drawing on McGregor's Theory X and Theory Y typology).

Mumford has developed a design approach that focuses on changing designers' values, from a Theory X to a Theory Y perspective of users, and increasing user involvement in design. Design effectiveness is evaluated as the extent to which systems are designed to restore and maintain organizational equilibrium, drawing on a Parsonian model of organizations and social relations. Developing shared values among designers, managers, and system users, and humanistic values in particular, is the suggested goal for effective system design. Design that reflects sociotechnical system principles is assumed if values can be aligned among all relevant parties.

At the same time, the technical system is relegated to backstage in sociotechnical analyses. Most of the focus is on specifying user participation and advocating more concern by designers with workplace issues (along the lines of the sociotechnical framework for work redesign). The empirical studies of sociotechnical design of computer systems, notes Olerup (1989, p. 60), "give very detailed accounts of the work design process, but next to nothing on the process of designing the computer system." In a historical review of sociotechnical theory, Mumford (1987) notes that very little of this research addresses technology design and suggests that one reason is the lack of engineering expertise by sociotechnical researchers (see also Cherns, 1987). Moreover, as Bansler (1989, p. 12) has written, "Although many of the sociotechnical ideas and recommendations have gained widespread acceptance among systems designers they have, however, only had little impact on how the systems actually developed..." Although the importance of job satisfaction is a cornerstone of sociotechnical theory, in practice sociotechnical researchers have not successfully convinced managers and designers to attend to the human factor in design. Sociotechnical theory provides principles for humane work organization and, in that way, provides indirect criteria for technology design.

Approaching the issues of technology design and use from a very different perspective are the new social constructionists such as those in England and France. Although perspectives on organizations and jobs differ, these studies follow in the same path as sociotechnical approaches in viewing the design and use of technology as the dynamics occurring within the scope of the user or individual designer. That is, design and use issues are largely, if not wholly, contained within the design space and action space. (In this view, the technology that emerges from designers is a subjectivist creation that seems to have few enduring attributes because the technology can be largely, if not completely, reinterpreted by the user acting within his or her action space. In each realm, technology design and technology use, individual values and perceptions are the determining

factors). These studies provide a number of important observations and insights but, because they tend to reduce technology-
related issues to highly individual values and perspectives, do
not examine the role of organizations and other structures on
technology design and use.

A very different perspective emerges in the Scandinavian
studies, which build on a sociotechnical perspective but take it to
the organizational rather than the individual level. The early
studies in Scandinavia identified a number of organizational
level issues affecting systems development and implementation,
shifting the focus of analysis of previous studies. For example,
one study found that an exclusive emphasis in design on achieving technical efficiency may be detrimental to user needs and
worklife as well as create "information systems dysfunctions"
(Bjørn-Andersen and Hedberg, 1977, p. 125). These researchers
conclude that improved designs will result from better communication between designers and users about "the value system
rather than the actual computerized system" (Hedberg and
Mumford, 1975, p. 58) and the "political aspects of designing"
(Bjørn-Andersen and Hedberg, 1977, p. 139). In terms of the
research in the 1970s and early 1980s, these studies provided the
groundwork for developing a broader perspective.

Recent approaches in Scandinavia have tried to move beyond
isolated participation of workers (users) in design, when it was
found that user participation was ineffective if not based on a
broader participation in workplace decisions.[24] Thus, the design
approaches being advocated are based on a more far-reaching
concept of workplace democracy. A number of design projects
have been undertaken in Scandinavian countries to develop
new approaches to design, to overcome what they view as
limitations in existing theory and practice. It is very much a
practical orientation, from which theory was then developed,
and it is shaped by the culture and social structure of those
societies. Significantly, the strong role of labor unions in those
societies and in corporations, the emphasis on, and government
support of, quality of worklife programs and a strong craft
tradition provide a different atmosphere for developing design
methods and approaches.

Pelle Ehn (1989) has provided the most detailed articulation of
the various dimensions of these approaches. He criticizes prevailing computer systems design approaches in several areas,

including the basic philosophy of engineering as bound by an overly narrow focus on design as a natural science. Rather, Ehn proposes a view of design as being craft or art as much as science and as crossing disciplinary boundaries between natural sciences, social sciences, and humanities. Perhaps what most distinguishes some of the Scandinavian approaches is that they see software design as supporting an explicit goal of industrial democracy. This perspective, then, frames their approach to the design process, namely participation by trade unions in a "collective resource" approach. The design process is structured to be compatible with the organizations of many Scandinavian companies in which there is a high degree of unionization and various forms of industrial democracy or union participation in management issues. Ehn and others address not only the design process but also the content of design, arguing that software design should support and allow for development of craft skills.

The objectives in a design approach reflect the larger organizational and social context in which it is developed and used. The contrast of design approaches in different countries illustrates how different factors are emphasized and how they reflect differences in organizational and social structure.[25] The differences in workplace organization can be said to reflect differences in industrial culture. That is, the combination of a country's or firm's economic market, employment practices, education system, legal system, social and engineering values, and other factors shape the way it will organize its production process or, for our purposes, technology design.[26] In the same way, proposals for changes in technology design processes and objectives will be constrained by the environment. The cross-national comparisons of design strategies illustrate both the possibilities and the constraints.[27] Building on this research we outline a model of technology design that includes the broader context of the organization-technology web.

A Schematic for the Study of Technology Design

The "seamless web" of technology, encompassing the full range of factors from individual values to the structure of the society in which it is created, may be so all encompassing as to include just about every social and technical factor. For our purposes we

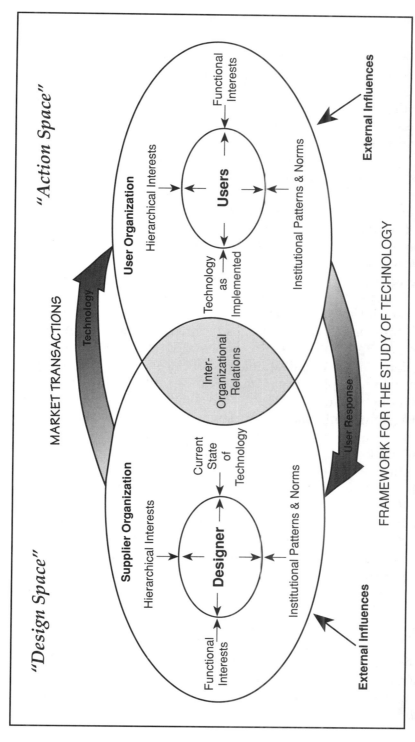

Fig. 2.2. Framework for the Study of Technology.

draw the net in a bit closer and sharpen our focus on a few dimensions of this larger web (see Figure 2.2).

Our model begins with the design space of the designer and his or her immediate environment. The values and decisions of the designer are significant in defining the technology Thus, understanding the design as an expression of the designer is important and we begin by seeing how individuals and design teams make decisions about design. We examine these explanations in context. (Designers may or may not explain their decisions as shaped by a broader set of factors, because they may believe they are determining a strictly technical set of specifications.)

Expanding outward within the organization, we focus on relations with other functional departments and hierarchical relations. Important here are the findings of organizational research on power in organizations and the limits to rationality in organizational decision making, as we have discussed in Chapter 1. The organization is not isolated but affected by its environment and thus it is also important to examine the external environments of the software design and user organizations. In the design organization factors that are important include pressures for competition with other vendors and selling its product to the user firm. In the user firm we view a similar range of factors. The action space of the user is shaped by the technology and other aspects of his or her position (e.g., degree of autonomy, responsibility, nature of the work tasks, etc.). The user's action space is also shaped by the overall type and structure of the organization and the way hierarchical and functional differences are negotiated. The user organization's market, as perceived by both the user firm and by the software designers, will shape design decisions and the viability of both the vendor's product and of the user organization's efficiency, effectiveness, and profitability and survival. This map of the terrain of technology design frames our analytic perspective as we move to the next section of empirical analysis of software design and use.

Endnotes

1. Industry has always been dependent upon information to coordinate and control operations. In this sense, Beninger (1986) argues that the information revolution was part of the Industrial Revolution, making possible the great

expansion of production and distribution in the late nineteenth century. To Beninger, the recent changes in information technologies represent a quantitative change rather than a dramatic qualitative change in the importance of information. However, Zuboff (1988) suggests that information technology goes beyond automating work activity by generating information about the work process that may add value to the production of goods or delivery of services. Zuboff also discusses the changes and experiences of "computer mediated work," in which work is performed as an abstract activity rather than a tactile skill. Another perspective on the meaning of computers in mediating activity and its perception by users is provided by Sherry Turkle (1984), in *The Second Self*.

2. Some of the first discussions and reports about how information technology has been and should be used to increase competitiveness in service industries can be found, for example, in Rockart and DeLong (1982), Ives and Learmonth (1984), Rockart and Treacy (1988). This has been a quite popular theme (e.g., Harris, 1985).

3. There are several problems with the term "user." From the software developer's perspective the term provides a generic label for people using the computer and there *are* many common aspects of computer use for all users. However, it is a problematic term for at least two reasons: First, the term tends to obscure the identities, roles, and functions of specific users in their jobs as bank tellers, accountants, sales managers, etc. Computer use becomes a common denominator that takes on greater importance than the specific application. Second, and perhaps more importantly, it emphasizes the importance of technology over people in which users are just adjuncts to the computer, thus inverting the relationship between people and computers. Instead, it should be recognized that people use the computer as a means of accomplishing their tasks. Related to this, and our point in this section, is that the term "user" decontextualizes people from their roles as workers. Agneta Olerup (1993) identified this issue in an earlier version of this manuscript and we agree with her in both these observations and in her conclusion that there is no good alternative to the term "user" for these discussions.

4. Those who are not fused and accepting of the common goals of the organization are "the confused, frustrated, and defeated [who] all suffer a common malady. They have not responded to the socializing process successfully...Lack of ability or lack of adaptation may have caused their problems" (Miller and Form, 1980, pp. 134-135). In Miller and Form's view, seeking satisfaction from work is futile for most people. Workers "are still encouraged to seek the values denied by the technical and economic realities of life. Failing to fulfill their social wants, they blame their failure on the organization rather than on the sociocultural orientation that leads them to look for security, satisfaction, and status, where they are in short supply." It is in "the approximately half the hours in each week for activities other than working or sleeping...[that] workers may exercise their options to engage in recreation, eating, participation in voluntary associations, sex, sheer idleness, and the like....Motivation generated in and toward out-of-work life can supply the will to work in factory or office." They go on to discuss, somewhat dismayed, that cultural changes in society make younger workers "much less willing to accept authoritarian influences at work or in the community" (pp.

154-155). Although the form of expression in these passages may seem a bit dated, it still represents a predominant underlying perspective about work organization and work: The issue about whether, and to what degree, work should be a source of satisfaction is still debated. This theme continues from early sociology of work such as Dubin (1956), to current social theorists such as Offe (1985) and Gorz (1980).

5. One of the notable articles is that by Meyer and Rowan (1991) and also discussed by Perrow (1984, 1986) and by Weltz (1991) specifically in terms of software. It is also discussed in studies of the workplace such as in Hirschhorn's (1984) work.

6. For example, Noble (1977, 1984), Gordon, Edwards, and Reich (1982) and Marglin (1974).

7. A number of management theorists have advocated notions of work humanization, participative decision making, improved human relations, and other forms of improving job satisfaction as a means of increasing worker motivation and thus productivity. The classic literature on human relations in the workplace was spawned by the Hawthorne experiments. These experiments were purported to show productivity increases from improved human relations factors. Despite considerable evidence over the years that the effect reported in the original experiments was unsubstantiated, the "Hawthorne effect" is still widely cited and a strongly held belief in management circles.

A number of reexaminations of the original Hawthorne data and of the original notes of the field researchers do not find the reputed associations. For example, one statistical analysis (Franke and Kaul, 1978, p. 623) of the experimental variable found that variables "accounting for 90% of the variance in quantity and quality of output...[were]...imposition of managerial discipline, economic adversity, and quality of raw materials provide most explanation, obviating the need to draw upon less clearly definable human relations mechanisms." Another study (Jones, 1992, p. 452) found that "whether the Hawthorne effect is defined in a narrow or a broad sense, the conclusion is the same: the original Hawthorne studies contain little clear evidence of a Hawthorne effect." (See also, Carey, 1967; Bramel and Friend, 1981; Sykes, 1965) Gillespie (1991) provides detailed examination of the "Hawthorne effect" and concludes it is "manufactured knowledge". He finds there was little in the Hawthorne results to support the interpretations but they did reflect a broader world view of Mayo and associates and other "academic and corporate interests."

Subsequent research has not provided compelling evidence that improvements in worker participation or involvement or other job enrichment changes lead to productivity increases. In fact, one recent study (Harrison, 1991, p. 74) finds that an employee involvement program "not only fails to help efficiency but actually appears to hurt it." A comprehensive review of research studies by the Texas Center for Productivity and Quality Work Life (1983, p. 3) found that "financial rewards were the most effective motivator, followed by goal setting and job enrichment, with participation clearly being the least effective." Other studies (e.g., Locke, Schweiger, and Latham, 1987) provide corroborating evidence that "there is no clear tendency for participation to result in higher productivity than authoritative decision making." Thus, in the past, a commitment to worklife improvements probably rested more on social and value choices than using it as an instrument of increased productivity. This view of worker participation programs as not leading to productivity increases is shared by researchers on opposite ends of the political spectrum, though some argue for it as a positive value choice while others argue against it as a distortion of the purpose of work and corporations (e.g., Locke and Schweiger, 1979; Locke, 1984; Schweiger and Leana, 1986; Sashkin, 1984; Wells, 1987).

8. See Salzman (1991, 1992) and Lund, Bishop, Newman, and Salzman (1993) for review of hardware design approaches.

9. From *Computer News* (1986), cited in Friedman (1989, p. 171).

10. The effectiveness of customer involvement in product design is discussed in Rosenthal (1992) and the equivocal findings about its effectiveness in software are discussed in Ives and Olsen (1984), King and Rodriguez (1981), Tait and Vessey (1988), and Friedman (1989). For other perspectives on limitations of user involvement, and how some of these problems can be addressed, see Robey and Farrow (1982), Franz and Robey (1984), Boland and Day (1989), Newman and Noble (1990), and Grudin (1991a, 1991b).

11. These books were all the textbooks being used in computer science and Management Information Systems courses at Boston University and a random selection of textbooks in the library. For overview and discussion of the technical and general problems of software development, see Cusamano (1991) and Friedman (1989).

12. These quotes are from, respectively, Hicks (1976), DeMarco (1978), Bowerman and Glover (1988), and also reflect statements in Davis (1983), Lucas (1985), DeRossi and Hopper (1984).

13. One text, Keen (1981), warns of "dangers of control by line users," consisting of users who can "squeeze out the DP department and demotivate DP specialists and DP managers." In this case the DP manager and staff need to "educate" the user about what they "truly need" instead of what they think they want and not relinquish control over design.

14. For example, a book on information systems by Lucas (1985) proposes active involvement of users during the entire design process, even to the extent of having a user in charge of the full design team. Some technical approaches to evaluating needs and making choices among different design options rely solely on cost criteria, using economic analysis as the basis for engineering decisionmaking (e.g., Boehm, 1981). Others (e.g., Turner, 1981) recognize that noneconomic valuation of tradeoffs is necessary and recommend techniques to help users develop consensus on systems requirements. For review of the literature on user involvement, see Friedman (1989).

15. There is no claim in this review or for our model of identifying or being the primogenitor. (Others such as Hirschheim and Klein, 1989, for example, have provided similar analyses of rationalistic models of organizations and systems development.) Rather, we attempt to draw on a few key concepts developed in various ways in a broad spectrum of research approaches. We do not attempt here a review of the different research and design perspectives that have developed over the past decade or so. A comprehensive review is provided by Friedman (1989).

The emergence of critical perspectives to the predominant approaches in software, and questioning of engineering in general, represents the culmination of earlier research into an intellectual zeitgeist of the late 1980s and 1990s, perhaps indicative of a paradigm shift that will lead to a consensus on how to examine these issues. However, the goal of developing a unified perspective is probably illusory. There are a number of articles that address different aspects of these issues. The Scandinavian approach (e.g., Ehn, 1989, for comprehensive overview) is a particular case, as we discuss below. A new approach, focusing on how users construct their reality and use computer systems, is part of an emerging body of literature (e.g., Woolgar, 1991) being developed in England by the Centre for Research into Innovation, Culture, and Technology (CRICT).

16. In a review of the research and literature, Kling (1987, p.3) notes that he did not identify any web models in the computer science textbooks. He found the predominant perspective of computers was one of discrete entities, unrelated to broader organizational dynamics.

17. For example, see Grudin (1991a, 1991b), Boland and Day (1989), Hirschheim and Klein (1989), Newman and Noble (1990), Franz and Robey (1984), and Robey and Farrow (1982).

18. For comprehensive overviews and reviews, see Attewell and Rule (1984), Kling (1980), and Friedman (1989).

19. A few representative studies are: Kling (1984), Bariff and Galbraith (1978), Markus (1984), Markus and Pfeffer (1983), Robey and Ferron (1982), and Boland and Day (1989).

20. See Markus (1984), Markus and Pfeffer (1983), Kling (1985), Danziger and Kraemer (1986).

21. Building on research in this area, Robey and Markus (1984, pp. 11-12) examine the politics of system design, challenging the rationalistic view of the development process. They find, for example, that most information requirements analysis methods "have an inherent bias to preserve the status quo, a beneficial outcome for those who already possess power," and "that systems which appear to be rationally justified also serve political aims," suggesting that the justification follows after decisions are made on the basis of politics.

22. In the U.S. political issues tend to be framed in terms of special interests of groups and coalitions representing pluralistic interests. There is a strong belief in mobility and class politics are not explicitly discussed nor is class position seen as an enduring characteristic. The perspective in the U.S. is shaped by experiences and folklore of a greater mobility in the U.S. than in other countries (e.g., Hamilton, 1972). For example, although the Democratic party usually represents organized labor, it is not a "Labor Party." In the U.S. there is a decline in the perception that there are particular interests shared by workers. This is reflected in declines in unionization and a declining influence and distinguishable political agenda by labor unions (cf. Domhoff, 1990, Chapter 4, on origins of the Wagner Act). This is a sharp difference when compared to the influence of labor unions in various parts of Europe and particularly in Scandinavian countries and it is reflected in differences in work organization, including technology policies.

23. Although influenced by U.S. human relations theory, sociotechnical researchers maintain a distinct approach, according to Friedman (1989, p. 195), because "they believe that once conflict has been built into a work situation only

structural change can remove it." The sociotechnical approach focuses on resolving conflict between management and workers by emphasizing "their common interests in the development of new technology, which is based on their mutual interests in preserving workplaces" (Bansler, 1989). Sociotechnical approaches tend to involve deeper organizational change than the U.S. Quality of Worklife and other programs. One exception in the U.S. is Pava (1983), one of the few researchers to address sociotechnical principles in office work who outlines a strategy that requires significant organizational restructuring to make best use of new technology and create satisfying jobs.

24. This is due, according to Bansler, to the "idealistic and inadequate understanding of the driving forces behind the technological transformation of work." Bansler's (1989, p. 15) critique is that the Scandinavian approaches (or, more accurately, the "critical tradition") reject "the harmonious view of social relations in the workplace, which imbue the systems theoretical and socio-technical research traditions." Instead, organizations should be viewed as "frameworks for conflicts among various interest groups with unequal power and resources. Social relations at work are characterized—not only by coopera-tion—but also by conflicts and struggles between managers and employees, and among different groups of employees...Since these conflicts are related to the class structure of the society, they cannot be `resolved' or abolished at the level of an individual organization, as the socio-technical tradition believes. The `participative approach' to systems development is not sufficient." Instead there needs to be a broader based change in the structure of work systems, if not in society.

25. One study of Canadian and Danish software designers' values (Kumar and Bjørn-Andersen, 1990) found systematic and significant differences. They found that although there was a dominance of technical and economic values (versus sociopolitical values such as concern about organizational and job satisfaction) in both countries, Danish designers were more concerned with the social issues than the Canadian designers. Other examples of the differ-ences in industrial culture and technology may be seen in the studies of Computer-Aided Design (Majchrzak and Salzman, 1989).

26. The concept of industrial culture as used here has been developed by Rauner and Ruth (1989).

27. For example, the Scandinavian approaches can provide a model for ways to reorient design but also show that their particular approach reflects a particular industrial culture shaped by, among other factors, a longstanding craft tradition, a workplace environment of 90 percent unionization, and requirements for labor union participation in many basic decisions that would be considered management prerogatives in the U.S.

The Structure of Software Design

The software industry really came of age in the 1970s and 1980s. This was a time of technological transformation in the workplace. The computer expanded from the backroom to the front office and evolved from simple data processing to integrated information systems. The growth of the independent software vendor led to an important change in software design. User firms began to purchase large, standard or semicustom systems from third-party vendors rather than purchasing software with hardware and having most applications software custom designed by an in-house programming staff. This added another dimension to the software design process: Software became the product of at least two organizations (the vendor and one or more user firms) and its design and production became mediated by the market. The organizational simplicity of software design occurring within one organization, as difficult a process as that may be, became relatively more complex organizationally.

This chapter examines one part of the process of technology design and use: the activities internal to the software design firm. It concentrates on the structure and dynamics of the design process rather than on specific design decisions. The findings presented in this chapter are based on a survey of vendor firms and may represent a different perspective than findings on software developed within a user firm.

By focusing on dynamics that transcend choices of particular individuals, we show how decisions are shaped and constrained by the structure of the design process itself. The three chapters following this one present case studies that describe specific choices of software features and functions and analyze the impacts of those choices on software users and customers. Taken together, this chapter and the case studies present the dual perspective necessary to appreciate how software is a socially constructed technology.

The business applications software industry for mainframes and minicomputers is composed of hardware manufacturers such as IBM and Digital Equipment Corporation, several large vendors, and numbers of small specialty firms. Our exploration of the design process began with extensive telephone interviews with the CEOs and vice presidents of 23 firms producing standard or semicustom software, representing a cross-section of size and applications areas (see Appendix 1 for details of the study). We focused on the range of organizational and social factors shaping the design process, particularly those issues they faced as vendors external to the user organization. Because vendor produced software is a product sold through the market and not developed by the user organization, the design process has several additional layers of complexity than design conducted internal to the user firm (though there may be many common issues). Issues of inter- and intraorganizational relations and the production of a commodity product developed as the software industry grew, which we describe below.

Emergence of the Independent Software Vendor

In the mid- to late 1980s, software became increasingly important as a distinct technology in the computer industry. This is evident in three developments: Software grew as a proportion of revenue for hardware companies; independent software firms obtained a rapidly growing share of the total software market; and standard software products were developed for particular application industry segments and specific functions, establishing informal standards for the delivery of services.[1]

The emergence of the software industry appeared to follow a familiar path of technological convergence in which an independent supplier industry arises to provide a generic technology for use in different types of production applications. This occurs when there is widespread demand for a new technology that originally provided novel capabilities to a particular industry and was produced by the user industry (Rosenberg, 1976).

Rosenberg's (1976) research identifies a pattern of vertical *dis*integration of an industry in which part of a specific industrial process becomes a freestanding industry that serves multiple firms and industrial segments. The user firm must then purchase the products through the market rather than through an internal procurement process. The vendor, as an independent industry producing a commodity product, or at least specializing in one area of production, generally has a greater pool of resources, knowledge, and skills to focus on producing a specific technology that will be widely used (Rosenberg, 1976, pp. 18–20). Because of this, the vendor is able to develop more advanced technology to serve a wide range of needs and becomes a center for diffusion of knowledge and techniques throughout the economy. A solution to one firm's problem or a new development, which might be proprietary if developed within a single user firm, becomes available to all firms that purchase the vendor's product. Thus, software vendors are positioned to diffuse "best practice" throughout the industry but may also need to design products that cater to mainstream preferences and practices; the vendor has to be responsive to a much broader constituency of users than the internal MIS department. These are just some of the dilemmas and pressures shaping software design.

Our survey, by capturing the actual practice of design by software vendors, provides an understanding of the important stages and responsibilities of software development and design in which the different sources of design preferences and influences become apparent in software development. This chapter presents findings on organizational dimensions that we found most central in the development of software and the effect of this structure on design choices. These general findings shape our analysis of the particular case studies of service sector software design presented in subsequent chapters.

The findings are grouped according to the following topics:
- The process and structure of software design,
- The software firm,
- The user organization.

The final section of this chapter summarizes the implications of these findings for the analysis of how design decisions reflect the organizational and social dimensions of the design process. It also discusses the competing claims by different user groups within an organization on what functions the software should serve.

The Process and Structure of Software Design

The first step in software development is to establish project objectives: the functionality and requirements of the software.

This involves making policy choices about the broad functions of the software, the market for which it will be developed, and the purposes it will serve. In the next step, the system specifications, or functional specifications, are determined. This involves more technical decisions about how to achieve the project objectives. The third step is to design programming specifications, which is a very detailed and technical process.

A software vendor faces problems that an MIS department in the user firm does not. The vendor works at a distance from the user or may be developing a product before a relationship with the users is established and the vendor must compete with other vendors and user firms' internal MIS departments. To address these issues, independent software vendors have marketing departments and produce a standard product in ways unlike formal descriptions of an MIS department's design process.[2] In most companies the marketing group has formal responsibility for the first phase of product design, defining the product requirements and necessary functionality. The marketing group outlines the basic product definition based on surveys of their users, informal discussions with users, and/or their own knowledge of users' applications.

The second phase of software design is largely directed by the development team, though a marketing person responsible for the product usually participates. At this stage the developers analyze the user and program requirements, establish the details of the particular functions of the software (what the inputs and outputs will be), and determine the overall structure of the program. In the next phase technical details are developed for program structure and procedures, including the responsibility for specific programming tasks.

During development there is ongoing discussion between development teams and the product manager in marketing to establish specific application requirements, such as how operational objectives should be implemented, the design of the interfaces, and other details of program design. When the development group in a larger company decides that the software has reached a sufficient level of completion, it sends the system to a testing group; in smaller companies, testing and debugging the software is done by the development group. After initial testing and debugging, the software is tested at a user site, further modifications are made as necessary, and then it is released for sale to customers.

When programming specifications are established, the basic functionality and structure of the software are defined. At the point of testing, most modifications are limited to fixing bugs (i.e., programming errors) and changes in interfaces; the orientation and product goals are well established and unlikely to be changed at this stage of design. However, because software may be used in different ways, its impact may be greatly modified in implementation as some groups or individuals make crucial decisions after the software is installed.

For the vendor, significant factors that affect design objectives are sharing of functions between marketing and development and being in a different position than an MIS department vis-à-vis users. These factors include different orientations between marketing and development groups within the vendor organization and the distance of the designer/vendor from the user organization and the need to build standard, or multiple user, products. At the same time, the variety of "users" in the user organization and the differing perspectives and influence of those who use and those who buy the software often lead to unexpected conflicts and shortfalls in software performance. These factors are of paramount concern in the consideration of organizational issues in software development and affect every stage of development, from initial conception to implementation by the user.

Software Development and the Marketing Department

The development process for vendors is different from that of MIS departments within the user organization. As noted previously, user requirements must be determined for a range of users, not all of whom are known during the development phase. Most vendors attempt to resolve the problems of user independent development by establishing marketing groups whose responsibility is to identify products, or features of products, that user organizations will purchase.

In all of the firms surveyed the marketing group had primary responsibility for the crucial connection between determining user requirements and defining the product. The evolution of marketing departments in firms differed, however. In the initial years in many firms the identification and definition of a product was done by the technical staff. In some companies, the principal of the company had been producing a system for one company or industry and decided there was a potential market for a standardized, often more elaborate, version of the system. In these cases marketing staff were "added-on" as the product definitions activity required more time and resources than the technical staff could provide. In a number of these companies the marketing function grew informally out of the sales function. That is, sales staff were brought in to sell the product a technical staff had built and then the sales staff became involved in customer feedback. Only later did the sales group develop a more defined marketing function. In a few companies a formal business model was used from the beginning, which required a marketing department to assess customer preferences and market potential.

Marketing staff are the liaison and interpreters between the user organization and the development team, converting the users' perceived work requirements into software specifications for developers. Formally, the marketing group determines user needs and translates them into product requirements. Marketing personnel have a central role in deciding which features and functions will be developed, how they will be implemented, and which aspects of users' work will be affected by the software. Marketing groups are generally composed of people with formal marketing backgrounds and/or with experience in the industry to which the product is sold. They usually have little if any technical software development expertise.

The marketing department has the responsibility for taking over one step in the development process that formerly was done by the technical staff. Thus, marketing staff fulfills a specialized role in the development process and should not change the process in any substantial manner. That is, specializing the marketing and requirements determination stages is expected to improve those tasks but not change the dynamics of the design process. However, nearly all the companies surveyed report that incorporating a formal role for marketing staff in the development process has significant impact not only on the development process but also on the requirements definition, as we discuss below.

After establishing overall product requirements and functionality, marketing works with higher level managers in the development group to formulate functional or external specifications. In the development group, the number of layers of positions is typically related to the company's size. The larger companies usually have a vice president of development, a manager of development, product managers for each software system or application, programming groups composed of different level programmers and analysts, sometimes an applications specialist with substantive knowledge of the user organization, and various technical specialists who affiliate with different product groups at different times. Smaller companies have fewer levels, often with just a manager and programming team. In some cases, the implementation and customer support group is part of the development group and at other times it is part of the marketing group.

Conflicts within the Software Organization

Separating the marketing and development functions creates an underlying tension between those who participate in establishing and those designing product requirements. The traditional functional tensions between marketing and research and development, regardless of industry, have been discussed in the product design literature.[3]

Although this relationship has been studied in the manufacturing environment, it is worthy of discussion here for two reasons. First, traditional software design methodologies do not explicitly acknowledge either the marketing department's importance and scope of responsibility or the systemic conflicts between marketing and development departments related to their orientations and functions. Second, the unique nature of software development differentiates it from traditional manufacturing in several important aspects.[4]

The requirements stage of software development is generally conceived as identifying functionality that can be built to serve particular production or information functions. However, the guiding criterion for marketing decisions about product definition is product salability. This criterion may be different from user effectiveness and from technical efficiency. The process of selling a product through the market introduces requirements that may not reflect operational needs of end users and brings other sets of demands into the design process. Commenting on this difference, one vice president of development at a very large software company said, "There is a tension between marketing requirements and technology; marketing focuses on what will sell in the marketplace but [customers] ask for things that can't be produced." There is a tendency to request features and functions that add "bells and whistles" to the product to give it an edge over the competition and to make the product appealing and stand out. Marketing is focused on selling the system, and thus on the buyer of the system, rather than the user and the day-to-day operational requirements.

This marketing orientation, which may be necessary to sell commodity products, is viewed by those who design and develop the software with attitudes ranging from skepticism to outright distrust. One executive in development said, "The product requirements process is by definition contentious." Another realized there had to be a balance between defining a product for sale and for users: "There are things that sell and things that get installed; the `glitz' and `sexy' versus the meat and potatoes." One executive felt the marketing staff encouraged a "have it your way" mentality among customers by promising them systems that could meet all their needs. Marketing, he felt, either promised more than could be delivered or else asked for feasible but complex flexibility that customers would not really use but that would help to sell the system.

Some executives and developers feel that marketing fails to provide a vital information gathering function for determining functionality requirements; instead, development receives information that is "shined by marketing" and staff must struggle to "get user input unfiltered." One lead systems analyst went so far as to have his group conduct its own surveys and assessments of user needs (though they did so surreptitiously).

In summary, we found that, overall, software designers and developers identified three major characteristics of the marketing department's approach that, in their view, impeded effective requirements analysis. First, marketing people do not have sufficient technical knowledge to define the product requirements that potentially can be developed. The product definitions are described as vague, without enough specification to be implemented. Second, functionality is defined without consideration of technical constraints and tradeoffs. Third, marketing has its own objectives and perspective that mediate its definition of user needs. Some development groups regard product requirements established by marketing of dubious accuracy in terms of actual user needs.

A View From the Marketing Department

Marketing staff naturally hold a different view of their relationship with development. They see themselves providing a vital role in shaping the technical goals of development in ways that are commercially viable. Marketing views the technical orientation in the software development team as leading to a focus on optimizing technical performance with minimal awareness or tolerance of user needs that require inelegant or suboptimal designs (e.g., extensive menus, displays, and procedures in the interfaces that slow performance). One marketing manager recalled arguments with a programmer about modifying a program to provide the user simultaneous access to two different screens of information. The programmer was adamantly opposed because it meant "patching together" two different databases and it was "inefficient and inelegant." The marketing manager said that he could not convince the programmer that this functionality was vital to the user and thus was more important than "offending his aesthetic of elegant design."

This difference between marketing and development emerged in our case studies of a software vendor. At a sales meeting previewing a new product with a major customer, the marketing representative described the system as having the flexibility to access and process an accounting task by any criteria the user wanted. The lead developer, who was attending the meeting, knew that the accounting procedure was flexible only within certain parameters and told the customer this, contradicting the marketing representative. In a subsequent interview with the developer, he said that this was typical of marketing, promising anything the customer wanted to hear. However, he felt his integrity was being compromised by such promises and was thus compelled to speak out, even at the risk of offending the marketing representative and, possibly, losing the sale.

In a separate interview, the marketing representative described his annoyance with the programmer for jeopardizing the sale. He said the programmers lived in an unreal world of technology and did not understand how the system would really be used. Of course the software was not infinitely flexible, the marketing representative acknowledged, but it *would* do everything the customer would ever want to do; in this sense, it was perfectly honest to promise the unlimited functionality he claimed.

This typical undermining of the sales effort by technical staff, the marketing representative said, was the reason that he avoided having technical staff meet the customer.

Such differing visions between marketing and development were described by many interviewees. Marketing staff often commented that they were not highly regarded by the technical staff, but marketing people knew they played a vital role in ensuring that their products were competitive and could be sold. They felt the technical staff functioned in an isolated world of technology and did not understand the reality of what customers wanted. Marketing staff told of "hiding" the technical staff from their customers for fear that they would undermine their sales. The technical staff often regarded marketing with distrust, or at least skepticism, feeling annoyed about the types of demands marketing expected from the technology and the claims that were made for the product. In the interviews, a company president who had a technical background said, "Discipline is an important factor in design. Programmers are very disciplined, but content people [in marketing] have no sense of discipline. It is a struggle to get nonprogrammers to be rigorous." The developers and programmers interviewed usually said they recognized a need for marketing, but varied in their views about its importance.[5]

In summary, the development staff are driven by technical possibilities and focused on operational functionality of the systems they build, including some consideration of the end-user of the system. The marketing staff are focused on the commercial potential of the product and the functionality necessary to make it a competitive product, which includes accomplishing the tasks defined by the buyer in the customer organization. The president of a financial software company said they learned it requires "proper marketing, not development, to break into a segment."

The structural position and function of the marketing department is an avenue through which political and economic factors are introduced into the software design process. Marketing personnel explain customer requirements to designers and are thus the interpreters of market needs. Marketing's assessment of the selling points or product preferences of buyers will influence tradeoffs among functions and features, but marketing's view of product preferences is often filtered by economic and political factors that shape the dominant ideology of user firms. For example, as illustrated in the case studies that follow, managers in some user firms may place greater emphasis on reducing labor costs and thus purchase systems that increase control and efficiency rather than enhancing service flexibility or responsiveness. In contrast, some managers take a different approach and view features and functions that enhance the user firm's own product development, sales, and delivery as more important than features and functions that reduce labor costs. It is marketing's function to assess these preferences when formulating specific design objectives for a new software product, even when the preferred features are not always based on adding value through operational enhancements.

The User Organization

The foremost factor guiding software design is attention to the requirements of the user organization. An organization's requirements are determined in part by the functions of the organization and in part by the activities, needs, and working conditions of individual users. Determining individual user requirements poses substantial, yet often unacknowledged (or not seriously considered) problems: Who are the users? What are the irreconcilable differences in their needs? How are tradeoffs made among conflicting needs of different users or user groups?

These questions are not explicitly addressed in the development process. In formal design methodologies the ability to determine user needs is usually assumed with little attention paid to the problems in developing a consensus about what the system should do and how these objectives should be accomplished. These issues take on a new dimension of complexity when systems move from large, centralized, batch processing mainframe computers to smaller, distributed, decentralized, interactive computers and systems.

While it was clear that under earlier systems the term "user" referred to the hands-on manipulator of the hardware (usually at a clerical level), users of integrative systems span the entire range of organizational levels. An earlier generation of banking systems, for example, provided batch account updating functions and internal functions such as payroll. Users were the back office clerks who input the data and the vast portion of business day activities in the branch office was conducted with no computer interaction. A modern banking system, in addition to back office operations, directly supports all retail customer interactions, from teller and ATM transactions to customer service functions ranging from account openings to investments. It also handles many commercial account functions, interbank financial transactions, and provides online operations information to management. In addition to the traditional users who input information, there are interactive users across many departments and many levels. The broad array of functions now computerized and information utilized interactively (in strategic management decisionmaking, for example) results in many other people becoming secondary users.

Buyer versus User

The person who makes the purchasing decision in the user organization is one of the more important parties in determining system requirements, according to our interviewees. This is a particularly significant issue for vendors building large, expensive, and functionally comprehensive systems. These systems often represent substantial investments for the customer, particularly if the company also needs to purchase new hardware to run the software. The vendors interviewed developed systems ranging in cost from several thousands of dollars to over a million dollars. When a system represents a major investment and when it performs mission critical functions, the purchasing decision is made by upper levels of management and, in some instances in smaller companies, requires approval by the board of directors. The "buyer" becomes a "user" of particular interest to the vendor and one who may have a different set of interests than hands-on users of the system.

Thus, decisions made by the buyer may not reflect the needs of actual users. The president of a company producing financial systems (with an average price of $100,000) for midsized investment firms said the purchase decision is made by senior level managers, often partners, in the customer's organization; the system, however, provides support for lower level personnel. The "senior people don't recognize the need to change their systems procedure," the president said, "but the midlevel people are dying," needing to change their procedures and having appropriate computer support. The president of a company designing manufacturing software reported that they cater to the central engineering group that makes the purchasing decision although the engineers' priorities are not, in his view, always functionally important for "getting the job done." Consequently, they "have to walk the line, not make enemies, and be supportive of the groups that are our allies" who will make the purchase decision even if their requirements are not realistic and are in conflict with needs of the hands-on users.

As the vice president of development in a very large, diversified software company said, you have to

> sell to the highest level of management that you can get to, even though these people have a superficial understanding of the technology. The higher level managers are susceptible to buzz words, the fancy features. They don't understand the day-to-day requirements of the job.

The president of this company, in a separate interview, also discussed company strategy as designing initial products to appeal "to the highest level in the company. It is in the *enhancements* [after initial implementation] that hands-on user needs are met."

In one of our case studies the lead developer of a comprehensive banking software system for midsized banks described how the buyer-user conflicts affect his software design:

> You're going to deliver this to the teller so you want to make it nice for the teller, but more importantly I have the guy who's making the purchasing decision and I have a board of directors who have a set of criteria that they want to run their bank as profitably as possible. This means that they want their policies enforced; they want their costs minimized. I want to deliver them tools that will enforce their policy better than the competition can and have to stay no more expensive than the competition.

He finds that tellers complain about the features that "enforce policies," such as requiring all transactions that are not "typical transactions" (e.g., customers who make three or more separate transactions or queries about their bank balance) to be approved by a supervisor, which is enforced by "freezing" the teller screen until the supervisor issues approval. They also limit the amount of information available to tellers because "the first guideline is that banks purposely and deliberately keep tellers ignorant of what the bank is trying to do [because] they believe this is their greatest protection."

The tellers complain that they don't like to have to tell the customer that they can't handle the transaction; they don't like the fact that the only information they get is that there is a problem with this account that can only be handled by a supervisor "over there". The first thing tellers ask for is the override function [to use] if they don't think they happen to need a supervisor.

However, very far down on the list of goals of the board of directors is teller satisfaction. It's very clear that the management, the board of directors, and the tellers have two completely separate agendas. The board of directors likes it when they find out our system will stop "bad" transactions.

Another respondent reported that upper level management in banking was almost exclusively focused on productivity. Although, he said, as much direct labor "productivity as possible was achieved in the '70s technology" and the advantage of the current generation of systems is in added functionality and other benefits, he found that "if we can show an increase in productivity, this is an `in'; it always sells." This software vendor executive believed that upper level managers in user firms were misguided by not placing more emphasis on improving their operations through enhanced software functionality. However, he knew that he had to emphasize productivity improvement as the most important feature even if the potential gains were minimal.

The consensus among software vendors was that buyers who are not from MIS departments usually do not have sufficient technical background to effectively evaluate software systems' performance. The result is that they make purchases based on promises of productivity gains or on feature comparisons, the widest range of features and functionality, rather than on effectiveness for daily operations. The process of software acquisition often tends to be regarded as just another capital acquisition based on traditional purchasing criteria. The important purchasing criteria may not reflect actual operations requirements and/or may reflect the goals of only some of the people in the organization and may reflect only their specific organizational objectives.

User versus User

The multiple functions of mission critical integrative systems result in different requirements for features and functions for different users and in different priorities when making tradeoffs in performance. The different interests were associated by interviewees with the function and level of the user in the organization. In broad terms, top management was concerned about achieving cost savings through productivity increases from workers and tangible and predictable bottom line benefits. Midlevel managers focused on the functions of information gathering, reporting, and sometimes aids for supervisory tasks (worker performance data and/or pacing). Among the lower level users, the interest was in functionality that would make task performance easier and service delivery more effective.

The specific objectives varied by the type of application and system. In a banking system, for example, the bank's marketing people were generally interested in the information-gathering features of the system (e.g., data fields they could add to the teller's transaction record that would require the teller to collect information from the customer during a transaction), managers were interested in security features that would minimize improper transactions, while tellers wanted a system that had good response time, required a minimum of keystrokes to process a transaction, and that gave them access to customer account information.

A company that produced software for programmable controllers (for machine tools) found each group in the customer's organization had significantly different motives for adopting automation. The vice president of the software firm found that "Central engineering has a list of what they want computerized, a `wish list' of what automation should do `because that's what automation is'." He noted that customers' engineers are enamored of systems with the greatest number of features and functionality for its "theoretical possibilities." At the "plant level and shop floor, they are more interested in getting the job done, less interested in `computers'" intrinsically as technology. This software vendor reported having a hard time convincing engineering management, who make the purchasing decisions, to buy "the product to do the job" rather than the one with the most features and functions.

Another vendor producing software for job shop and inventory control also commented that managers make requests that are inappropriate for their needs. The president of this firm said that "half of the management [in their customer firms] don't know how to manage, half don't know their company's business, and a third have both problems. To deal with the needs of the customer, we go into the bowels of the company and determine what the needs are and tell management what those needs are." In general there was a common view among vendors that "users don't know what they need," and "what they want is not what they need."

Users seem to suggest a substantial portion of the ideas for software enhancements and added functionality *after* the basic system has been designed. User groups were identified as an important source of ideas. However, we found that middle management or staff specialists, not lower level end users, were most likely to attend user group meetings.

Not surprisingly, the different functions of users and their different uses of the software system led to conflicting needs requirements in the cases we investigated in depth. The conflicts that we found among users could be characterized as arising from either vertical interactions with supervision, control, access, and level of decisionmaking, or from horizontal interactions concerning workflow, scope of activity/tasks, and responsibility for different functions.

In one bank we studied, horizontal issues involved the distribution of tasks between the centralized back office and the local branch offices. Tradeoffs among alternative software designs determined such matters as how much sorting and processing of transactions (e.g., credit card payments, different types of loan payments, etc.) was done by tellers or in the back office (where nearly all of it had been done previously), and how much information customer service representatives in the branches were allowed to change on an account and which aspects were reserved for back office personnel (who wanted to exercise greater control). Specific features and functions of the software system determined the splits in processing activity and responsibility between alternative horizontal functions, creating a sense of winners and losers. Different software design decisions could have forced a different allocation of work activity and therefore a different balance of responsibility.

Vertical organizational issues in the same case study included the degree of autonomy or decisionmaking power allowed tellers. Features of the software were designed to restrict the types of transactions that tellers could process, requiring a supervisor's override for types of transactions and conditions specified by the bank's programming staff in accordance with formal company policies. The result was to constrain not only the tellers' autonomy, but also flexibility and adjustment to branch or transaction-specific conditions. Again, the particular configuration of software features and functions clearly affected these vertical working relationships and, ultimately, the overall effectiveness of the software used in this service delivery operation.

Decisions on the final features and functions in software design often require making direct tradeoffs among different users' needs. Even when requirements are not in direct conflict, vendors find they must limit the temptation to incorporate all requests. Some vendors experienced severe development and financial problems by trying to build systems that were too large and complex, driven, in part, by trying to make them be all things to all users. At one very large company, they "took every customer request during the designing process and implemented it, resulting in a `tower of babel' which was a collection of functions without a central architecture." One common lesson learned was not to be overly ambitious in new product development; this meant choices had to be made and some user requirements would not be met. In making those choices, they would respond to some users more than others and the "user" they paid closest attention to was the buyer.

There are also strategic design choices about the degree of change and innovation both the user and vendor firms have to make. These are choices about whether one should engage in incremental or radical innovation and the pitfalls of listening too closely to current users. If a choice is made for more radical innovations, a problem arises about deciding which new features serve organizational goals of innovation and those which are just bells and whistles. Making these strategic choices involves carefully sifting through the implications of each choice and finding criteria that balance operational needs of the user firm with sales and marketing concerns of the vendor.

Making Strategic Choices

The differing organizational and functional roles of different groups in the user organizations lead to different types of preferences and needs for system requirements. Our survey examined the consequences of these different structural positions for the *content* of software specifications. Two types of requirements were found: incremental or a more visionary orientation. The incremental view focuses on satisfying users' current needs by improving upon previous software or a noncomputerized process. The alternative software design perspective is to develop a product of the future, embodying long-range goals and managerial objectives, but sometimes this involved development of bells and whistles guided more by developers' imaginations than by users' work requirements.

Incremental Software Development

The interviews and case studies indicate that user defined designs tend to be built around existing job requirements for the work "as is" rather than around work processes that are reconceptualized to make use of advances in software design and hardware technology. In the view of one vice president of development, users "just want to computerize existing functions and procedures, even when they are not efficient." Interviewees often cited the example of user specifications for a program that merely reproduced on the computer the exact same paper forms previously used. The vendors often experienced user resistance to using new technology as an opportunity to reorganize existing procedures and processes. Other, more consequential examples included users' perceived needs to preserve existing workflow steps, procedures, and reporting requirements that could be eliminated or changed with new software systems. Such software development may be described as bounded or incremental. The changes requested by users mainly focus on increasing speed and efficiency, generally small changes that do not change work procedures.

Because many new systems simply replicate features and functions of older technologies, the limitations of the older systems are built into new ones. Technological advances often are not utilized in designing the new software. In one example from retail operations, hardware limitations of previous generation computers limited the size of numbers in a field, requiring customer account numbers to be broken into two parts and entered in two fields. Although this is no longer necessary with new computers, one vendor reports that their clients require new software to have multipart account number capabilities, even though the feature is actually a drawback, requiring two entries instead of one. In another instance, a vendor introducing new systems to banks found that banks resist adopting software that changed existing procedures. The proposed changes were for different screen layouts, different sequencing of transactions steps, and displays including more information. Consequently, the company designed powerful new banking workstations to replicate the screens, features, functions, and structure of technically obsolete systems developed in the mid-1970s and that they were trying to replace. There is a tendency for users to preserve existing procedures with limited critical appraisal of the rationality of existing procedures. One software designer termed this phenomenon "limitations turned features."

Development that was bounded by incremental changes requested by users was recognized as a drawback of user-driven design. If users drive the direction of product development, executives in several companies said they would "miss the needs of those who aren't yet customers," and if "you don't expand your customer base may be lost to the competition" which may be developing more advanced systems. Importantly, marketing and engineering personnel in the software company see this as an example of users' limited vision and consequently may discount user input. One vendor commented that "you can't be literal about customer requests," and another said the "user doesn't have the vision of how the product could be developed. It is the vendor who can assemble a broader view because of contact with many users." A common complaint of the software developers we interviewed is that users want their work tasks on new computer systems to follow the same procedures found in manual or previous computer systems. It was pointed out that most users have limited technical knowledge about computer systems, an area in which they are not trained or educated, and users usually lack the broader view of the organization that allows them to evaluate the overall requirements of service or production.

The advantage of incremental development is that it preserves existing work procedures and may be more conducive to preserving existing working conditions. User-driven design approaches provide greater assurances that software designs will meet the needs of users and the requirements of the work process. As discussed above by the president of one software firm, the central engineering group had a wish list based on the theoretical possibilities of computerization whereas the plant and shopfloor users "just want [functionality] to get the job done." Moreover, users are more likely to accept and use a new system if it reflects actual operating conditions. User-defined systems are less likely to be dysfunctional for existing service delivery or production.

The resulting dilemma is that although looking beyond the immediate work requirements is necessary to advance techno-logical development and work systems, ignoring end-users may lead to dysfunctional systems. It was not evident from our interviews or case studies that there are standard methods or guidelines to distinguish between incremental development that serves the needs of users and that which leads to merely enhanc-ing an obsolete system.

Bells, Whistles, and "Visionary" Development

Software developers and designers often try to develop more visionary products than suggested by users. In addition to the developers' own contributions, we found that input is solicited from managers in the user organization and is shaped by the public and industry news media. Managerial influence from the user organization is obviously important in the development process because of management's position and power; if nothing else, management makes the buy decision. However, vendors reported that input from high level managers is also sought because they are seen as having "more global vision, a vision of the future, and of the potential of the system, while the user just wants it to fit into existing operations." Vendors, therefore, turn to managers who are removed from the detail work of the production process for broader views of effective new processes, organizational forms, and service orientations.

Visionary software development may also lead to emphasis on bells and whistles. Focusing on the theoretical potential of the technology may lead to developments that excite developers and managers but have little relationship to optimal work require-ments. The trade media were discussed as an important factor influencing visionary software development. Obvious journal-istic considerations tend to direct the focus of both vendor and user on the new, the next generation, the bells and whistles, rather than the mundane. The media exert a powerful influence that shapes the expectations of marketing people in software companies and managers in user companies. One executive said that there was mutual responsibility for media hype because the vendor promotes the most advanced features, or potential features, to differentiate the product and to attract the media. Vendors "are looking for the next new technology, one that is not well understood, and they highlight the `sizzle' through their sales force." A vice president of development said, "It is a double-edged sword; you need the press to get your story out, yet they present it with hype and create unrealistic expectations."

The result of a technology emphasis and futuristic focus of media and marketing is that software development may be guided by spectacular imagination with little correspondence to actual work requirements. The "focus on technology," an interviewee commented, "may result in something slick but useless. It leads the customer to want things that are not possible to develop." For example, when evaluating new software systems, managers often rely on media accounts of cutting-edge capabilities as a basis for comparing features of existing systems and writing purchase specifications for many bells and whistles. This has led to what one software executive described as "features that sell the product and features that are used."

User requirements are not just operational needs, but also the "selling requirements." The success of the system, for a vendor, depends first on its salability and, second, on its performance. In the case studies we found that when the development team and marketing mangers met to discuss user requirements, the important requirements were those that would attract users to purchase their system instead of a competitor's system or instead of using an internal MIS department or a custom software house. Discussion often centered on functionality: What features and functions did users want and what features and functions would make this system competitive?

One systems designer commented:

> We spend a lot of time putting features into our system that the customers use to make their buying decision, but that I never see implemented in actual use of the system. It's always a struggle between installation and marketing concerns, between what to put in as marketing code versus installable code. Marketing code is code that makes the buyer continue to talk to you

whereas installation code is that which the customer will likely want to install. There are different programming issues with each. If I know that some code has very little likelihood of ever being installed, I don't believe it is a sin to make the wrong program worse.

As a vendor we have different pressures than an internal MIS department. An MIS department in a firm knows exactly what to deliver and you have some control over what your end-user will take. In our case we have a bunch of people [from the user company] who aren't technical and they want to know, "Is it zippy?" "Does it paint the screen quickly?" all sorts of things that should have no bearing on the criteria for making a purchase decision.... We have a customer who doesn't understand all the technological issues.

The bells and whistles aspect of visionary development is evident in many artificial intelligence (AI) applications, development of expert systems, and addition of natural language capabilities to applications software. These are not necessarily frivolous developments, *per se,* but may distort products in particular applications. For example, one developer of banking software discussed his plans to incorporate natural language capabilities in the next release of their system because executives and buyers like the ability to make inquiries of the system without learning specific commands. However, the system is actually used regularly by lower level personnel in several departments. These regular users learn the necessary commands, which are much faster than natural language queries. Natural language query appeals to executives who are enamored of the idea of access to information without training. In practice, however, the developer predicted it would rarely, if ever, be used beyond the first few months after adoption. A vice president of development in another company said, "nobody currently uses AI in business, but we have to make the promise to include it `tomorrow' in order to sell our products." There was widespread recognition among the interviewed software executives and developers that part of what they build is necessary to satisfy media-shaped expectations of the office of the future, even though the features are seldom used.

In another company, one executive found that customers wanted the flexibility to customize nearly all of the system features. He believed that the users would not use such broad flexibility, but, to sell the system, he felt compelled to include it even though it would make the system needlessly complex and difficult to maintain across sites. These customers, he complained, "want bells and whistles, things they don't need; they are often going toward `automation' without having an idea of where they are going or what they want. They want customizing functions that are used less than 10 percent of the time. Why are they willing to risk the success of a project [because of the added complexity and unreliability of customization] for something that contributes less than 10 percent to their goal?"

Vendors said they incorporate bells and whistles in their software design because these features sell the product by differentiating it in an increasingly crowded marketplace. Vendors find that "since customers don't really understand the technology, they look for the minute differences between products, for more spectacular features and functions." Our survey respondents readily acknowledged that designing features and functions to make their products competitive in the marketplace is an objective that may differ from user effectiveness.

Thus, in vendor produced software, the commercial nature of the design and selling process can lead to distortion of requirements analysis based on user needs. There are also strategic choices that vendors need to make about the direction of software and for users to make about the degree of innovation in technology and organization they wish to undertake with new technology.

Software Development for a Commercial Market

This chapter discussed a number of factors that shape software design, focusing on how the structure of the design process shapes design outcomes. In the next chapter we focus on specific software design decisions. We find that design decisions are shaped by the interplay between the organizational structure, individual preferences and values, and the influence of the market. When taking the broad view of design, it becomes clear that an individual designer's or design team's decisions reflect an array of factors. It is for this reason we argue that solutions to design problems are limited if they focus only on individual designer decisions. Our survey identified three important dimensions of organizations, structure, and product development (see Figure 3.1):

- the imperatives of developing a product for a commercial market;
- the varied interests and functions of users;
- the inherent conflicts in organizations related to power and hierarchy.

Each of these dimensions poses organizational issues requiring tradeoffs in the design of effective software for service sector applications. It is important to understand the dynamics involved in each set of issues and how organizational structure and the relationship between vendor and user organizations shape and bias design outcomes.

The necessary commercial orientation of the software vendor adds a market dimension and product imperative that is not addressed in the current literature on software design (although there may be similarity in some of the issues to internally developed software). Software development by vendors must not only fulfill widespread operational needs but also be commercially viable, and sometimes these are divergent requirements.

The process of determining design requirements is significantly shaped by the marketing department of the vendor and the buyer in the user firm. The marketing function is created in vendors to address the problems of distance between software users and developers and to assess commercial requirements to make the product competitive. The problems arising from adding marketing staff to the development process include the different orientations between marketing and development groups and the tensions that result.

Conflicts between marketing and development groups are often attributed to personality differences. Although our interviewees confirm this type of difference, we find the essential tension is not personal but functional. The marketing department role is to introduce the commercial requirements of a generic product into a software development process that is focused on technical achievements. This functional difference is frequently exacerbated by the marketing staff's lack of technical expertise and the technical staff's lack of commercial orientation and considerable distance from the end-user. The marketing function is the agency through which managerial objectives in the user firm and the dynamics of market competition confront

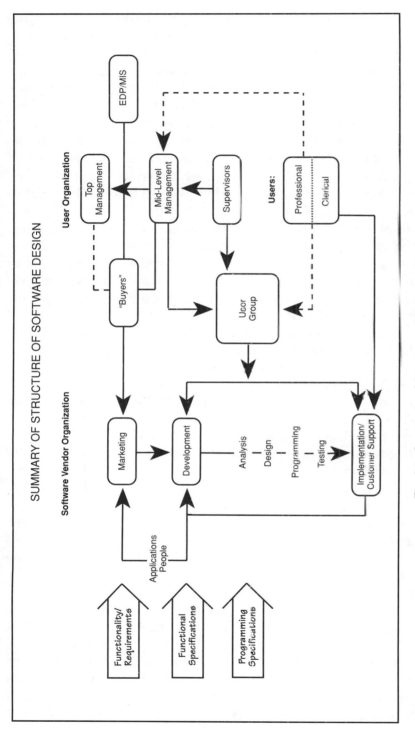

Fig. 3.1. Summary of Structure of Software Design.

engineering objectives. The influence of marketing over technical objectives will likely increase as software matures into commodity products.

Features and functions for commercial viability diverge from user effectiveness of the product in part because of the procurement approaches of the user firm. In many firms our interviews and case studies revealed that the mission-critical functionality and expense of new software (usually significantly greater than the existing system) moves the purchase decision to higher levels of management. In terms of organizational structure, they tend to be far removed from operations though below the executive management ranks involved in strategic decisionmaking. (The buyer is not discussed in formal models of user requirements analysis in part because in internal organization decisions the buyer is often the user or from the user department. In purchases of large systems from vendors, buyers are often senior level managers though procurement evaluation may include people from the MIS department.)

According to software vendors, buyers who are not from MIS departments usually do not have sufficient technical background to effectively evaluate a software system's performance. Through their role in handling software procurement, these individuals become the source for expressing ultimate user preferences (see Chapter 8 which discusses software procurement issues for the user organization). The result is that they may make purchases based on comparing the range of features and functionality rather than on effectiveness for daily operations, leading to a "bells and whistles" bias in the system and emphasis on management functions that may detract from operational performance and service delivery. Software designs may incorporate the concerns of different users, but ultimately the system must exhibit those particular features and functions requested by the buyer. When conflicts arise, in the words of one developer, "the guy who signs the check wins!"

This chapter has focused on how organizational structure leads to conflicting views on design. This discussion also illustrates the theoretical points made in earlier chapters that organizations must be viewed as a conglomeration of different groups with divergent interests. Understanding the structure of design provides a road map of interests but requires detailed analysis of how design decisions are shaped by these structural characteristics. In the cases that follow we show how these different issues came into play in the design and use of software. The common thread in each case is how decisions were socially shaped and how they represented tradeoffs among different groups. The cases also illustrate a range of different types of decisions made in design.

Endnotes

1. Packaged software accounted for 70 percent of total software revenues in 1988 (U.S. Department of Commerce, 1988) and in 1985, 79 percent of all packaged software revenue was for medium to large-scale (non-PC) systems (U.S. Department of Commerce, 1986). A growing proportion cf packaged software was being produced by independent software vendors. By 1985, software sales by independent software vendors equaled software sales by hardware vendors, each with 40 percent of the total market, the remaining 20 percent held by systems integrators (U.S., Department of Commerce, 1986). Employment in the prepackaged software industry grew dramatically from 87,000 employees in 1988 to 133,000 by 1992 (U.S. Department of Labor, 1992). Hardware companies such as IBM and DEC also increased their sales of software, developed new applications packages, and commercialized internal proprietary products. It was estimated that for the five largest hardware manufacturers, software sales accounted for 27 to 35 percent of total revenues in 1987 and that by the mid-1990s the majority of these firms' revenues would come from software sales (Field, 1987).

2. Although internal MIS departments generally do not have a distinct marketing group, some have people who serve marketing functions. These people conduct user requirement assessments of the "customers" in the organization and may try to "sell" the services of the MIS department to other departments in the organization. Some of the issues raised here may be relevant to internal MIS departments; it is an area we did not address but is in need of further research. Some of the issues particular to software vendors are also discussed by Ling(1988).

3. These issues in product design have been discussed by Rosenthal (1992) and Souder (1987). In manufacturing situations, new approaches suggest that design begin with marketing notions of customer requirements, but that they then be linked to particular choices about the product's design. One such technique, called "the house of quality" (Hauser and Clausing, 1988), has been adopted in several industries.

4. It is generally recognized that there are significant differences in managing software and hardware research and development. However, Cusamano (1991) argues that software development can be successfully organized and managed in factories similar to manufacturing.

5. Most striking in our findings are the reports that senior management in the software firms does not always recognize the significant differences and inherent tensions between the two groups. Some CEOs report no apparent

problem between the two groups and assume that marketing barely controls product definition, while their development group may report much greater conflict with marketing. The executives interviewed expressed sometimes contradictory views about the relative importance of marketing and development groups. The majority of CEOs felt the problems that existed between the two groups were the result of the overly technical orientation of development people. There is strong consensus that a marketing orientation should drive product design. At the same time, the CEOs interviewed felt that the limited technical backgrounds of marketing personnel restricted the contribution they could make to the development process even though they were formally charged with defining the product.

Thus, the professed importance of the marketing role does not appear to be fully supported by actual practice. It is clear that, although formally the marketing *function* drives product innovation and development, the technical staff are valued much more highly than the marketing staff. (In very large companies, however, marketing executives were usually more active in company management.) A contributing factor may be that 21 of the 23 companies surveyed were started with a single product focus for a specific market niche with which the CEO was familiar and marketing executives paid little attention to formal marketing strategies. Establishing their product success initially required only technical strength and market opportunity. As the product and the market mature, they are aware of marketing's increased importance but, in practice, the CEOs appear hesitant about giving the marketing department substantial authority over design (particularly to overrule decisions by the development group). As discussed in these chpaters, it is also not evident that marketing departments have the best means of determining user needs.

II

CASE STUDIES
OF
SOFTWARE DESIGN

II

Case Studies of Software Design

Part I positioned us to understand social shaping of software design by reviewing the relevant literature and developing a set of organizing concepts and frameworks. The core of Part II is Chapters 4, 5 and 6, which present case studies of software designed to enhance service delivery in three different industries: transactions in retail banking, field service of equipment, and medical care in hospitals. Each of these case studies presents considerable detail about key features and functions of particular software systems and their impacts on the workplace and service delivery. We also include relevant background on the industry being studied and discussion of underlying operating objectives and constraints of the organization adopting the software systems.

Chapter 7, which presents our analysis of each individual case and selected cross-case comparisons, draws on the concepts and frameworks from Part I. We concentrate on the organizational issues, particularly the role of workplace dynamics over control of work and use of power in the organization as it influences software development. We also address additional issues, such as the role of producing a commodity product in a commercial market, to demonstrate other aspects of the social shaping of technology design. Chapter 7 also presents conclusions about how one may proceed to map the social context of software design to, perhaps, more directly shape technology in ways that are more effective.

4

Banking and a
Tale of Two Systems

The 1980s were the worst of times for many in the banking industry. Following the deregulation of the early 1980s, the industry nearly went into shock as more than 2,000 banks and savings and loans failed. Banking could no longer be characterized as a staid enterprise of blue pin-striped suits and "banker's hours." Deregulation and competition made traditional ways of doing business obsolete and, in many cases, disastrous for banks that failed to adapt. A record number of banks were unable to make the transition successfully and, among those that survived, it was a difficult period that required them to reassess their operations.

Software developed for the banking industry during this period reflected the contradictions of an industry in transition. Some banks tried to maintain their traditional values and operating procedures in their system design requirements. However, some software developers found that changes in the banking environment and their own software market required them to consider different values and methods of service delivery in their designs for new systems. A brief account of the industry's evolution with computer systems sets the stage for the cases presented in this chapter.

Banks are large users of computer systems and were among the first large commercial institutions to use computers. Design of banking systems has been affected by changes in technology, external regulation, competition, and the labor market. These changes have combined to define the operational objectives of new computer system designs.

During the 1950s and 1960s, banks installed large mainframe systems for back office transaction processing, such as account updating, on a batch system mode. By the 1970s large banks had invested extensively in mainframe computer systems and smaller banks were beginning to adopt computer systems as prices dropped and smaller computers became more powerful. In both large and small banks, computer applications were increasingly introduced to support front office transactions of tellers and customer service representatives in branch offices. Because these systems make data instantly available for a variety of steps in processing transactions, they integrate people throughout the banking organization.

Traditionally departments of banks have little direct interaction with each other. The three major divisions or offices, back office, central office, and branch office, are usually in different locations. An online computerized system provides direct linkages among all departments, providing a degree of organizational integration. For example, an account change entered by a teller is immediately available to everyone in every location in the bank. Some systems also allow individuals to communicate directly when one department posts information to other departments (see Figure 4.1).

In the retail banking industry nonmanagerial employees perform mostly transaction processing tasks. Teller systems are tied into central databases on mainframes to check account balances and track cash deposits received by each teller, but the system does not allow tellers to alter the database nor does it support other branch office operations. Prior to the 1980s, there was little variability in markets. Banks were organized with a high division of labor, highly formalized procedures, and rigid rules of authority. Little emphasis was placed on employee initiative and management saw little advantage in trying to be more competitive, particularly for consumer demand deposit accounts. As one commentator observed: "banks usually hired people who were good at taking orders and accomplishing well-defined, routine tasks . . . people who want a less demanding career." This was characteristic of employees at all levels of the bank. "The role of `the three 3s' summed up the challenge of being a bank executive: Borrow at 3 percent. Lend at a 3-point spread. And be on the golf course by 3 p.m." (Meehan, 1992, p. 86).

The two cases in this chapter examine a traditional banking system in use and the design decisions in the development of a new system.[1] The cases illustrate why features that may be dysfunctional for end users are developed, how software vendors must negotiate among competing interests (and ultimately

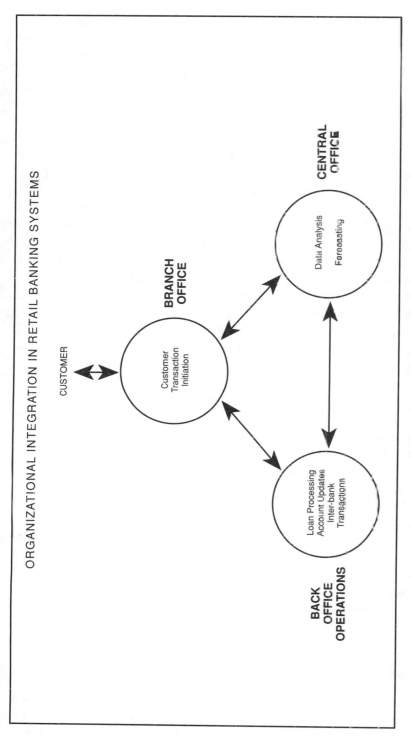

Fig. 4.1. Organizational Integration in Retail Banking Systems.

respond to the preferences of those who make the purchase decision), and how software design decisions partially reflect the values of powerful constituencies, and thus may not correspond to the functional needs of end users or their customers.

Computerizing Tradition

"Big Bank" followed the rather traditional practices of New England banking. It invested conservatively and ran its operations in a hierarchical fashion, with policies, procedures, and decisions issued from its central offices with military-like authority. It was a well-established bank that historically saw its primary focus on commercial accounts. State banking regulations did not permit banks to have branches in more than one city, which limited the size of a bank's retail operations. Thus, Big Bank regarded its retail operations as a necessary part of its operations as a full service bank but not a major source of revenue. In the mid-1980s, after this regulation was repealed, the bank expanded its retail banking operations by acquiring several smaller banks and increasing marketing efforts for retail accounts.

The software systems at Big Bank were purchased in the 1970s as a shell, which was then modified by the in-house programming department. The system handled most teller-customer transactions, many of the customer service representative transactions, such as address change and account history inquiries, and back office transactions such as account updating. The bank's systems department modified the software over time to handle new functions and integrate new branch offices acquired in its expansion. Big Bank's operating policies and procedures and their information systems were clearly designed to achieve four essential objectives: accuracy, efficiency, security, and customer service. We examined the functionality of the systems, design considerations and developments made by the bank, and the actual use of the systems.[2]

Operating Objectives in Banking

Four objectives proved to underlie the essential characteristics of the system and banking in general: accuracy, efficiency, security, and customer service.[3] The relative importance of each, however, may vary from one banking activity to another. Tradeoffs among them also may be necessary (e.g., accommodating some customer requests may compromise security or accuracy). Each of these objectives needs to be appreciated in terms of the kinds of requirements that it sets for the design of software-based systems.

Accuracy   Accuracy is nonnegotiable in retail banking.   All accounts must be correct and kept fully up-to-date. Transactions must be verifiable. A considerable amount of cash is handled at each teller window and regular or significant discrepancies in cash balances cannot be tolerated. Periodic cash tabulations and reconciliations are necessary. The bank must also keep accurate information on the names, addresses, social security numbers, and other items for every account held by each of its customers.

Efficiency   Retail banking is highly competitive and there is strong pressure to reduce unnecessary costs, particularly after deregulation led to intensified competition. Efficient transaction processing is, therefore, important and is facilitated through automation of teller functions. The speed with which data can be entered into the computer-based system and inquiries made through it depends on both the response time of the technology and the skill of the tellers who use it. To the extent that the system is designed for ease of use, skill requirements can be reduced. Nevertheless, with turnover in the teller ranks being frequent, training is an important prerequisite for achieving efficiency through automation.

Security   Tellers deal with money and information about money. Both of these dimensions call for security measures. Someone must be made accountable for the security of the cash that flows in and out of retail banks. When there are questions about the legitimacy of customer requests for withdrawals, someone must be authorized to approve or deny requests. Account information needs to be available to tellers and to customers but not to unauthorized parties.

Customer Service   In branch banking, service to the customer includes the ability to execute requested transactions in a smooth and courteous manner, provide account information as needed, and to have the flexibility to respond to contingencies as they arise without unduly inconveniencing the customer.

The skill of good management is achieving the proper balance among these objectives. For example, achieving absolute security and accuracy might require extensive checking and rechecking of each transaction by tellers and extensive supervision and surveillance of tellers. This, however, might result in long delays for customers and low productivity of tellers. The ways these different objectives are balanced depends upon the values within the organization (as reflected in organizational structure and operating procedures) and pressures from the external environment.

Approaches to assuring accuracy and security may vary according to the degree of trust managers have in tellers, the amount of autonomy provided to the tellers, and the skills of tellers. The extent to which customer service can be compromised may depend upon whether customers can find better service at other banks and the pressure on productivity is partially determined by profit margins. Both of these can reflect the degree of competition in the market.

The design of the banking software is the formal specification of how these objectives are to be implemented in operations. As we set forth in the first two chapters, this is not always an objective assessment and may reflect the needs of some users over others. Thus, design tradeoffs may also reflect assumptions and values about tellers, the market environment, and the day-to-day operating environment, as well as the power relationships within the organization.

The banking system at Big Bank was designed to implement the four traditional banking objectives at all of its branch offices. The designers at the central office had continually updated and modified the system over a decade. The software designers and managers were satisfied that they had a system which achieved their objectives and carefully regulated transactions in the branch offices uniformly.

Automation and the Teller

Big Bank's IBM system recorded a wide range of payment, withdrawal, and deposit transactions. The terminal, specially designed for these banking functions, had separate keys for each of the different kinds of transactions. The software and communications network allowed tellers to view certain account information. System access was controlled by plastic identification cards that were issued to tellers and their supervisors and passed through a card reader attached to each terminal. The bank provided training to all new tellers, including hands-on training. To be a teller, one must be conversant with the features and functions of the system (as well as having other proficiencies such as the counting and handling of cash).

Each minute aspect of the teller system has some effect on each teller, but most are likely to be imperceptible because they are quickly perceived as "the way the job is done." The terminal and the software that process the transactions do not fundamentally change the job activity or level of responsibility or skill of the teller. Furthermore, the teller system had remained basically the same since its introduction at the bank over a decade earlier. Some branches had an older terminal, while an updated model was installed in others.

Routine Use of the Teller System

Typical actions, aside from entering the transactions themselves that are required by the system, include:
- signing on at beginning of the day using the teller's plastic identification card.
- using the teller card to override hold status messages (discussed in the next section).
- settlement of the daily transactions at each teller's window, which requires "batching out" work according to several standard categories (cash in, checks in, savings deposits in, cash out).
- verifying the cash balance at the teller's window at the end of the day (teller counts cash, then compares it with the amount that the computer has tallied from the day's starting balance, inflows, and outflows.

More specialized use of the system includes activities such as: making account inquiries, correcting transactions, tabulating and transmitting transaction information ("batching out"), and various types of incoming items (cash, checks, savings deposits).

Tellers reported that the system was very reliable and easy to use. No troublesome operating errors were detected. When the host system was down, withdrawal transactions could not be verified for adequacy of funds through the online connection with the centralized account database. However, tellers could continue to process transactions on the teller terminals to generate receipts for customers and keep track of the transactions.

When, on very rare occasions, the "controller system" went down, the terminals could not function and tellers conducted transactions manually (customers did not get a computer-generated receipt) and later entered all the transactions when the system service was restored and time permitted.

An experienced teller could use the system to complete the end of day "settling" function in as little as five minutes by monitoring cash early and "batching" throughout the day (these are considered tricks of the trade that the tellers learn informally from each other). Less experienced tellers may take a half-hour or more to settle.

Nonroutine Uses of the System

Unannounced cash audits of each teller are conducted every month. The head teller may use any of the terminals to audit a teller's balances at any time. Certain types of audits (e.g., a teller's use of the "correct deposit from savings account" feature to correct an error) could signal possible irregularities.

The teller system was designed to provide a certain amount of allocation of responsibility between tellers and their supervisors. Under a specified set of exceptional situations (defined by management at the bank through the setting of software parameter settings), the teller's terminal will freeze with a message about the account on the screen. At this point, the requested transaction can be completed only if an officer's authorization card (as distinguished from the teller's card) is passed through a card reader on the terminal. The purpose of this procedure is clear. When, for example, an account shows an exceptional amount of activity on a single day (more than three transactions), or a stop order condition is already on an account, a deliberate decision must be made by a responsible employee before more withdrawals are executed on an account. For example, a flashing message appears on the screen whenever a withdrawal over $50 is entered for a new account (less than six months old). If a withdrawal is being entered for over $50, an override using the officer's card override is required. For a larger attempted withdrawal on a new account, a customer service representative (CSR) must check the activity on the account before an override is attempted. Operating policies established at the central office state that officer's cards are assigned to only CSRs and branch managers, neither of whom is regularly stationed behind the teller windows.

The System in Use

Retail banking is a service and all aspects of automation, including the teller system, must be assessed in terms of customer impacts. In the case of the teller system, impacts on the customer are minimal compared to having no automation at all. In either case, the customer gets a receipt for the completed payment or deposit. With regard to the time of transaction, assuming the system is functioning properly, processing time depends more on the exchange of paper and currency between the teller and the customer than the time to key in the transaction itself.

The functionality requirements of the teller system are: to keep account of teller cash balance; check current customer transaction against account status and provide customer history; provide immediate access to recent checking account information, print customer receipts, identify customers with special account privileges; and keep track of all transaction types and amounts. The system does not change account information, it only records and monitors transactions; all account changes are entered, verified, and processed in the back office operations of proof and transit each night.

The features and functions for the implementation of these system requirements are for accounting and monitoring systems. Functions are provided to track the cash balance for the day. At the end of the day the teller must verify cash in the drawer against system accounting; initially there were no online editing capabilities (that is, there was no provision for the teller to correct mistakes without a supervisor's approval).

The designers saw very little latitude in making these decisions about the system. They saw themselves as designing the system to enforce the bank's policies that were established by bank management. However, in implementing the formal rules and procedures of the bank, the designers had to anticipate contingencies that the system would be able to handle. Unlike procedures and rules that are established through policy manuals and depend on enforcement by humans, the computer system must be designed with preestablished priorities for handling all conflicting conditions and necessary tradeoffs between the different objectives of the bank and the user job requirements.

For routine banking operations, the system enhanced operations. It was faster, provided more information, and eliminated paperwork previously required. However, for nonroutine situations, such as multiple transactions in separate visits to the teller by the same person in a single day, the system was designed to enforce formal banking procedures with emphasis on security rather than operational ease as the primary goal.[4] The result, as we observed and is the general case in organizations, was that the bank did not operate in the way it was envisioned by central office management and systems designers. This became strikingly apparent on our first field visit to a branch office.

In one large downtown branch the customers streamed in the moment the doors were unlocked. A young man in work clothes, looking a bit out of place among the men and women in freshly pressed business suits, waited his turn in line and then ambled up to one of the seven teller windows. He was met with a cheery, "Good morning, Bob!" Bob greeted her by name and asked for his account balance, made a withdrawal, and then purchased a money order made out to the local utility company. His business completed, he left the window to address the envelope for the money order.

A short while later Bob had again made his way to the front of the line and to another teller window where he was greeted by name again. The first teller said to us, *sotto voce*, "Watch what happens." As we looked on we saw Bob begin the same routine, first asking for his account balance and then trying to make a withdrawal. However, the teller's screen froze because the withdrawal was Bob's fourth transaction of the day (he made two separate transactions in his first trip to the teller). As we looked around for a customer service representative (the officer) to come investigate and brandish her privileged plastic card, we instead saw the teller reach over to her neighbor's station. Picking up a plastic card, she unfroze her terminal and provided Bob with his withdrawal and money order.

This was only the second of five trips to the teller that Bob made that morning, each with the same routine. The tellers all knew Bob well and were accustomed to his biweekly routine for paying the bills for the small painting company he owned. (No one seemed to know the rhyme or reason for his routine, though one teller thought perhaps he was illiterate or learning disabled and could not keep a checking account balance.) The tellers also knew Anna, who was withdrawing $15,000 from an account she had opened only a week before. (A successful businesswoman and longstanding customer at the bank, she had just recently opened another account for a new business venture.) And they

knew Pielar when she made her fourth and fifth separate transactions of the day (the tellers thought that either she was not
accustomed to the routines in U.S. banking or was not very
organized).

Throughout the morning, every 5 or 10 minutes, one of the
tellers sought out the sole officer's card that would unlock her
"frozen" terminal. Only once or twice an hour would a teller
inform an unknown customer (or a known customer with an
unknown circumstance) that her terminal was not working
properly and that she needed the assistance of her supervisor.

If tellers operated the computer system as designed, it would
slow transactions significantly and be an almost constant inter-
ruption to the supervisor. To maintain efficient operations, the
managers in all the branches we visited had given the officer card
to the tellers to use at their discretion. Instead of requiring a
supervisor to make the override decision, tellers were expected
to assess the situation and decide whether to override or call a
supervisor.

The operating realities of the bank thus resulted in branch
managers circumventing the system design. Moreover, although flagging multiple transactions is just one feature of the
system design that is a significant problem, overcoming this one
feature undermines *all* security provisions in the system because the officer card is now freely available to the tellers. The
result is that supervisor oversight is entirely dependent on the
teller's discretion and local branch manager's policy. This
implementation of the system increases the responsibility of the
teller although, at the same time, the *design* of the system is
reminding the teller that, formally, the bank management does
not trust him or her to make even routine decisions. The result
of the system's design is the worst of both worlds: negating all
security features *and* providing tellers with a constant reminder
that although they have some important responsibility in the
performance of their job, it is not recognized and they are not
thought to be capable or trustworthy enough to have that
responsibility as part of their formal job assignment. Nevertheless, this is a system designed, approved, and still accepted by
the bank's management and systems developers. This was only
one of a number of problems tellers experienced with the
system design. Although it appears to be a small problem, it had
significant consequences.

Designing for a New Banking Environment

Banking deregulation presented some of the most significant challenges banks faced since the Great Depression of the 1930s. Competition, consolidation, and opportunities for product innovation required dramatic changes in services of banks and operational requirements. The functions of banks expanded and the nature of banking operations changed at an accelerating pace. Moreover, changes in the financial environment in the United States, such as double digit inflation and interest rates, transformed formerly staid banking operations into a dynamic industry.

This dynamism shook up the industry and left many banks reeling. Profit levels began a decline that was hastened by a combination of market competition and unforeseen national and international events (See Figure 4.2.).[5] These events precipitated sweeping changes that had been building throughout the decade and made it clear that the banking industry was now subject to the same competition and volatility of other industries. (Many banks, under extreme pressure, made broad changes and increased profitability dramatically in 1988. Much of the change, such as restructuring and selling off unprofitable units, led to one-time profits that did not stem the overall downward trend in the industry.)

Fig. 4.2. Bank Profitability: Return on Assets & Equity.

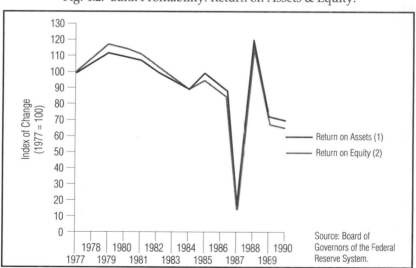

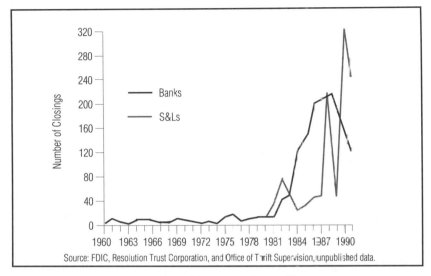

Fig. 4.3. Bank and Savings & Loan Closings.

Not all banks were able to succeed by restructuring and offering new services and products; they suffered the consequences of increased competition. By the late 1980s, the changing environment coupled with poor investment decisions resulted in a postwar record of bank failures, numbering 1,319 from 1981 to 1991 (compared to a total of 91 failures in the preceding decade), and 1,022 savings and loan failures (see Figure 4.3).

To compete more effectively, many executives began to seek a competitive edge through technology and software was often the centerpiece of a technology strategy. By 1989 banks were spending more than $10 billion a year on electronic technology and, as one writer observed, "In the battle among banks for retail customers, the victors are likely to be those that use high technology best" (Quint, 1989). Designing software for this market became a different kind of enterprise, leading to a change in the types of criteria used in designing an effective system.

Changes in computer hardware and software expanded the potential applications and capabilities of computerization. Lower cost hardware, more powerful computers, and advances in programming languages extended the range of possible banking applications. Thus, the potential uses of computers expanded, allowing them to be used to achieve a wider range of banking objectives.

Finally, deregulation of banking allowed banks to merge and larger banks to acquire smaller banks. Bank acquisitions often brought together institutions with large existing investments in incompatible computer systems. Integrating systems posed technical and training problems.

Shifts in Banking Objectives

In deregulated markets, new objectives developed and increased the importance of existing objectives. Banks were permitted to offer more services and products such as certificates of deposit (CDs), different types of mortgages, interest bearing checking accounts, and other financial services. Regional boundaries on retail banking became less restrictive, allowing banks to compete in larger geographical areas as well as acquire and merge with other banks.

The volatile economic conditions of the 1980s also placed new demands on banks. Interest rates fluctuated rapidly, daily for some products, and terms and conditions of products, especially mortgages, changed constantly. Such changes in the systems processing the products needed to be rapidly entered. Keeping current information available to everyone responsible for selling the products became an important objective.

In deregulated banking, therefore, new objectives arose: responding to competition, responding to changes in the financial environment, developing and marketing new products, and managing and strengthening the customer's relationship with the bank.

Competition Deregulation enabled banks to compete with each other by offering new services, with noncommercial banking institutions such as investment funds and savings and loans, and with institutions outside regional boundaries. Responding to the competition required banks to quickly match the products (e.g., certificates of deposit, money market funds) and conditions (e.g., interest rates, services, accessibility of funds) offered by other institutions.

Environment Volatile interest rates, changes in regulatory reporting requirements, changes in tax laws, and other external environmental changes required banks to adjust their services and procedures quickly. These changes also changed the informational needs of different departments in the bank: New reports were required and different restrictions and procedures were needed to process transactions.

New Products The types of products and conditions of existing products that could be developed depended on regulations, customer base, and resources of the bank. As traditional banking regulations were eliminated, opportunities arose to develop new products or modify existing products. The need to continually create new products resulted from increased competition following reductions in banking restrictions.

Marketing and Sales Marketing and sales grew more important during the 1980s. New products and competition made market analysis of products and services necessary to identify what customers would purchase. Banks also had to develop an effective means of selling the new products and services.

Customer Relationship Banks had to begin managing and strengthening their customer relationships. This involved using customer contacts to sell new products, increasing the amount of funds customers maintained at the bank, service existing products (e.g., renewing certificates of deposit), and increasing the customer's commitment to the bank (e.g., transferring funds from demand accounts to long-term products such as certificates of deposit). Tracking all of a customer's relations or accounts with the bank, therefore, became vital.

In summary, this newly competitive environment pressured banks to seek ways to determine customer needs, develop new products, and offer new services. Information had to be updated quickly and to be readily available to bank branch personnel. Management and marketing departments sought better analyses and support for strategies to expand their customer base and increase the yield from their existing customers.

Computerization Strategies

Whereas traditional banking systems were used to process and track large amounts of data and to monitor tellers' activities and cash, new systems were considered competitive tools. As such they were utilized to analyze management, provide online support to many operations, and help banks in offering products and services that gave them a competitive advantage. In addition, the expanded capabilities of new hardware and software increased the role of computers in achieving the traditional banking objectives of efficiency and effectiveness of operations. The greater flexibility and power of the new generation systems reduced the degree of limitations in tradeoffs between efficiency and security.

The greater range of functions and importance of computer systems increased the complexity and requirements for effectiveness of software. Direct and indirect consequences of this were the emergence of more third-party vendors, standard or semicustom software, and the diffusion of comprehensive computer systems into smaller banks.

As the range of functions required in a banking system increased, inhouse MIS departments often did not have the capability to produce effective systems. Third-party vendors were able to develop systems more effectively. Because development costs would be shared by a number of users, vendors could invest more in developing highly sophisticated and complex systems, could sometimes spend more time on debugging, and generally could produce a more comprehensive and higher quality system than that produced by a bank's MIS department.

Although a bank may not obtain extensive customization from a third-party system, it gains more extensive functionality and often more effective and less defective software. Also, the lower software costs of standard systems produced by a vendor can be afforded by smaller banks that cannot afford the initial development costs of a custom system or the cost of an inhouse MIS department. In addition, the dramatic decrease in the cost of computer hardware makes it possible for even small banks to use sophisticated software.

To provide such new software applications, an industry of independent software companies has arisen. These companies differ from internal MIS departments in their objectives and strategies. Internal MIS had only one customer and was part of the user organization. Vendors have multiple customers, must make systems that are built on a standard shell, require minimal customization, yet address a broad range of banking requirements. A significant influence on development is that vendors, unlike internal MIS departments, must sell their products in competition with other products.

Responding to the new requirements of banking and building on the capabilities of a new generation of technology, the Banking Systems Corporation developed a state-of-the-art teller system as part of a larger new banking system. The design process of this system illustrates the factors that shape design decisions during the development process and how the software came to embody the contradictions of an industry in transition.

The Banking Systems Corporation

The Banking Systems Corporation (BSC, a pseudonym) was founded in the mid-1970s to produce a retail banking operations software system that was a standard design but could be customized by each client. The principal officer of the firm was a consultant to the banking industry and recognized a need for a system that could handle mortgage lending and financial reporting. He founded BSC with financial backing from a venture capital group. The company grew to over 200 employees largely on the sale of the two systems.

In the late 1970s and early 1980s, the president of the firm felt its products should be designed for a deregulated and dynamic banking environment. The central feature of this design approach is that the systems can be changed by customers. The BSC built a standard system with a wide range of features and functionality with parameters that can be modified by the client. Many of the features, such as screen configurations, can be changed by a client with little computer experience. BSC's system handled nearly all aspects of banking transactions and information storage and retrieval. Several major functions of this system are outlined in Figure 4.4.

BSC's guiding philosophy in design was that, optimally, nothing should be hardwired; every feature and function should have parameters that could be modified by the client. Although this type of approach resulted in complex designs, it proved to offer an important competitive advantage. For example, during the early 1970s when interest rates were stable, as they had been for decades, most systems allocated only single digits for interest rates. BSC's system was designed with broad parameters instead of fixed or hardwired features. Thus, when inflation and interest rates soared to the double digits, the BSC system was able to compute double digit interest rates without modification of the source code. In this and many other design areas, BSC was foresighted and/or fortuitous in anticipating a number of changes that occurred and designed its product with the flexibility to respond to them. In an industry dominated by

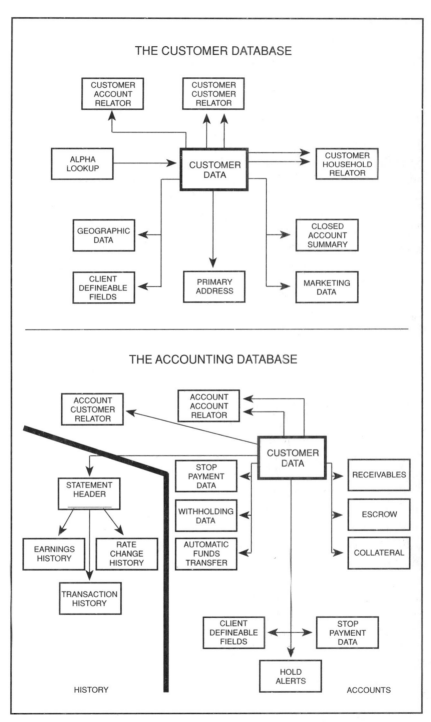

Fig. 4.4. Customer and Accounting Databases.

large companies that sell hardware and software, such as IBM and Unisys (formerly Burroughs), BSC succeeded by finding a niche and designing products with flexibility and functionality, thus giving BSC one of its important competitive advantages.

The management and development staff of BSC decided to design a new system with much greater functionality than their own existing systems and their competitors' systems. The design task BSC faced was more complex than any system either it or its competitors had ever designed. The reasons were the rapid change in banking operations, with little certainty on its direction, and changes in technology even more rapid as the lower cost and higher power of minicomputers allowed smaller banks and savings and loans to purchase mission critical systems. Because most operational banking tasks were conducted through computers, the software played a central role in defining how those tasks would be structured, how jobs within the bank would be defined, and the responsibility required of different users in the bank. The system had to improve the competitive position of smaller banks using the system in order for them to survive. Also, for BSC, the system had to provide clear competitive advantage over other vendors' systems and over systems designed by a bank's internal MIS department. Furthermore, BSC had to consider that its vision of cutting edge technology might be beyond the range of change that current traditional bank managements, who were used to a stable environment, might want in their organizations and in their comfortable banking procedures. Thus, a system that had clear technological superiority would not necessarily succeed if it could not be sold to current bank management.

As the chief programmer for the system described the challenge, it was that:

> We have a customer who doesn't understand all the technological issues. Moreover, their own industry is evolving and they haven't realized the impact on their way of doing business. Banks are organizations that are designed to keep overhead low, labor costs low, which means they hire people at the lowest pay levels. As a result, they don't have people with a lot of expertise, they need things kept very simple, very straightforward, and very much the same.

To illustrate how a small development staff confronted the issues, we describe how they set out to design the teller station, a standalone module of the larger system BSC was developing.

The Teller Station

The Teller Station had several significant design features and functions. First, the software for the screens, unlike the existing fixed-screen teller stations, allows the screen format to be customized by each bank. Thus, screens can be set up to meet each bank's particular procedures for handling transactions and preferences for displaying information. Second, the teller station can be integrated with many different computers. Thus, the teller station can operate across different systems without changing its features or functionality.

Third, "intelligent capabilities" provide better and more flexible decisionmaking options. This allows the system to handle more contingencies without requiring either a teller decision or a supervisor's oversight. The teller stations are linked to supervisor stations so that tellers can consult them about an account problem electronically instead of requiring the supervisor to walk to the teller station to discuss the situation. Thus, the consultation is invisible to the customer.

The system was developed to analyze characteristics of the customer's account for sales purposes. For example, while the teller is processing the customer's transaction, such as a deposit, the system will analyze the account characteristics for products the teller might be able to sell to the customer. If the customer had $10,000 in a low-interest bearing savings account for six months, the system would prompt the teller to give the customer a brochure on certificates of deposit or a money market fund. To aid tellers in selling these products, they will be able to access a database about product information such as interest rates and terms.

Design History

The Teller Station design was developed by a small group within BSC. When the project was first proposed, the company decided not to fund it. However, the chief programmer and one of his programmers went ahead and spent several weekends building a prototype. The prototype impressed the president of the company, who then decided to approve and fund the development.

The chief programmer and one programmer designed and

built most of the teller system with help from another programmer in designing interfaces with the company's other systems.
All of the code was written by the three of them, working over a
period of 18 months. As the chief programmer described it, they
designed "the underlying software to be as flexible as the state of
the art would allow," incorporating the latest cutting edge technology. They enjoyed a high degree of autonomy because they
were outside the established programming groups. They reported to the president periodically, but otherwise worked independently of other groups in the company. When the system's
basic functionality was established, a product manager reviewed
the designs for compatibility with banking operations and emulation of existing systems.

Design Objectives

The Teller Station development group had three design goals:
- To utilize the increased power of computers and new programming languages to improve the use of computers to
  achieve traditional banking objectives (efficiency, accuracy,
  security, and customer service);
- To support the new banking objectives of responding to the
  competition, responding to environmental changes, developing innovative new products, marketing and selling new
  products, and managing the customer relationship with the
  bank; and,
- To preserve their customers' investment in existing equipment and training by designing the new system to integrate
  existing systems and emulate the teller stations being
  replaced.

In carrying out the first set of objectives, the designers created
teller station features and functions that would "enforce the rules
as the primary objective." The significance of this objective,
particularly as a selling point, was shaped by the client's view of
the attributes, experience, and training of tellers. Tellers have a
very high turnover rate, with more than one year of tenure
considered substantial. Banks generally do not invest significant
resources or time in training tellers. The tellers tend to be young
and with high school educations. The view expressed by one
of the system's designers was that tellers are "mostly kids,"

"stupid, have little interest in the job, are careless, error prone, and not trustworthy, and thus a security risk." This view of the end user clearly influenced design of the Teller Station. For example, if the teller's only interest or preference is seen as wanting to dispose of the customer as quickly as possible and not be burdened with unnecessary information and not restrict transactions if a customer is overdrawn or missed a loan payment for example (so that customers do not become angry with the teller), a system should have the teller refer the customer to a supervisor without disclosing the nature of the problem. The designers also learned that bank management does not want the teller to become involved in customer problems. Tellers, again according to one of the designers, will be "kept in the dark because they are not trained in human relations that are necessary to interact with the customer; you can't afford to do that because of the high turnover, and tellers are just not that discrete."

The system design was intended primarily to satisfy those who make the purchasing decision. As one designer said:

> You're going to deliver this to the teller, so you want to make it nice for the teller, but more importantly I have the guy who's making the purchasing decision and I have a board of directors who have a set of criteria, that is, they want to run their bank as profitably as possible. This means they want their policies enforced, they want their costs minimized. I want to deliver them tools that will enforce their policy better than the competition can and I've got to stay no more expensive than the competition.

Eventually, they hope to achieve these objectives by designing systems that allow little, if any, discretion by the teller.

As this designer explained, the tellers expressed dissatisfaction to the developers with this aspect of the design:

> The tellers complain that they don't like to have to tell the customer that they can't handle the transaction; they don't like the fact that the only information they get is that there is a problem with this account that can only be handled by a supervisor over there.

The tellers say they want to be able to handle a wide range of transactions and have the information and authority to serve the customer without being required to consult a supervisor. "The first thing tellers ask for is the override function so that they can make the thing override complaints if they don't think they happen to need a supervisor."

Features and functions to aid the teller were not considered the highest priority by systems designers because:

> Very far down on the list of goals of the board of directors [of the bank] is teller satisfaction. The banks take a stab at making sure someone from the teller line (the head teller often, who is someone who has been away from actual teller operations for maybe five years) is involved in the process [of establishing system definition]. It's very clear that the management, board of directors, and tellers have two completely separate agendas. The board of directors likes it when they find out our system will stop "bad" transactions (i.e., that pose risks to security).

When deciding which information to make accessible to the teller, the designers noted:

> The first guideline is that banks purposely and deliberately keep tellers, and others in the branch, ignorant of what the bank is trying to do. Banks believe that their greatest protection is in keeping the teller and everyone else, including the branch managers, purposely ignorant. The less your people seem to know about the actual reasons behind the actual policies and details about how you are operating your institution, the better off they seem to think they are.

When the users within an organization have differences about how the system should be designed, "The guy who signs the check wins. That's the bottom line."

All decisionmaking was to be built into the Teller Station software so that no discretion would be left to the teller and there would be few instances when consultation with a supervisor would be necessary. In previous systems, there were limitations in the types of nonstandard transactions that the system could evaluate and little flexibility to respond uniquely to an individual situation. This resulted in regular supervisor intervention or increased decisionmaking autonomy by tellers. Because this was considered a negative condition, this new system was developed to evaluate a much broader range of conditions and to allow more flexibility.

Parameters for decisionmaking using the BSC Teller Station can be set according to each bank's policy and multiple factors can be used to evaluate individual situations. If a customer tried to cash a check for an amount greater than the balance of his or her account, the computer can check for funds in other products, such as savings accounts, so that the transaction can proceed. The system is also designed to monitor all of the customer's relationships with the bank, such as loans and credit card accounts. Depending upon the bank's specifications, the system could require the teller to refer a routine transaction to a supervisor if there was a problem, such as a missed payment, with one of the customer's accounts.

The system was designed to assess nonstandard transactions and individual situations, rather than merely display information for the teller or supervisor. This was intended to simplify the teller's task, eliminate discretion, and increase security. In the words of the chief programmer, the system was built to give the teller just three responses for a transaction:

- "Yes, proceed with the transaction,"
- "No, do not proceed with the transaction," or,
- "Call a human" (for those few situations outside of the system's decisionmaking capability).

The system was intended to be so flexible, powerful, and "intelligent" that its operators would require none of these characteristics. Thus, when a problem arose, the only role of the teller, beyond pressing the proper keys, was to give voice and action to the system's command to "call a human," a category which evidently excluded the teller. These design objectives applied the latest in technology to implement the banks operating policies which reflected traditional banking objectives.

At the same time, the Teller Station was being designed with functions to support the new banking objectives. To respond to the new banking environment, banks would have to give greater consideration to competition, financial environment volatility, innovation pressures, and "customer management." These were objectives that designers saw as important and they designed new modules of the Teller System to respond to these needs.

Marketing and sales departments in banks were growing in importance and size as their role became crucial for improving a bank's competitiveness. Profit could be increased by increasing the amount of funds a customer deposits and the types of products he or she maintains with the bank. Although a customer might have a longstanding account with one bank, he or she might respond to an advertisement and mail in a check for a Certificate of Deposit (CD) at a competing bank. Banks thus tried to use any contact with their customers to strengthen the customer relationship to sell them new services and encourage them to transfer funds from demand deposits to long-term products such as CDs.

These objectives require a greater investment in, and utilization of, teller skills and knowledge. The Teller System's functionality to meet the new objectives of banking in competitive market conditions was designed around this new concept of the teller's role. The system analyzes the customer's accounts during a routine transaction. The system prompts the teller to hand the customer a brochure on a particular product. suggest a new service, or inform the customer about the status of his or her funds, such as the need to rollover a CD. In many cases it is expected that the customer may then ask the teller about current interest rates, terms, and product comparisons. The system provides teller support for some of these requests with a function to query interest rates, for example.

The increasing capitalization of the retail banking industry (ATMs and teller systems) change the marginal benefit of increasing teller efficiency. Productivity in routine transactions is primarily increased by ATM use but transactions handled by tellers produce limited productivity gains because the bulk of the teller's discretionary time is spent interacting with the customer, not in the tasks of transaction processing. Consequently, the potential for increasing profits is less from minimizing transaction time and/or the cost of labor (i.e., the skill level) and more from changing the nature of the encounter. Rather than trying to decrease a five minute encounter to four minutes and 30 seconds, it is more profitable to maximize the potential value added by the teller.

To assist in achieving this objective, the system is designed to be a marketing *tool* for the teller and a resource to provide product information about complex and changing products. This set of design objectives leads to features and functions that are tools *for* the teller rather than a means to enforce operational objectives of management. The implicit view of the teller in this role is key salesperson for a particular market segment, thus as a revenue generator rather than a labor cost.

Concluding Comments: Contradictions and Conflicting Values in Design

The cases illustrate a number of problems designers confront in designing large-scale systems that are integral to the day-to-day work of users. At Big Bank systems designers were confronted with a relatively straightforward task: Design a system that reflected formal policies and procedures governing banking transactions, most of which were well documented. The system, as designed, did this rather effectively. However, in practice we observed that the informal or real work practices were incompatible with the formal procedures of the organization and thus the system design as well. A few dysfunctional system functions resulted in branches implementing the system in a way that undermined much of its promise to regulate teller transactions. In this way, the informal work practices were preserved and branches continued to operate in many areas on the basis of judgment exercised by managers and tellers. At the same time, the formal reality, as presented by the various policy manuals and description of the system design, continued to reflect the officially prescribed methods of operation. Business-as-usual continued with the banking system adding some improvements in efficiency and tracking of information but it was far from achieving the promises of some of its key selling features. A system design that did not reflect the formal policies and procedures would require system designers to confront a much larger set of organizational issues.

In contrast, the designers of the Teller System (and of the larger new banking system) were faced with a number of contradictory requirements and with specifications that reflected value choices by some users rather than the needs of others. Not all of the contradictions and conflicts were apparent to the designers nor did they always recognize that accommodating the requirements established by management (one group of "users") would produce a system that was clumsy and have features that were even irrelevant to the day-to-day operations of the bank.

The designers at BSC felt they had to accommodate the traditional banking objectives such as those that defined the system at Big Bank. In fact, the designers' own attitudes about the "worth" of tellers and their work was consistent with a traditional banking philosophy. Central to this philosophy was an approach to reducing costs and increasing profitability by reducing labor costs and increasing security. These objectives shaped the focus on using the most advanced technology to eliminate every last refuge of teller autonomy and decisionmaking. It was assumed that not only would this be successful, but that whatever constraints on the teller's actions this introduced, they were less significant than the advantages for achieving security and efficiency. Never did BSC system designers consider that teller discretion and skill might add to the efficiency of the bank.

Because the attitudes about tellers were expressed by designers as values consonant with their own views, it might be easy to mistake the resulting software as reflecting value choices by these designers. However, as is also evident in the rationale they articulated, these designers were also expressing their assessment of what features would best sell the system. Salable features and functions often reflected the values designers and marketing staff believed were held by bank managers who would be making the purchase decision. The designers also assessed the employment situation of tellers and identified these end users as having a low level of commitment to the organization because they were a low paid workforce with very high turnover.

The contradictions and value conflicts in design came from responding to the requirements of the new banking environment without assessing the conflicts with the traditional objectives of banking. (Even if the designers had reassessed their design approaches, they might have been constrained by bank managers who were trying to maintain traditional operations by only grafting on a few new innovations. Had the designers been more aware of this problem, they might still have proceeded with a similar design fearing that survival of their own software company could not wait for major changes and a more enlightened management to develop in the banking industry.) Thus, new features and functions for the new banking environment were added on to an old system. The design included contradictory elements in an attempt to respond to the expressed preferences of most bank managers and to offer new features and functions that would appeal to managers trying to improve the competitiveness of their banks. The latter features and functions would also allow BSC to stand out among *its* competitors.

Decisions about how to design a software system are shaped and complicated by factors far beyond technical procedures of determining optimal system requirements. It is a process that, as these cases show, involve tradeoffs among competing objectives and values and, for the vendor, decisions to ensure their own survival even at the cost of producing systems that may not be best for the end user.

Endnotes

1. We conducted case studies of two banking software systems. The first case study was of a system shell that was purchased and customized by the MIS department of a large commercial bank. We learned how to use the system and interviewed its designers at the central office of the bank and then observed its use and interviewed tellers, supervisors, and managers at four branch offices. The second case involved a series of interviews over two years at a software vendor as the firm was enhancing a recently released product and developing new modules of a software system for banks.

2. We interviewed the systems designer, managers of systems development and operations planning in the central office, and the tellers, supervisors, customer service representatives, and managers in four branch offices.

3. These were not explicitly identified as objectives nor were they identified as formal principles of design. Rather, based on our interviews we believe that this set of objectives implicitly shapes existing operational policies and procedures of the bank and decisions made by managers and systems designers.

4. A small number of people make a number of separate trips to the teller window each day and many of these people do so regularly. Over a two-hour period (in the morning) in a large city branch office, each teller had four to five customers who made three or more transactions that day.

5. For example, the sharp drop in profits in 1987 reflected banks increasing their cash reserves to offset potentially large loan defaults by Third World countries, particularly Latin American countries such as Brazil which stopped payment on its loans. Federal Deposit Insurance Corporation chairman William Seidman thought the "vast majority of the decline" in banks' profits "was because of problems with their Brazil loans" (Nash, 1987, p. 5; Berg, 1987; McLaughlin and Wolfson, 1988). Profits also fell because of the stock market crash in the last quarter of 1987. The sharp changes in savings and loans closings were probably a reflection of political maneuvering and problems in leadership of the agency overseeing S and L closings (Thomas, 1989a, 1989b, 1990; Skidmore, 1992; Pine, 1988; Mahar, 1990; Yang and Glechman, 1988). The banks responded by restructuring, laying off employees, cutting costs, and raising fees, and Brazil, a large debtor, resumed interest payments on its loans in 1988 (Miller, 1989; Nash, 1988; Bennett, 1988).

5

Keeping the Customer Satisfied: Field Service and the Art of Automation[*]

The "Maytag repairman" is the familiar image of field service. When servicing electronic equipment such as computers, however, the job is significantly more demanding than fixing washing machines. Not only are computers more complex than most other machines, they are also more central to the ongoing operations of an organization. Increasingly, everything an organization does depends upon electronic equipment in some way. Large computer systems are often expected to run 24 hours a day, 365 days a year. When computers are such an integral part of an organization's operations, maintaining the equipment is tantamount to keeping a person's heart beating and blood circulating. Thus, unlike the idle television caricature, field service engineers are increasingly viewed as the paramedics for electronics who can quickly and ably respond to system crashes.

At the same time that field service has become more demanding, the complexity of the job has increased. The "machinery" of the modern organization is less often composed of gears turning, typewriters clattering, and paper being shuffled. Instead, the sights and sounds of the modern organization consist of screens glowing, keys clicking, and, to the uninitiated, an assemblage of opaque, "black boxes." Inside these boxes is a miniature world that gives no clue as to the nature of its inner workings.

The field service engineer's (FE) job and function have been growing while the size of the technology itself has been shrinking. His or her skill is less often exercised as a skilled craftworker in the repair of a part and more often as a skilled analyst who can

---

[*]This chapter was written with Frederick Van Bennekom and is based on his field research and case study.

understand the abstract workings and nature of electronics to identify the problem and trace it to the malfunctioning component. The required manual skills are often minimal, just enough dexterity to swap out a bad part for a good one usually suffices. At the same time, the scope of field service has expanded from just repairing worn and broken or defective parts to collecting information about design defects and debugging equipment that may have been released prematurely. Rather than working as a lone gun, riding from call to call, the FE has become one node in a field service network of many linkages.

Field service requires a coordinated group of people to analyze problems, ensure delivery of the required parts (the hundreds or thousands of parts of a large computer cannot be carried in one repair truck like the few dozen parts of a washing machine), track equipment reliability, and collect information for engineering design. The integration and support of field service increasingly comes from new software systems. This case study focuses on the design of software for the automated management of field service calls. We ask how this field service management system affects,

- accountability and control of service delivery,
- the integrity of historical data on product failure and repair/replacement,
- the allocation of work among the field engineers,
- changes in the structure of jobs,
- relative responsibilities of related groups of workers,
- relative power through "ownership" of the technology.

Background to the Field Service Industry

We begin by describing the role of field service organizations and the transformation of field service during the 1980s.

The Role of Field Service Organizations

In an integrated firm, the field service organization must function in concert with new product sales and other divisions of the parent company. Field service organizations are generally regarded as cost centers within the overall firm. The business mission of a field service organization within an integrated firm is to ensure the customer's satisfaction with a product after the sale, focusing on repair and maintenance of the capital good at the customer site. In accomplishing this mission, the field service organization ensures its own revenue stream by retaining customers for its services and also leverages the entire firm in its efforts to sell more products.

The field service organization in an integrated firm historically played a secondary role in the firm's overall business mission. Field service supported the primary role of manufacturing and marketing of the firm's tangible product. To a great extent field service, regarded as a cost center, was considered a necessary evil required to install the product and deliver service during the warranty period. Field service also helped stimulate sales of the tangible product by increasing the company's goodwill, supporting marketing objectives, and gathering data for product engineering. Goodwill was improved by keeping the customer satisfied with the company's products through responsive support service. The company's good name was kept before the customer with each positive service encounter.

Field service support also allowed the parent firm to introduce new products quickly. Following a strategy of either being first-to-market or rapidly responding to a competitor often meant that the product had engineering or manufacturing deficiencies. The field service organization could resolve such problems of premature release by subsequent installation of Field Change Orders (FCOs). Consequently, it was usually the field service group that bore the brunt of the customer's dissatisfaction with the performance of the product.

Field service had a secondary function to collect data on product reliability for the product engineering organization. Field engineers made field service reports that were sent to the engineering organization for analysis. Each service event on a product in the field was an opportunity to understand how the product could be engineered better.

The dominant objective of field service management was to deliver a high level of service that met the expectations of the customer. Customers typically emphasized response time (how long it took for a field engineer to arrive at the equipment site) and down time (how long for the problem to be solved). During the 1970s and early 1980s, a period of rapid diffusion of electronic goods, management's primary challenge was keeping up with the service demands of the quickly growing customer installed base of products. Cost containment and increasing revenue growth were not key concerns because service delivery was more important than cost issues and revenue was growing proportionally with the installed base. Moreover, an absence of severe price competition in the marketplace allowed field service to maintain high profit margins (averaging 35 percent) and the revenues from servicing hardware in the field appeared to be on a growth trend.

More recently, in the late 1980s, field service in the computer industry began to face increased competition. Revenues from servicing hardware declined as a percentage of total service revenues (which also includes activities such as systems integration services and software support). The Ledgeway Group, a Division of Dataquest, projected that the hardware service fraction of total U.S. aggregate revenues in the computer industry would be 41 percent in 1994, a significant decline from the comparable 1989 figure of 48 percent. The decline in potential revenues from hardware field service is occurring just at the time when the role of the field service organization is changing and when parent organizations are looking to them to be self-sustaining profit centers. Simultaneously, effective field service operations are becoming necessary prerequisites to the successful sales of new equipment and for maintaining the loyalty of customers.

In summary, several issues typically face managers of field service organizations:

- How to be responsive to customer needs for service without letting the service costs (investments plus operating expenses) get out of line with projected revenues,
- How to design field service operations to promote customer satisfaction with the company's products,
- How to structure the field engineer's work and supporting information systems to collect valuable data on product reliability without adversely affecting either the efficiency or effectiveness of the field service activity.

To begin to appreciate the complexity of these issues, one needs to look at various options for organizing the delivery of field services. Only then can one assess the efficacy of software systems designed for such applications.

Accordingly, in the sections below, we provide background information on the traditional field service organization, changes in the field service environment, and an introduction to systems that automate aspects of field service delivery. We then summarize the experiences of two companies that adopted the same field service management software. Finally, we draw some conclusions about how social choices shaped software design in both its initial design and in implementation.

Traditional Field Service Organization

The process of field service delivery involves: (1) taking customer requests for service, (2) sending technicians, spare parts, and service equipment to the equipment site, and (3) correcting the customer's equipment problem (see Figure 5.1). A traditional field service office with a simple set of responsibilities and a small customer base to support might meet these tasks with a relatively unstructured organization. The smaller the operation, the more likely that job responsibilities are loosely defined with people doing what needs to be done.

Figure 5.1. Service Call Model.

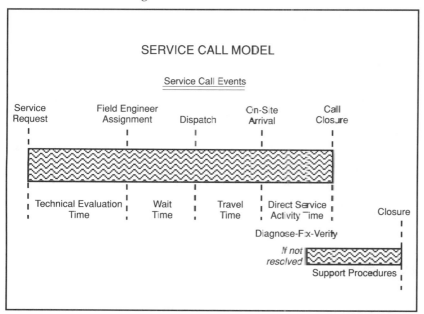

The logistics of servicing equipment located across the country requires a common operational design of geographically dispersed service resources (spare parts and field technicians) in local branch offices. These field offices are part of a formal command hierarchy, but traditionally they acted as independent businesses with an entrepreneurial spirit. Each local manager could decide, for example, the mix of technical skills on his or her staff, how dispatching would be done, and how backup technical specialists would be applied to problem situations.

The field service organization's loyalty to its customers conflicts at times with loyalty to the company. For example, to fix a valued customer's equipment, arrangements might be made with another branch office to fly a spare part to the branch in need even though this would go against stated company procedures. These decentralized field service offices held such power because they constituted the heart of the service business. The nature of field service involves responding to numerous contingencies and was thus an operation that required immediate decisions in each local office and at the site of service. Allowing people delivering the service autonomy to do what was needed to get the job done meant that formal procedures were "loose," they left some decisionmaking power at lower levels. Those policies that did exist were not necessarily enforced if the office was running smoothly and customers were not complaining.

Although networks for sharing ideas and resources developed among the company's local field offices, these networks were not intended to facilitate control by a central organization. In addition, and very importantly, field service traditionally was ignored as a revenue source by the parent company. The performance of the field service organization was largely evaluated on how well it was keeping the customer satisfied. Coincident with changes in technology were changes in the role of field service. The technology is thus being shaped by a new set of objectives as well as the traditional ones. After describing field service operations we explore how two companies implemented a new automated system.

The Dispatch Decision

Typically customers call the local field service office to request a response when their equipment malfunctions. Although one individual might have formal responsibility for taking customer calls, a secretary, the field engineers, or the manager of the local office might also record the necessary information about the service request on a form and post the form on a board on the wall. In a very small office the local manager usually made assignment and dispatch decisions. A moderate size office might have a designated dispatcher to assign an appropriate field engineer and then notify him or her by phone.

The dispatching decision contains several significant logistical considerations. Primary among these is to maintain continuity in the relationship between an FE and a customer. Efficient and effective field service also requires that some problems be attended to by a technical specialist who can quickly fix the problem. The most rapid response is achieved by assigning FEs on the basis of proximity and availability.

The dispatch decision, therefore, is based on an assessment of the particular customer, the specific problem, the assignment of an FE, and a judgment about which objective was most important in that situation and how to best meet that objective. "Dispatching by account representative" provides continuity of service. Under this approach an FE is assigned primary responsibility for specific customer accounts so the customer sees a known face when the service provider arrives on site. If the specific problem is known at the time of dispatch, then a technical specialist might be assigned. An FE at a nearby customer site might be dispatched once he or she is available. Alternatively, if the service contract requires response within a specified period, then the next "warm body" would be dispatched. The manager of the local office usually would be involved in some of these dispatch decisions and an engineer who was physically in the office might occasionally choose the calls he or she would take. Sometimes the motivation of the engineer was to "cherry pick" a call he or she wanted to take for individual reasons (e.g., liked the customer, it was an easy call, it was located in a convenient place).

Responding to the Service Call

Once the dispatch decision was made, it would be telephoned to the appropriate FE. With assignment in hand the field engineer would go to the stockroom in the local office and sign out a kit with the spare parts for the customer equipment to be repaired.

The FE then traveled to the customer site, diagnosed the problem with test equipment, performed the repair, and verified that the equipment was functioning properly. Then the service call would be closed. The FE might talk with the contact for the customer site about the problem and how it was resolved. He or she would also record any required information about the work performed and call the dispatcher in the local office to take another assignment. On the next visit to the office the FE would sign in the defective parts from the customer's equipment and return the rest of the kit.

Not all service calls go smoothly. The FE might not have the spare part needed, he or she might not be able to isolate the problem, or the repair might take longer than expected. A call to the office might be needed to have a spare part delivered or to get assistance from another field engineer. Toward the end of the workday an engineer in the office might take the initiative to go to a customer site to assist a fellow technician who had been on site for some time or with a difficult problem.

The first-level manager focuses primarily on operational control and functions as foreman as well as manager. Because service operations occur at remote locations, the manager must track the FEs' whereabouts and the status of unresolved calls. A good manager constantly tries to keep aware of the status of requests for service and frequently has to expedite service calls that have problems. Traditionally, planning decisions were made more by "seat-of-the-pants" than based on analysis of hard data, drawing on the manager's closeness to and experience with the operation.

The entrepreneurial structure of the local office and the culture it engendered created branch offices that were relatively autonomous. In a well-run office, work was done through a group effort with many decisions left to individual judgment. Camaraderie was commonplace with strong interpersonal ties during and after the workday. Individuals in the local office identified strongly with the service objectives of the local business. People did what was right to satisfy the customer simply because it needed to be done.

This structure and culture, though effective in many respects, had its inefficiencies. The lack of a systematized assignment procedure led to less efficient dispatch of FEs, resulting in low utilization of this key resource. The short spans of control needed for this type of decisionmaking and logistic support provided the field offices more autonomy and allowed them to focus on establishing a personal relationship with customers with little regard for efficiency or profitability. In short, the corporate objective of service delivery traditionally dominated that of cost containment, which had not been a major concern because of the growing revenue base from service contracts on installed customer equipment.

Changes in Field Service Environment

These traditional methods of conducting field service have been challenged by several changes in the industry environment, primarily technological advances in the capital equipment that field service organizations maintain. Electronic equipment is much more reliable and sophisticated in its hardware and software than previously. These products also have a shorter life cycle and thus new products are introduced more frequently. Simultaneously, the applications environment in which such equipment is used has become more complex. As these new environmental conditions have combined to dramatically change the demands placed upon the field service operation, the mix of people, assets, and procedures had to adapt accordingly.

More reliable products require less service and thus annual service contract revenues have declined dramatically. Despite the continued growth in the installed base through new sales, absolute revenue from remedial maintenance services is declining and operating profit margins are a fraction of their previous level.

The nature of the service task has shifted from skill in repair to skill in diagnostics as electronic products have become more complex but simpler to repair. The diagnostic task is increasingly more complicated because the application environment in which these products function has become much more complex. Electronic products no longer function in isolation in the customer environment; increasingly, they operate in conjunction with the firm's other products, for example, in a manufacturing process control system. Furthermore, a customer's technology network might span multiple facilities around the globe.

Customers want service organizations that can support this more complex environment. While offering more powerful capabilities to users, this environment is more dependent than ever on a high level of service. The repair of the failing device must be coordinated among multiple vendors in multiple locations. Geographic dispersion triggers new challenges: Large nationwide customers want consistent service levels across their entire account.

Finally, product life cycles continue to decrease, accelerating other changes in the service organization's environment. The service organization must continually update its service resources, its stock of spare parts, and the new technical skills required to service the latest products. Servicing in this networked integrated environment is a complex task requiring a different set of organizational capabilities from the traditional field service organization.

Diagnostic programs and tools must be more sophisticated. Effective field service delivery is increasingly dependent upon the ability to manage and coordinate customer accounts. Software service skills must be developed as a set of skills distinct from hardware service delivery. Resolution of software problems frequently requires recreating the problem in a controlled environment in centralized support centers. Implementing the identified fix seldom requires a physical visit to the customer site.

Requirements of the field service organization have changed dramatically in conjunction with new technical developments. The flattening of revenue growth has created a new management objective of cost containment to be achieved through higher utilization of technical resources and larger management spans of control. The use of scarce specialized resources must be carefully coordinated and scheduled. Achieving these goals raises new challenges for field service organizations pursuing the dual objectives of service responsiveness and cost efficiency.

Automating Field Service

Field service management software (FSMS) applications have been developed in response to these needs for increased control and coordination. The FSMS application is primarily an administrative or adjunct technology because it coordinates and controls the delivery of service but does not enhance the direct service task of diagnosing or repairing the malfunctioning equipment. An FSMS application is usually composed of a series of modules that serve different functions. The core modules are the logistics module, the contract module, and the dispatch module. Other modules can be added if the field service organization needs additional functionality (see Figure 5.2). Examples of additional modules are: repair depots where customers can mail damaged parts for repair in lieu of onsite service and a remote technical assistance service center from which specialized technicians can support FEs at field sites.

The logistics module manages the spare parts inventory. The module also tracks the parts as they are dispensed to FEs for use on service calls and the damaged parts the FE returns after completing the call. Inventory levels are tracked by the module and emergency orders of needed parts are monitored.

The contract module contains all the data about the contractual level of service the customer has purchased for each piece of equipment as well as data about the equipment itself. This module must be designed to allow for the variety of service levels the field service organization markets. Data from the contract module will be used for periodic billing of service contracts and it is used by the dispatch module to determine the level of service to be provided.

The dispatch module is the heart of the FSMS because it tracks and controls the sequence of events that occur during a service call (see Figure 5.3). When a customer calls the dispatch center, information from the contract module is retrieved on the terminal screen to verify that the contract exists and to access data needed by the FE, such as the location of the equipment. The logged service call can be assigned to an FE if the person who answers the phone also serves as a dispatcher. Alternatively, the FSMS system can be implemented so that the logging and dispatching functions are separated. In that case, the dispatcher's terminal will display the service calls that have been logged and the FEs in that service area who are available for assignment and dispatch.

Typically, the FSMS system has programmed logic to identify potential service administration problems before they occur. For example, calls for which the promised response time is about to

Welcome To

SERVICEMASTER

by

The SMC Corporation

OPTIONS

1. Dispatch	6. TAC
2. Billing	7. Host–Remote
3. Logistics	8. RCM
4. Reports	9. Scheduling
5. Report–Writer	

99. Logoff System

Choice: 01

MASTER MENU
For
Dispatch Functions

01. Customer File Maintenance	17. Skill File Maintenance
02. Contract File Maintenance	18. Closed Call Utilities
03. Mass Call Generation	
04. Dispatch	
05. Call Tracking	
06. Employee File Maintenance	
07. Kit File Maintenance	
08. Manual Call Close	
09. Mass Change Rules File	
10. Mass Sites Change	
11. Message Inquiry and Update	
12. Parts Master Maintenance	
13. Product File Maintenance	
14. Password File Maintenance	
15. Code File Maintenance	
16. Site File Maintenance	

Selection: 04

DISPATCH MAIN MENU

Dispatcher: Dispatch Functions

1. Customer Initiated Incidents	6. Call Tracking
2. Uncommitted Call Display and Employee Selection	
3. Employee Initiated Updates	
4. Message Inquiry and Update	
5. In-Transit Inquiry and Update	

9. Exit from Dispatch

Selection: 0

Fig. 5.2. Initial Screen Sequence.

be missed are flagged. When an FE has been at a customer site for prolonged period, a "customer outage" situation, it will be visible to the first-level manager's attention through the information displayed on a terminal. The FSMS also can be programmed to automatically invoke a sequence of events. For example, if the primary FE (the account representative) does not answer a page to receive notification of a logged service request, then a secondary FE can be paged automatically after a specified period of time.

The data files in the FSMS application also can be used for purposes other than the immediate service delivery concern. The contract module contains data that the marketing department can use for research when developing new service programs. During the course of the service call, data collected automatically by the system combined with data collected by the FE can be used by service managers to redesign service operations and to measure individual performance. These data also provide information to product engineering groups about systematic problems with products in the field. This information can be used to redesign products still being manufactured or to design new products.

The general flow of a field service call and the lines of direct contact in a nonautomated field service operation are shown in Figure 5.4. In Figure 5.5 the changes associated with an FSMS are illustrated. In terms of the overall flow of field service operations, the greatest impact of an FSMS is in three areas: the integration and involvement of groups in the central office in the dispatch and monitoring of field service calls, the loss of local autonomy of the field service engineer and a new accountability to central office groups, and a change in the role and functions of the branch manager.

Field Service in Action: The Cases of Zeno and Trident

We studied a field service management system in use at two companies, both integrated manufacturing firms that serviced their own products. The companies were computer manufacturers, but differed in the types and breadth of the products they manufactured. The companies differed in age and in their organizational designs.

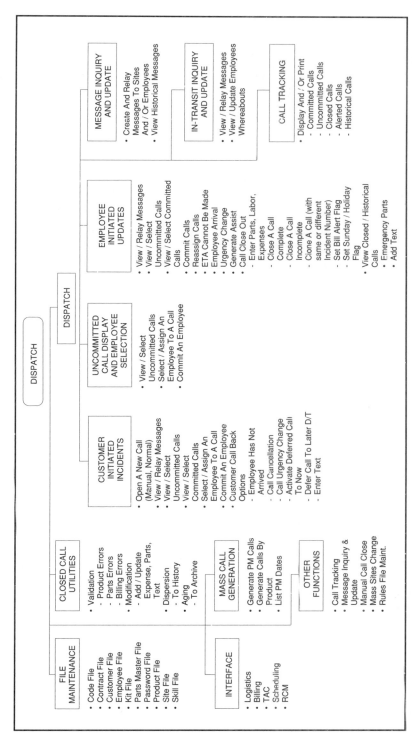

Fig. 5.3. Dispatch.

Zeno

Zeno (a pseudonym) is a large computer manufacturer with a broad product line. Zeno is a mature company and had been in business over 20 years at the time of our study. The company is procedurally oriented in its organizational design but has a history of a brightly entrepreneurial and decentralized decisionmaking structure that was being challenged by the requirements of the new marketplace.

Zeno had begun developing its own FSMS applications over a decade earlier and had gone through several generations of more sophisticated, internally developed FSMS applications. The features of these systems were designed to fit the particular service delivery procedures at Zeno without concern for general applicability to other firms. As the approach to service delivery evolved, the FSMS was modified to be compatible with these changes.

Calls were handled initially in the branch office but the function was continually becoming more centralized. At the time of our study, dispatching was performed by regional offices. The dispatching logic was a combination of the account representative program and specialization. Centralized diagnostic and support capabilities had been developed to help isolate the problem prior to FE assignment to allow for dispatching specialists. Both the FEs' and the first-level managers' roles were increasingly focused on customer management.

Zeno tried to combine cost efficiencies and customer effectiveness in its service operations design. The centralized support resources were seen as a means of gaining efficiencies while providing a competitive edge through improved service level. The size of Zeno provided the capital resources and critical mass necessary to support this investment.

The change to a more specialized and integrated operational design was accompanied by more sophisticated mechanisms to exercise operational and managerial control. The data captured by the FSMS about each service transaction were part of a sophisticated information system used by many departments in the organization in support of each of their needs. The data were used to monitor and evaluate the performance of the field engineer.

Accompanying Bert, one of the field engineers, on his calls one day, we observed the system in action. Leaving the local field

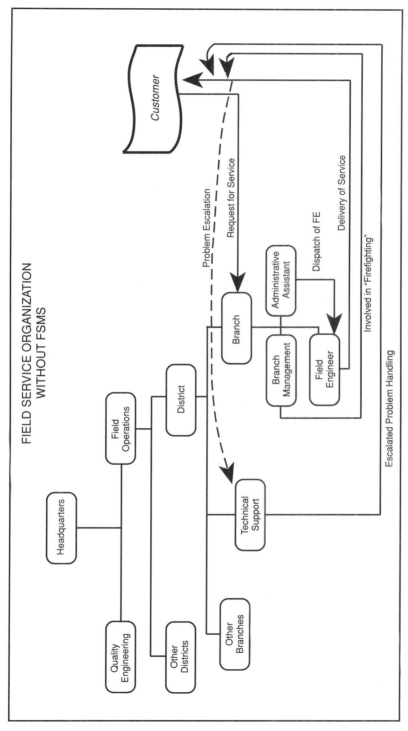

Fig. 5.4. Field Service Organization Without FSMS.

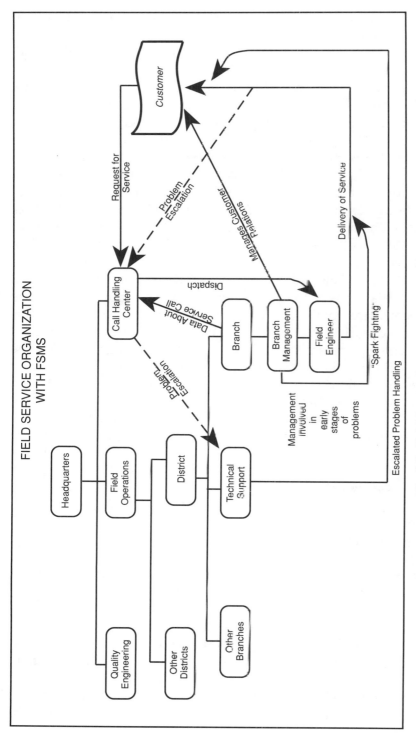

Fig. 5.5. Field Service Organization With FSMS.

office early in the morning, Bert called the regional call handling center to get his assignments for the day (he used to pick up his assignments from the field office). His first call was to a local manufacturing plant to install a new disk drive on one of the company's mainframe computers. Arriving at the site, we checked in with the security guard and our "customer contact," the data center manager, escorted us to the data center. The disk drive was quickly installed and the computer rebooted without problem. However, while running diagnostics for a final check of the system, a problem occurred intermittently. After another 30 minutes of diagnostics, and no small amount of cursing, Bert finally found the problem: a logic board he had replaced only the week before had a version of systems software that was incompatible with the new disk drive.

Bert disconnected the disk drive and explained the problem to the data center manager. The problem was technically with the logic board not the disk drive and, because this service call was logged as disk drive installation, the data center manager would have to place another call for repair of the logic board. The tracking by the FSMS would not allow Bert to make a significant repair without record of a service call; not only did he need to account for his time (this was much too long a time to spend on disk drive installation) but the quality engineering (QE) department would want a record of the logic board problem. As the data center manager started grumbling about "just getting the damn thing fixed," Bert explained that he did not have the correct software with him and would have had to make a separate return trip in any event. Bert assured him he would have it fixed on his return visit, though Bert knew that with the automated call assignment he could not really guarantee that he would be the FE assigned to the call. Bert reminded the data center manager that when he made his service call he needed to be sure to place *two* field service requests: one to fix the logic board and another for installation of the disk drive which was now disconnected because of the logic board problem.

After packing his tool kit, Bert called the dispatch center to report on the service call. The FEs were required to update the status of each call so the FSMS call handling system would close the service call. Rolling his eyes, Bert explained that he also had to provide a list of other data which, he derisively characterized as "feed for the bean counters," namely a number of management reports.

Barking his answers into the telephone, Bert answered questions from the dispatcher as though he were suffering through an interrogation: "8:15" (time arrived on site); "3 hours" (time spent on installation); "11:15" (time left the site); "9484" (type of system worked on); and so on, finally ending with "P," the installation code. The last piece of information was one of 25 codes to identify the specific problem encountered. (It was a recent change in the system requested by the company's quality engineering group so that equipment could be monitored according to the categories they used. QE found the coding previously used by field service inadequate for their purposes.) Responding to a query from the other end of the line, Bert repeated his last answer, saying, "That's right, it's a `P'." He then said, "I gotta go now to take care of this next call," and hung up the phone.

Bert said, "One of my big customers has a system down. I've gotta call him to tell him we're on our way. Then we gotta go, pronto." While he was on the phone, we grabbed Bert's FE manual and looked up "installation codes," finding "P": "Paperwork missing."

Riding in the van on the way to the next site, we asked Bert about the installation code. He replied,

> Look, I've got a critical customer down. You think I've got time to figure out which one of those silly codes to give? Hell no! "P" I can remember, and it covers everything. QEs always telling us to give them this data and that data, but do we ever see anything come of it? I'd like to get one of those Ivory Tower guys out here on a call so they could find out what the real world is like.

Travelling across town, we got to the next customer site after lunch. After checking in, Bert ran several diagnostics, isolated the failure to a problem in the memory part of the system. Bert thought it was probably a logic board, but he noticed a few connectors appeared loose and several other minor problems. The customer also pointed out a sticky switch on another part of the system and asked Bert if he would fix that as long as he was there. Bert replaced the failed board with a new one from his spare parts kit and attended to the other problems. It was now going on 5 pm. He once again called the dispatch center to report on the call. Following their conversation with the FE manual in hand, we noted that he gave the "Customer Request Time" for the call as 1 pm. He also listed the "Option

Type" worked on as "System" with "Repair Time" as two hours.

On the way back to the local field office, Bert answered our questions before they were asked.

> Yeah, the customer called in the problem at 8:30 this morning. But, the customer has a four hour response time guaranteed in the service contract, and our regional office monitors our response time also, so we ask the customer if it's OK if we show up at a certain time. If they say "yes," then that becomes the request time. The dispatcher then erases the time the customer called in and puts in this later time. No wonder our response time numbers look real good, eh? According to the [FSMS system] reports, we're there before they put down the telephone!
>
> Now you want to know about "Option Type." I said "System" because listing all the things I worked on just takes too damn long. And you want to know why I reported about half the time actually spent on the repair. Well, I got beat up last month for long repair times on this kind of system so I shortened it a bit. Let the next person try to beat my record, huh? I do gotta watch it though. If I report too few hours working on calls then my direct labor utilization is too low. So I bump up the hours on installations or preventative maintenance calls. They don't look at those numbers much. It's called "pencil whipping" the data.
>
> [After a pause, Bert added:] You know, you'd think with all the numbers they get from us they'd figure out what we're doing, but they don't.

In subsequent interviews with managers we discovered that they were, in fact, well aware of FEs "pencil whipping" the data. The central office managers and the QE engineers had discussed the problem and were determined not to capitulate to the FEs whom they saw as trying to shirk their responsibilities. To this end, they were about to implement a modification of the software that would more closely monitor each FE's performance and data provided. Although the managers anticipated a struggle, they were certain that eventually they would be able to collect accurate data for monitoring performance and for the quality engineering department's needs.

Trident

Trident (a pseudonym) is a small computer company that manufactures workstation computers. The firm was young, growing rapidly, and had retained the entrepreneurial spirit of its days as a very small firm. Trident's corporate culture placed great emphasis on individual accountability and responsibility. Accordingly, Trident established an Account Representative Program as the heart of its field service delivery strategy.

Trident initially attempted to develop its own FSMS application for its own hardware platform, but its systems were not powerful enough to handle the number of interactive users required in an FSMS application. The company then purchased an FSMS package and implemented most of its software modules. Trident deliberately chose a package that meshed with 80 percent of its current operational design, recognizing that the procedures embedded in the FSMS design would have to be adapted to some extent.

Trident's field service operation is highly decentralized with the branch or local offices acting as independent businesses. Previously, all customer calls came to the branch office which did the dispatching. With the FSMS, dispatching is centralized but Trident tried to retain its decentralized focus within the context of the new operational design required by the FSMS. Communication of the dispatching decisions to the FEs is done by telephone and all the FEs carry pagers. The branch office administrator, whose previous job had been 80 percent dispatching, was given the broadened responsibility of handling both contract administration and logistics functions. About once an hour she checks her video terminal for the status of open calls and the FEs' whereabouts. A senior field engineer was trained as her backup for these functions.

Riding with one of Trident's FEs, Hank, we followed him through his day, responding to calls and repairing computers much like the way it was done by Bert at Zeno. However, we noticed that after each call Hank reported a minimal amount of information and he reported exactly what occurred, that is, the actual time spent on a call and a broad but accurate description of the repair. Driving to a customer in the afternoon, we asked Hank about "pencil whipping" the data. He looked baffled and asked what we meant. We asked if he ever changed the numbers to make his performance look better. "No," he replied, "they don't use the data from these reports for my evaluation. Most of our performance is based on customer satisfaction."

Hank did not find the new system particularly intrusive or an impediment to his work. However, it did change some aspects of the job. Under the old system the dispatcher performed the technical evaluation. When the FE spoke with the dispatcher, they could discuss the customer's problem before going to the site, sometimes making an initial diagnosis and picking up parts if necessary. Now, the technical evaluation and dispatching functions are specialized. The calls are logged and evaluated by technicians who enter into the system a brief description of the problem and a dispatch code. The call is automatically queued for the dispatcher. The dispatcher does not have any information about the problem except what the technicians have entered into the system. The dispatcher reads the technical evaluation to the FE but is unable to discuss it. Another disadvantage, from Hank's perspective, is that at the end of the day he used to be able to ask the dispatcher what calls were open and pick one close to his home. Instead, the centralized dispatch assigns whatever open call is next in line.

In the field service office we discussed the new system with the branch manager. He spoke very favorably of the call handling system, stating that the "burden of dispatching" had been removed from his responsibilities. He views the FSMS as a "four star tool" to help him track incidents and give him time to focus on customer management. He used to spend most of his day dealing with dispatch assignments and fire fighting problems. Now he is able to spend most of his day meeting with customers to discuss more general issues of maintenance schedules, contracts, and selling additional services, which, he said, is what his job is supposed to be.

This manager changed certain design features of the FSMS to meet his particular objectives. When an FE is assigned to a service call, he or she is paged by the FSMS. The system was originally designed so that after a certain time had elapsed, if the FE had not responded to the page, the backup person assigned to the account was automatically paged. Trident specifically disabled this feature because managers felt it would hurt the personal relations the branch office had with customers and both quality and efficiency would suffer. The local branch manager and administrative assistant knew their accounts, which FE had an established relationship with the customer, and whether they should provide special services to a particular customer (e.g., they might increase the priority of a call for a large customer, or for a minor but repeated problem, or just as a personal favor to some customers). They were also concerned that it might allow the FE who was the primary account representative to pass off work by not answering the page, or by calls being handed to an FE not experienced with a particular customer or system. Instead, unanswered calls are routed to the field office. The field office manager then makes the decision about alternative call assignments.

While the branch manager viewed the FSMS as his tool, the new capabilities it gave the central office created contention over ownership of the tool. The central and branch offices had debated the amount of detailed data the field engineer would be required to collect. The quality engineering organization needed data about product performance in the field. The input codes of the FSMS were seen as a feature to support their task. However, the field organization saw this as an extra burden on the field engineers and inconsistent with its objective of efficient delivery of a high level of service. The complex and extensive coding took considerable time and no immediate improvement in customer satisfaction could be determined. Consequently, the first set of input codes proved counterproductive to the goals of quality engineering. There were so many codes (more than 100 for all the input categories) that the FE used only a few, about 15, rather than selecting the code whose nuance best matched the situation. The result was that QE received misleading information. Later, the input codes were greatly simplified and a template was created to help the FEs determine which code was appropriate. QE claimed that the codes did not provide the richness of detail it needed. QE asked that the FEs, in return for a shorter list of codes, enter more detailed *textual* explanations of the situation.

In general, branch managers and FEs at Trident were quite positive about the FSMS. They recounted problems during the initial implementation, such as the excessive number of codes for QE, but felt most were being resolved without too much problem. However, they did note that they had not anticipated a number of issues that arose with implementation of the FSMS. Although they expected a change in technical aspects of the operations, they were surprised by the amount of negotiation over turf issues such as responsibility for calls and changes in roles, for example, the QE data the FEs were expected to collect.

The field office manager felt that ultimately the needs of the field office and the FEs would prevail, though compromises would have to be made. He found that the system was brought in to fulfill a different vision of each group in the entire organization, that, the system

> ... was a lot of things to a lot of people in the company. They all wanted the system to serve their needs, but I had to push hard [during the implementation] to keep the focus on its primary objective: to serve the field office's needs for providing field service.

He noted that he had lost the autonomy he had enjoyed as a field manager under the old system when the central office learned about the potential of the system. The central office managers and engineers wanted to keep modifying the system in ways that increased their control. He saw the potential for the field office to become "slaves to people inside the home office." Overall, however, he thought the system was more of an aid than an impediment to delivering effective service. As long as he could continue to keep his customers satisfied, he thought the system design would continue to reflect the priorities and preferences of the field office.

Observations on Field Service and the FSMS

At both Zeno and Trident the design of the FSMS changed the structure of the organization and delivery of field service and the working conditions in several significant aspects. Some new roles were created to maintain, administer, and transact business with the new software process technology. Also, many of the jobs changed due to the structured procedures that the software application overlaid on organizational processes. New capabilities were supported and created by the FSMS. New and modified inter- and intraorganizational relationships developed as the rules changed. However, the two companies each handled the situation differently.

Changes in Job Structures

Because of alterations in the service delivery process, the roles of the dispatchers, field technicians, and managers changed. The dispatcher's job was greatly altered. The dispatchers, along with the initial telephone receptionist, perform virtually their entire work through the FSMS. The dispatch function overall is more specialized and centralized with an FSMS. This removes the daily face-to-face interaction between the dispatchers and the FEs. Centralization also makes it less likely that the dispatchers will become acquainted with service customers.

With dispatching centralized, local office personnel are freed to focus upon other areas of concern. In Trident the branch administrator acquired broader responsibilities and the senior engineer had his job enriched in business procedural areas as backup for the branch administrator. The first-level managers in both companies were focused more heavily on developing improved relationships with customers and became involved in service operation matters only when the FSMS flagged a potential problem.

The specialization and centralization of the dispatching function also affected the field engineer. The dispatching task that determines much of the day-to-day schedule of the FE is in a central office and the more structured FSMS dispatching logic removes most of the FE's ability to influence his or her schedule. Although there was a certain time efficiency of the FSMS in call allocation (e.g., based on proximity to the next call location), there was the danger of not providing the best qualified FE or one with an established relationship with the customer. Overall it was felt at Trident that this feature would reduce satisfaction and it was disabled. At Zeno, however, evaluation was based "on the numbers" and thus time efficiency became more important than other less quantifiable criteria such as customer satisfaction.

Changes in Intergroup Interactions and Control

The FSMS application changed the nature of field service operations at Trident and Zeno in two ways. First, the new capabilities that the FSMS added to the organization created contention over whose objectives the system should serve. Second, the structure needed to execute the operational task required that groups interact in new ways. These interactions were complicated by changes in the business environment that the FSMS was not originally designed to address. In Zeno, the source of contention between the field offices and the headquarters groups focused on the level of detail that would be collected, raising the issue of whether the FSMS serves the field's or central office's purposes. QE was determined to use the system to support its function. Because the central office groups were focused on productivity measurement and they were the more powerful groups in the organization, they were able to claim priority in determining design choices. In Trident, this controversy was not as pronounced because the field and QE management were able to negotiate more openly and recognize the tradeoffs involved in collecting data for planning purposes and its effect on the efficiency of FEs. Moreover, they did not try to use data collection for control and monitoring purposes.

The data collection features of the FSMS were also used differently in Trident and Zeno, with different effects on FEs working conditions and the accuracy of the data collected. In Trident, because FEs were evaluated qualitatively on the degree of satisfaction expressed by their customers, there was no incentive to manipulate data. At Zeno, however, the data were used to evaluate and monitor the FE. The FE thus had a disincentive to report accurate data. Rather than elicit the cooperation of the FE to assist in data collection, Zeno chose to modify the FSMS software with tighter control and edit procedures in an attempt to eliminate manipulation (pencil whipping) of input data or to catch those who did.

Organizational Values and FSMS Design

We have seen how the FSMS software developer must create a product that will function in a broad spectrum of business and operational environments to give the product a broad market appeal (issues discussed in Chapter 3). This requires great flexibility in how the features and functions of the FSMS can be implemented in various operational settings. We found in our field sites that the user organization made choices affecting individual jobs, group responsibilities, and headquarters versus field "ownership" of the FSMS as a management tool. The FSMS designer set the stage for implementation, but it was the user organization that either used or modified the system design according to its prevailing values about job and organizational design.

By automating many tedious procedures, some jobs were

enhanced. The branch administrator in Trident and the senior engineer had variety added to their jobs. The new responsibilities gave each a broader understanding of the business, although the branch administrator was initially fearful of what her job would entail without dispatching. The local manager gained substantial time to spend with his customers to gain a better understanding of their needs. Presumably, increased contact strengthened Trident's relationship with its customers, thereby promoting increased product sales.

Power Shifts

Power relations in the user organization often determined which features and functions of the FSMS were implemented or modified. The locus of power in the organization became more centralized when the FSMS was implemented. Central organizations saw the new capabilities of the FSMS as supporting their objectives, providing information for quality engineering, for example. This resulted in new procedures for conducting business in the field.

The FSMS alters entrepreneurial qualities of the local office by imposing new structure and discipline for coordination and control. Jobs can become more specialized and narrowly focused. People have less opportunity to decide what is right to satisfy the customer's problem. At Zeno, they more frequently do what they are directed to do. The divergence between individual goals and corporate objectives becomes greater as the FSMS tool is used to monitor and measure individual performance. When, in Zeno, the input data were used for operational control, including performance appraisals for the field engineer, FEs had the incentive to "pencil whip" the data. Rather than fostering responsible autonomy to achieve common goals of performance, stricter bureaucratic controls were implemented and the FEs' reaction was counterproductive for the organization as a whole.

Concluding Comments

This chapter has presented findings about how field service management software affects workers and their service customers. Vendors designed software that appeared to the user organization be a cost-effective investment. The desire for more effectiveness through software in this case was traced to growing pressure in the computer and electronics industry for responsive and efficient handling of service calls, coupled with a need for more accurate tracking of related items, such as component inventories and field failure rates. However, those groups that were more powerful, QE and managers, had their requirements designed into the software with little consideration of conflicting requirements by other users such as the FEs.

This type of applications software presented design issues similar to those from the banking industry presented in Chapter 4. The FSMS changed job structures by largely replacing discretion with prespecified options and other procedural requirements that were built into the software, through which people perform their daily work. It also involves:

- fundamental changes in the nature of the interactions among workers with related jobs,
- value choices in the use (or nonuse) of features contained in the software, and
- shifts in the locus of power in the organization.

Thus, automation for field service delivery turns out to have workplace implications beyond the cost of service delivery. Its impacts on the effectiveness of field service delivery transcend those easily anticipated by software designers.

6

The Computer System and the Hospital: Organizational Power and Control of Information

Ross Koppel*

Although information may be the lifeblood of a business, in a hospital, information can literally determine the fate of its "customers'" life. Designers of hospital computer systems confront many of the issues addressed in large business information systems: security, speed, differing user skill levels, billing, accounting, coordination of many departments, accessibility, and imposition of the computer system on existing structures and processes. Hospitals, however, offer some notable dissimilarities that alter many of the usual procedures and safeguards. *Denying* access to data in a hospital can be catastrophic. Accessing the computerized record of a patient in a medical emergency should not depend upon finding the person with the authorized code or card. Essential patient data must not wait on system down time. Hospitals, moreover, are 24-hour institutions, with several shift changes and a constant influx of new personnel. Some errors cannot be corrected post hoc and losing one's "customer" is more than an issue of losing market share. In hospitals, the emergency must be seen as routine business and the issue of data access takes on a new perspective; response time is not only money, it can mean a life.

Hospitals and hospital computer systems also confront unusual administrative and personnel arrangements. Hospital administrators do not have conventional hierarchial relations

*This chapter was written by Ross Koppel based on research by Ross Koppel, Albert Crawford, and Robert Cort. The author thanks Joel Telles and Harold Salzman for their many insights and suggestions.

with most of their physicians and departments. Computer system design and procedures cannot be dictated by administrative fiat. The system designer must negotiate with powerful departments and independent professionals, all of whom have what they view as nonnegotiable demands.

As we have seen in the preceding cases, the computer system is often one of the more malleable constraints on installing a computer information system. The demands and logic of the organization affect the system design as the logic of the new system affects the organization.[1] This chapter examines the interplay of the hospital's stakeholders, the design of the new computer system, and a key value of the institution, confidentiality of medical data. We argue that powerful organizational stakeholders, attending physicians, powerful medical service departments and the nursing department, determine the allocation of access to data, not the technology or the technicians. The Information Services Department, initially the critical player in the game, is relegated to a service function as soon as the doctors and nurses learn the system's capabilities and structure the negotiations.

Most of the literature on the installation and operation of a hospitalwide information system focuses on productivity and return on investment. Little research is available on the social and organizational implications of medical information systems (Aydin, 1989). Here, we ask how the computer system with its integration of tasks and information will affect:

- maintenance of professional position or autonomy,
- alteration of skill levels,
- confidentiality of records,
- quality of patient care,
- organization and department conflict, and
- productivity.

Background on Hospitals: External Environment and Internal Communications

Trends Affecting Hospitals in the United States

Economic and labor force needs have spurred sales of medical information systems. Hospitals throughout the United States are installing integrated medical information systems that allow point-of-care (bedside) data entry and retrieval (Herring, 1989).[2] St. George's Hospital (a pseudonym), a nonsectarian teaching hospital[3] in a large Eastern city, was part of this trend. In the period from 1989 to 1991 it installed a hospitalwide information system that included a computer terminal in every patient room, nursing station, laboratory, and office. The hospital hoped that automation and integration of information (e.g., data from patients, physicians, nurses, pharmacies, and laboratories) would provide clinical and economic benefits. Integrated medical information systems are particularly attractive to hospitals because they help address many of the problems that emerged during the 1980s. Hospitals are forced to become more business-like to deal with declining reimbursements from third party payers, increasing competition, new forms of reimbursement that do not reward inefficiencies, and demands for tighter government oversight. In addition, hospitals face an aging population (thus sicker people) and a nursing shortage. We consider each of this issues in turn.

Reimbursements Hospital care is the largest single category of the nation's annual $750 billion health expenditures, representing about 38 percent of the total. To reduce costs, government, and increasingly other medical payers, no longer pay on a cost reimbursed basis. The most common payment scheme now is Prospective Payment Systems (PPS) in which the hospital is given a set fee for each patient discharged based on illness category. PPS has succeeded in dramatically reducing the average length of stay (which has decreased 9 percent in 10 years) and in shifting much of the care to outpatient services (which increased 46 percent in a decade). In response, hospitals have increased their outpatient departments and have sought to expand their businesses to nontraditional hospital services, such as buying nursing homes, selling home medical equipment, and opening satellite clinics. The hospital computer system is needed to service the maze of cost accounting systems, billing procedures, organizational links, record keeping requirements, and insurance regulations. (There is, in fact, a related software industry that optimizes patients' illness categories so that hospitals can bill for the highest remunerated illness categories.)

Competition and Aging Hospitals have also come under

competitive and other economic pressures. In the 1981-1991 period, 8 percent (or 471) of the nation's community hospitals closed. The total number of beds has declined and the occupancy rates have fallen 12 percent.[4] In addition, the population is aging, which results in greater illness and much greater demand for hospital services. Compared to ten years ago, hospitals are more likely to be filled with sicker and older patients.

In response to these factors, hospitals have refocused their orientation to management as running a business. They advertise for market share of the insured or affluent population, engage in elaborate market research and strategic planning, and seek allegiances with physicians who can refer and admit insured patients. Integrated hospital computer systems provide administrators crucial information on costs and markets. The systems allow analysis of admissions data for each physician, of geographic distribution of patients and probable patients, and of costs and reimbursements on illness-by-illness, department-by-department, and even doctor-by-doctor bases. In short, the computer systems allow the temples of care and technology to understand their operations and to market them with the same fiscal tools and techniques used by shopping malls and department stores.

Accountability The most recent decade has also seen a significant increase in demand for hospitals' technical accountability through utilization reviews, mortality reports, infection analyses, tighter audits, and prospective fee schedules derived from a Resource-based Relative Value Scale (RBRVS) which seeks to gauge the value of the resources required to deliver specific services. Moreover, fear of malpractice suits is pandemic. Hospitals look to accurate patient records as central to oversight, documentation, and legal protection. Integrated hospital computer systems directly serve these needs. A study of several hospital information systems (Herring, 1989) found that with computerization:

- Medication errors were reduced by 34 percent.
- Patient calls were reduced by 26 percent and repeat calls by 50 percent.
- Discharge teaching documentation was improved by 14 percent.
- Intravenous (IV) site assessment was improved by 4 percent.

More generally, the study found that the computerization:

- decreased errors of omission,
- provided greater timeliness of tests and procedures, and
- improved charting.

In addition, the ability to immediately transform patient information into databases and statistics makes these systems particularly attractive.

Nursing Shortage Last in the litany of hospitals' recent troubles is the shortage of allied medical personnel, most especially nurses. The problem is caused by a tremendous increase in demand, not a decline in supply. More nurses are entering the field but even more are needed. Dramatic increases in nursing salaries have gone a long way to alleviating the shortage, but the pay increases have greatly added to the cost of medical care.

Many of the new machines used in hospitals require nurses, increasing the demand for more nurses. Thus, rather than reduce the need for nurses, the new technologies increase it. Hospital patient information systems, however, are designed to reduce labor input. Research by Tribulski (1989) found that the systems allowed nurses to devote an average of about one-half hour per shift more to addressing patient needs and one-half hour per shift less to paperwork. Perhaps equally important, Koska (1990) reports that hospital information systems improved job satisfaction among nurses. Hospitals, thus, have sought computer systems to reduce nursing costs and to end their constant search for new nurses.

In sum, the past decade has been one of great challenge to hospitals. Some of the difficulties reflect the successes of medical science and art. Many of the drugs and techniques that prolong life also bring lingering costs and more people in need of long-term care. Many of the forces on the medical system have been external, such poverty, insurance regulations, and government oversight. Hospitals have turned to integrated computer information systems as one way of addressing the needs brought on by these forces. As we shall see, however, the computer systems change as well as serve the organizations that install them.

The Impact of Information Systems on Hospitals

Hospitals require extensive documentation of all medical plans and treatments and of all patients' signs, symptoms, and diagnoses. This documentation is required because services must be provided at all hours and under extreme conditions, because of the various medical and nonmedical personnel who deal with each patient, because of the complexity of medical treatment and the need to coordinate disparate elements, and because of invoicing, legal, and regulatory requirements. Central to patient documentation is the patient chart, the record of the patient's medical history, diagnosis, treatment, and laboratory reports. It is the basic document of hospital practice and is the linchpin of the hospital's other record systems.

Information flow in a hospital is traditionally unidirectional. For example: Attending physicians give orders to nurses, the pharmacy, and technicians; labs send reports to doctors; radiologists review X-rays and send reports to the attending physician; nurses record information in the patient chart for review by doctors. All of the information is reflected on the patient's chart, but the chart is kept at the nurse's desk or near the patient's bed. It is unlikely for someone not immediately involved in treating the patient to request the chart. Typically, there is little feedback to the departments or individuals that provide medication, special foods, medical equipment, or laboratory reports.

With computerization of patient data and patient care programs, the flow of information can be made omnidirectional. Many hospital stakeholders can review (and sometimes alter) information previously unavailable or requiring significant effort to obtain. An electronic patient record allows different professionals immediate access to a wide range of patient data.

What can we anticipate about the introduction of a computer system in a hospital?

- We might expect hospital data computerization to exacerbate departmental rivalries and fragmentation and to aggravate contrasting professional perspectives (Cockerham, 1986; Aydin, 1989; Flood and Scott, 1987).
- Alternatively, the potential for more and immediate information and feedback might increase the awareness of other professionals' concerns and obligations, reducing conflict and rivalry.
- We may expect faster and more complete information to improve the skills and understanding of workers who, before, could not so easily observe the results of their efforts.
- We can anticipate that increased access to patient information would result in fewer errors and better medical care.

- We can predict that the effort to control the computer software design will be intertwined with the power distribution of the hospital.
- We can speculate that the formal rules required by computer logic will force the hospital to confront the informal structures and methods of operation used with paper-based systems.
- Last, we may predict that the widespread availability of patient data will raise questions of confidentiality.

Research from other hospitals reveals a mix of benefits and conflicts associated with the new systems. Aydin (1989) finds that acceptance and use of information systems differed significantly by department and by occupational group. A study by Packer (1988) shows the contrasting anticipated benefits of hospital departments' perceptions of computer systems. Nurses and data processing professionals had profoundly different expectations for the point-of-care computer system. Nurses ranked "improved patient care" and "reduced risk of improper care" on the top of their lists. Data processing professionals listed these items at or near the bottom of their ranking and placed "improved productivity" and "better service scheduling" at the top of their list. Nurses, correspondingly, put these two items at or near the bottom of their lists.

Koska (1990) reports that administrators at a Midwestern hospital were shocked when physicians were not eager to review the monthly practice reports generated by the new information system. The practice reports provided data on admissions, length of stay, diagnoses, charges, and the hospital's reimbursement for each physician's Medicare and Medicaid patients. The administrators viewed the reports as the successful cost accounting product of their new system. The doctors apparently did not share that view, and many "threw the reports right into the wastebasket" (Koska, 1990, p. 32).[5] It is not clear from this report if the physicians were annoyed that administrators could use the information system to examine their practices, but it illustrates how computers allow nonmedical staff access to data that otherwise would be difficult to obtain.

A more striking example of the alternative perspectives can be seen in the way the computer system was presented to the many occupational groups at St. George's Hospital. Each occupational group was made to feel that the program was specifically designed for them. While true in a sense that, for example, one can customize a car at time of purchase, the presentations seriously downplayed the system's focus on integration with other departments inherent in an integrated hospital information system.

A good example of this tilt is seen in the presentation of the MAGIC System software by its designers to nursing staff. The MAGIC System company executive asked if the nursing staff subscribed to what is called the standard American nursing practice plan or "nursing philosophy," a code of beliefs and practices that emphasizes a nursing care plan somewhat separate from the physicians' orders. This plan focuses on treatment of the patient as a whole rather than only the specific disease. The nurses responded that, indeed, the nursing care plan exactly reflected their orientation. The MAGIC System executive seemed delighted and perhaps surprised by what appeared to be a fortunate coincidence, exclaiming that the MAGIC System's nursing software was built around exactly that plan or philosophy.

This "coincidence" was highly probable because almost all U.S. nurses subscribe to the orientation reflected in the software. The MAGIC System leader's question assured him of a winning response; he must have known that the nurses would feel particularly favored by the system. It seemed that the software vendor's practices appeared to favor the prevailing beliefs and practices of each of the involved departments.

Medical Magic: The Design of St. George's Hospital Computer System

St. George's Hospital's new computer system produces an electronic patient chart. The computer system replaced a system of paper records. The new system incorporates all medical orders (e.g., orders for medication and treatment), a chronicle of signs, symptoms, and results (including, for example, blood pressure measurements and laboratory tests), and the set of practitioners' notes on diagnoses and treatments. With integration into the hospitalwide computer system, relevant data from all hospital departments and personnel are electronically and instantly inserted into the patient chart. This information may be automatically displayed, graphed, and analyzed in different formats and combinations. Also, the chart may be simultaneously viewed (and altered or added to) from the patient's room, the nursing station, the doctor's office, or from any computer equipped with a modem.

The greater access to patient records enabled by this system has a cost. Patient records contain much confidential information. The patient's willingness to confide in his or her health care provider requires that patient information be seen only by those with a need to know. Legal obligations of confidentiality also reinforce the need to protect such information. The electronic system changes the process of viewing patient records. Because it is not a physical chart at the nurses' station, it cannot be guarded in the same way to protect confidentiality. Protecting confidentiality and providing ready access to patient charts were key issues in design.

The electronic chart project began by selecting a software development contractor. St. George's assembled a task force from representatives of the medical and nursing staffs, the administration, and the information systems department. The task force examined the several hospital software systems available or in advanced design stages. Consensus on selection criteria was quickly achieved; everyone wanted state-of-the-art technology that could do everything. The "final" criteria were: electronic chart capability, bedside (or point-of-care) data entry/retrieval, and flexibility of design and use.

St. George's signed a multimillion dollar contract with MAGIC Hospital Information Systems (a pseudonym), the vendor with the most highly developed system and with the most exultant promises of software programs and services. The MAGIC System is an integrated patient care system that supports almost all aspects of documentation by nurses, physicians, and ancillary department personnel. To support this online record keeping and automatic information transfer, St. George's installed six minicomputers and 500 terminals throughout the hospital, including terminals in every patient room, in all ancillary departments and other supporting areas, in physicians' offices, and in clinics. Essentially, the hospital agreed to place a terminal wherever it would facilitate the work of clinical staff.

Basic computer system security is achieved with magnetic cards (personnel badges with a magnetic strip) and with password security codes. Every terminal has a magnetic card reader attached to it. To use the system, an employee must insert his or her badge and type in his or her password security code. The MAGIC System computer contains a file which lists every employee and his or her type of access. The initial menu screen that each employee sees upon entering the MAGIC System is specific to that employee's type of access.

Most of the documentation in a medical record, either paper or electronic, falls into one of three categories: orders, results, and notes. *Orders* In the conventional paper system, orders (medication or medical treatment) are written on the chart by physicians or other health care providers. Although physicians are the only ones who can order medication or other pivotal medical interventions, many clinicians, such as nurses and physical therapists, also enter orders into the chart. Moreover, students in several fields and at various levels of training also enter orders. On occasion, doctors will telephone in oral orders which they must countersign during their next visit to the patient's room.

With the MAGIC System at St. George's, orders are almost always entered (typed) directly by the clinician generating them. The order entry portion of the MAGIC System is designed to be very easy to use. Once the clinician enters the order, the transaction is complete. If appropriate, a copy of the new order is transmitted directly to the department or individual who must act on it (e.g., the pharmacy to prepare medication, the dietary department to alter meals). Regulatory constraints require that other forms of documentation remain in paper form. For example, patient consent forms (with signatures) must be maintained in paper form even though they could be recorded electronically.

Results Results are usually defined as information that documents tests or procedures. Results range from temperature readings to radiology reports. In the conventional paper system, nurses or other medical personnel wrote results directly on the chart. Laboratory reports were inserted in the chart when they arrived at the nurses' station after what was sometimes a very long and circuitous journey. With St. George's MAGIC System, observations and measurements derived at a patient's bedside are immediately entered in the record (e.g., the nurse takes a temperature reading and types the number into the electronic chart). Laboratory results are entered directly from the lab where they are produced. There is no waiting and all authorized participants can view the results immediately.

Notes With the paper system, notes and other textual material were written in the chart. Extensive comments by physicians were often dictated and inserted later. The notes functions of St. George's MAGIC System were not yet completely developed at the time of our study, but some processes were emerging in response to need and experience. It was already clear that the degree of automation of textual commentary will vary in relation to the complexity and predictability of the material.

Three types of notes software were being implemented. Each reflects differing demands and types of care:

- Menu-type choices are used to offer statements that can be expressed in a phrase or two. That is, rather than taking the time to write a note, the clinician selects a prewritten note from a list of options. A physician, for example, can select "S.O.B." from an onscreen menu and the notation "patient exhibits shortness of breath" appears in the chart.
- Somewhat longer or less standard comments are typed at the terminal by the clinician. Frequently, the clinician combines new material with prewritten menu choices. For example, a notation might read "In the early mornings 'patient exhibits shortness of breath'."
- Very complex textual comments, such as discharge summaries, still rely on dictation and transcription. The transcribed notes are incorporated in the electronic record in free form.

Also, the electronic patient chart allows several different formats for task-specific notes. These include: operative notes, progress notes, and nursing care plans. Each has its own format and system of menu choices. As with all information entered in the computer system, the notes are immediately accessible to all appropriate health care providers.[6]

Looking at the Information: Confidentiality versus Access

Integration of information allows many professional and para-professional workers to obtain more data about their tasks than was possible with the paper-based system. Laboratory or radiology technicians, for example, may view patient data that would have been unavailable to them when all patient information was maintained in the chart near the patient's room. Such information facilitates technicians' performance and understanding of their work.

Similarly, doctors and other medical practitioners need not wait for lab or other reports to be received by the nurses and placed in the chart. The information can be viewed from any location. Thus, their work is facilitated and enhanced by the computer system.

On the other hand, designers of the system have intentionally limited what many personnel see when they turn on their computers. That is, the initial menu screens reflect only the authorized level of access and functional activities of each employee.

According to its designers, the advantages of these system features are:

- A simplified screen and menu increases efficiency and may reduce user confusion.
- There may be literally hundreds of users on the system at any time. Anything that reduces the amount of information presented improves computer response time.
- Clerks and other users might be frustrated by a computer screen (menu) filled with choices and actions they are not permitted to select.
- Staff viewing a range of forbidden choices might besiege the Information Services Department with requests for greater access to the system. The programmers and systems analysts do not want to be in the role of approving or disapproving access requests. Access-related policies are determined by interdepartmental committees.

Several disadvantages to restricting initial menus, however, were acknowledged by the Information Services Department. They were:

- By limiting the user's view of the system's possible functions, the hospital limits that worker's ability to find new uses for the computer system or to improve his or her understanding of the system (e.g., if you do not know about a computer system function, you are unlikely to suggest a new and valuable use for that function).
- The hospital is, thus, foreclosing productivity enhancements that might be generated by users' experimentation with the MAGIC System.
- The possible negative motivational consequences of restricting job and career development via restrictions on

enhanced learning and experimentation are suffered by both the hospital and the employees.[7]

Issues involving confidentiality of patient records existed with the old paper system, but St.George's staff discovered that the MAGIC System forced them to change many policies and procedures, both formal and informal. Specifically, formal procedures ensuring confidentiality of patient information needed to be modified because of the greater availability of electronic records.

Hospital staff, administrators, and computer system designers must determine who will have access to the system. That is:

- What information will be accessible and by whom?
- Where, when, and under what circumstances can this information be seen and/or altered?
- What manipulation (addition, revision, deletion) of that information will be allowed?
- How will the system track access to and alterations of records, and who will oversee the ledger of activities (the audit trail)?

It became clear that no simple answer could be found. The original assumption of the software designers, "whoever has the `need' shall be granted access," proved insufficient amid the large volume and variety of claims of "need." Also, not surprisingly, some of the more powerful stakeholders in the organization perceived and advocated reasons for allocating access that are not universally accepted.

Illustrations of these conflicts are not hard to find. Some top administrators, for example, believed that they should have access to patient data because the information is needed to assess general operations of the hospital. Physicians, however, saw no reason for nonphysicians to review their cases except in extraordinary circumstances. Somewhat similarly, physicians were sometimes unsympathetic to access claims of the service departments (e.g., dietary) or the less prestigious professional departments (e.g., physical therapy). Some physicians felt that the other departments should follow the directives as stipulated by the doctors and had little need to review the entire patient chart.

White Coats, White Lies, and Instant Information

Before the introduction of the hospital computer system, the speed of information was usually determined by interoffice mail.

Doctors' gained access to information by visiting the hospital or by a phone call to a laboratory or nurse. While the information was moving around, or before it could be read, there was slack in the organization that allowed the routine practice of medicine. Newly trained doctors would administer the experienced physicians' treatment guidelines, doctors would cover for each other, and doctor's secretaries would sign forms following their bosses' instructions.

The computer system reduces nearly to zero the time required for the distribution of information. It alters or tightens the record keeping process. These changes significantly affect the way doctors deal with their younger colleagues, with each other, and with clerical staff. We observed the effects of the system on interactions of physicians with their colleagues and with residents.

Modern medical practice, with its myriad, high tech laboratory tests and diagnostic tools, is sometimes criticized for what is called "treating the chart and not the patient." This refers to physicians who concentrate on laboratory and other data and fail to observe or interact with the patient. Some doctors at St. George's fear that the MAGIC System facilitates such practices. Indeed, at the extreme, physicians could conceivably avoid even visiting the patient's room.

To address this concern, the doctors at the hospital ordered that the original remote order entry procedure be redesigned to restrict the practice of "treating the chart and not the patient." The new protocol requires that any medical order entered into the computer system from a terminal other than the one at the patient's bedside must be countersigned (reapproved/reentered) within 24 hours at the terminal in the patient's room: A remote order will be treated as the equivalent of an oral order under the old paper record system and must be countersigned by the physician in the vicinity of the patient.

St. George's hospital, like most hospitals, has a symbiotic relationship with its attending physicians. Attending physicians are powerful organizational stakeholders over whom hospitals have only limited authority. They are fully credentialed practitioners who have been approved by the hospital to admit and treat patients, in contrast to residents, who are medical school graduates receiving additional training. The financial viability of the hospital depends heavily on its patient base and thus on its attending physicians' good will. The hospital must provide services to these physicians. Now more than ever before, these services include access to sophisticated computer resources.

St. George's administration is particularly eager to maintain good relations with its attending physicians because it has an open practice plan that allows physicians to admit patients to other hospitals. Thus, St. George's must provide ongoing satisfaction to the "attendings." In designing the computer system, the hospital was eager to accommodate their wishes. As revealed below, however, the needs of confidentiality and the desire to satisfy attendings are not always compatible.

Each time an attending physician views one of his or her patient's chart, the computer provides a list of all access events to that chart. Thus, the attending physicians could perform a post hoc review of all those seeking access to the charts. Attending physicians, however, do not see themselves as cops and seldom wish to use their time calling around the hospital to find out why an unauthorized individual viewed their charts.

A second confidentiality review option, also in use, is a warning system. If a physician seeks to view the chart of patient to which he or she has not been given programmed authority, the computer flashes the message: "ACCESS TO THIS RECORD IS UNAUTHORIZED, A RECORD IS BEING MADE OF THIS ACCESS AND ALL ACTIONS."

A third option, also in use, involves restricting access to specific groups of professionals. Doctors and nurses, for example, are usually allowed to see all parts of the patients' charts (although a record is made of the access events). On the other hand, other groups, such as the dietary department or the physical therapists, may not be allowed access to all patients' charts. Moreover, only sections of charts to which they have access will be displayed on the computer system.

In addition to their roles as independent practitioners with control over much of the hospital's client base, attending physicians are responsible for training the residents or house staff (physicians who are completing specialized medical education). At St. George's Hospital, as in other teaching hospitals, there is opportunity for conflict between these two strata of physicians.[8] The new computer system sometimes facilitates that conflict. House staff (also called residents) are supposed to be guided by the attending physicians, dutifully executing the established doctors' orders. However, house staff are also the physicians in charge of the hour-to-hour care of patients, including routine and emergency care. Conflict arises about autonomy and access to the patient records. With the old paper-based system, attending physicians who were away from the hospital could not view patient charts or new patient data. They would have to come to the hospital or call a nurse to have the new data read over the phone. The new computer system, however, allows attending physicians to monitor their patients from their offices or homes. Attendings, thus, can alter their original orders and in this way deprive the house staff of an opportunity to learn by exercising their emerging authority.

The house staff, beyond executing the attending physicians' general directives, are eager to act on their own insights and on the most recent test results. They are, similarly, eager to observe the effects of their own orders on a patient's condition. Thus, the electronic chart becomes an element in a controversy of house staff autonomy versus computer-assisted long-range control by the attendings.

During the day, for example, an attending physician may outline a strategy that calls for continued use of a particular medication to be followed by a reevaluation of the patient after two days. That first night, however, the patient's condition may change in ways suggesting that the medication is ineffective or counterproductive. The resident, monitoring the patient on an hour-to-hour basis, may be tempted to alter the medication. With the old system, the attending physician would probably be inaccessible and certainly would not be able to view the new data. The resident would probably issue new orders, responding to the changing conditions. However, with the electronic system, the attending could review the chart from his or her home and alter the medication orders. The house staff, thus, are obliged to surrender some of their autonomy to the greater but more distant expertise of the attending physicians. Note that from the patient's perspective, the best solution is not clear. Presumably, an experienced attending physician will provide the better care, even from the distance of the office or home. However, there is an obvious value to having the doctor on the scene make the decisions immediately and perhaps in consultation with the patient.

Physician's Agents, Group Practice, and the Electronic Signature

Attending physicians may wish to delegate certain access rights to residents, medical students, and office personnel. Some of these physicians argue that their agents should have the same security clearance as the attending physician. Occasionally, attending physicians want their agents to have identical identification badges and security codes.

Most probably, doctors who request such privileges are reflecting experiences with procedures under the previous paper-based system of record keeping. By allowing a few trusted workers to sign for them, these doctors avoided paperwork. Undoubtedly, they felt that they could oversee the actions of their underlings. As one attending physician insisted at a computer system design committee meeting, "I want my secretary to be able to [electronically] sign my charts just as she has always done. If she messes up, I'll fire her." Others in the committee pointed out that the secretary could be granted the same level of permission as the attending physician, but that she would be given a different identification badge and password. Thus, the secretary would have the access level the doctor determined but her actions would be accountable to only her use of the system.

A similar situation arose in relation to group practice arrangements and the electronic signature. Doctors often form group practice arrangements, treating each others' patients. In such arrangements, for example, all the cardiologists in a group practice may have a need to see the records of all of the patients in that practice and would demand reciprocal access rights to all patients within that group practice.

Some group practice physicians, again, perhaps reflecting the earlier paper-based methods, wanted a single identification badge for all members of their group. Here, the solution was easily handled by the system designers: The computer would be programmed to allow all members of a particular group practice to receive access to the charts of patients being treated by any member of that group.

Department Conflict and Professional Ethos

The introduction of the computer system generates conflicts among departments that were dormant or perhaps nonexistent.

The new system also highlights professional norms and concerns about professional status. The two examples, below, illustrate these points.

What's in a Day? Nurses and the Pharmacy

Nurses are currently in conflict with the hospital pharmacy over the definition of "what's in a day" or, more specifically, "when do you start counting a day's worth of pills that are ordered in the middle of the day?" The conflict arises in large part from the increased integration of information generated by the MAGIC System. MAGIC System designers are being asked to help solve the problem. Under the old system, a physician told the nurse that a patient was to be given a medication, for example, four times a day. The doctor recorded that information in the chart but the nurse requested the medication from the pharmacy. Now, the pharmacy receives the order for medication directly when the doctor enters it in the electronic patient chart. The nurse does not place the order but only administers the medication when the pharmacy sends it to the patient's floor.

The dispute arises because the pharmacy has a different definition of how to handle orders issued in the middle of the day (very few medication orders are issued exactly at midnight). The pharmacy believes that, if only four pills are needed per day, it should supply a prorated number of pills the first day. Thus, if the medication order were placed at 11 A.M. the pharmacy sends only two or three pills for the first day. The nurses respond that they well understand the issues and that they will do their best to space the administration of the medication. That is, the nurses say that "four pills per day *is* four pills per day" and that they will continue to exercise professional judgment about distribution.

The pharmacy, in contrast, points to the time and date stamp that the computer attaches to every physician order and claims that they are responsibly calculating the appropriate medication for the first day. The pharmacists add that the old noncomputer system, wherein the nurse mediated the information, was merely inefficient and wasteful.

Nurses have often mediated information between doctors and others. For example, in addition to the medication schedule on the first day of new medication, experienced nurses often question doctors' orders if they think them ill-considered. The questioning may be polite but firm. A nurse will ask a doctor, for example, "did you know that this patient was also taking medication `X'?" Or," did you remember that the patient is scheduled for a `Y' procedure tomorrow?" On rare occasions, when a doctor is half-asleep or unfamiliar with the case, an experienced nurse will refuse to carry out an order. Two points should be noted here. It has been estimated that up to 20 percent of prescriptions are misfilled due to doctors' illegible handwriting. The computerized system reduces the probability of errors due to illegible handwriting. However, it is worth remembering that a misspelling in context is easily interpreted by a human but will totally befuddle a computer. Similarly, a slightly confused but basically sensible order will be corrected or clarified by the nurse. The computer is seldom that helpful. Thus, while the benefits of direct computer communication with the pharmacy and the billing office are appreciable, there are also risks and liabilities.

Where to Put the Terminals? Different Views

As we have seen, the flow of information within the hospital is altered by the new information system. The system, however, also alters the generation of information. Much of the data on patients are collected by asking the patient or by taking various readings from the patient's body, for example, temperature and blood pressure. These data are entered into the computer system from the patient's bedside computer terminal. The most obvious location for bedside computer terminals, one would assume, is by the bedside. That is not where the terminals were placed. This decision was made by the nurses after considerable debate. In each room, the computer terminals are several feet from the bedside, on the nursing server/sink cabinet at the entrance of each patient room. The process of determining the computer terminal's placement is instructive.

Much of the interaction between a clinician and patient benefits from face-to-face observation. Doctors, for example, are trained to observe the way patients use their hands in pointing to sources of pain. A patient's flat palm moving generally over the belly may indicate a different sort of problem than a patient's finger pointing to a specific spot in the area. (The former may indicate a dull, generalized pain whereas the latter may indicate a sharp specific pain.) Similarly, when asking about personal activities or medical histories, a doctor or nurse would want to see the patient's facial expressions and other gestures. In terms of efficiency, one would expect that nurses taking blood pressure or temperature measurements would want the computer as close as possible to the bedside to allow convenient data entry of the information (nurses are unquestionably the most frequent users of the bedside computer terminals).

However, the nurses decided to have the terminals placed away from the patients' beds despite attempts to convince them otherwise. The nurses' first objection was that the computer terminals would occupy too much space, preventing emergency equipment from approaching the patient. This was dismissed after the use of a tape measure and the offer to purchase a retractable stand (the type on which hospital TVs are placed). The second objection was that the retractable stands could not hold the weight of the terminals. This objection was dismissed with a scale; the computer terminals weigh less than the TVs. The third objection was that the retractable stands would be too expensive. This objection was dismissed by comparing the cost of the multimillion dollar system with the trivial cost of the retractable stands. The nurses' fourth objection was that typing is noisy. This was dismissed with surprise, for hospitals are seldom quiet.

Eventually, the nurses simply demanded that the computers be placed by the nurse server/sink cabinet. That is where they are. Perhaps the nurses' objections to placement of terminals near the bedside was that they did not wish to display their lack of familiarity with computers to the patients. Their unstated concern may have reflected a professional ethos for the patina of competence potentially blemished by the learning process being viewed by patients.

Computer System Effects

Early in this chapter we listed several factors that would probably be affected by the computer information system. We suggested that in addition to its impact on confidentiality, the new computer system would likely affect the quality and productivity of medical care, the skills and autonomy of the workers, and relations among departments and professionals. We now consider these issues in light of what we know about the computer system and the hospital's operations.

Quality and Productivity of Medical Care

The computer system has significant potential for enhancing quality of care within the hospital. Immediate and greater information generally reduces errors and provides opportunity for greater understanding and better coordination among health care providers. Information can be graphically displayed and statistically correlated in ways that would have taken hours and required long-forgotten skills (and probably would not have been done). With the MAGIC System a radiologist or lab worker can review the patient chart to observe the context of the data (i.e., view previous test results and suspected diagnoses). The MAGIC System also provides a constant reminder of medication times and repeated procedures.

Productivity is enhanced by faster information flow, enhanced access to information, routinized note taking procedures, efficient documentation of records and measures, and the instantaneous graphic and statistical presentations. The new system should eliminate the time wasted looking for notes or worrying about lost papers. Interdepartmental relations, while not necessarily made more harmonious, are facilitated by systematic transfer of data and automatic reconfiguration of data into desired formats or protocols.

On the other hand, this case also illustrates the unintended consequences of immediate transfer of information without the mediating role of nurses or others. While the MAGIC System generates significant efficiencies of time and effort, it may sacrifice oversight by skilled and experienced information gatekeepers. Moreover, to the extent that data on a computer screen may be granted greater legitimacy and accuracy than information in a paper chart, the MAGIC System may engender an uncritical acceptance of data.

Autonomy, Conflict, and Power

Use and perception of hospital computer systems reflects the differing social, functional, and political positions within the hospital. While many of the conflicts antedate the new computer system the design of the computer system brings them more into focus and creates some new potential and rival sources of tension. The computer system engendered conflict between nurses and pharmacists, for example, by removing the slack in the system, establishing a level of control that did not exist previously. With the old system, the nurses controlled the amount and administration of medication on the first day of a new medication. With the new system, the doctors and pharmacists regain control but at the cost of the nurses' mediating or gatekeeper role. Lost is their hands-on experience with the patients and the possibility of nurses catching errors before the prescription order enters the pipeline.

Conflict between the attending physicians and the residents may also be heightened by the new computer system. The new system may diminish the learning process of the younger doctors. The system may be used in ways that enhance the care of some patients or, alternately, provide a remote and technical kind of care that fails to meet the real needs of the sick.

A different example of contrasting department perspectives can be seen in the way the computer system was presented to nurses at St. George's Hospital. Each occupational group was made to feel that the program was specifically designed for them. While true in a sense, the initial presentation to each department emphasized the special accommodation to that department rather than the need for integration with other departments. The need of the vendor to "sell" the system to each constituency can distort the functionality of the system. Thus, the power of the departments and professional groups, in concert with a vendor seeking acceptance and cooperation, may reduce the total worth of the integrated system.

In computerization at St. George's we see how organizational power can shape the implementation of an organization-wide information system. The case examines the roles and activities of attending physicians, who may be viewed as independent agents with power over the hospital's client base. The interplay between attending physicians and other stakeholders provides an unusual view of competition and of the emergence of computer system knowledge by a previously computer-illiterate group. The process of allocating access to the computer system (determining who may view and manipulate the system's information) is the forum in which the stakeholders' priorities emerge clearly and in which the contests among those stakeholders are most transparent.

Even attending physicians, however, are subject to limitations to MAGIC System functions. Although integration of information and tasks is a key goal of the system's designers, restrictions are often placed on the technology to ensure conformity with medical norms or with values associated with good practice. In a key debate, one group of physicians argued for restricting their own use of the computer system to ensure that they visit patients on a daily basis. The doctors were concerned that some physicians would employ the technology to neglect their patients and, instead, focus on their patients' laboratory and other data.

Nurses' decisions regarding placement of the computer screens exemplifies the need for the appearance of professional expertise. Nurses seemed to observe the medical ethos that full-fledged medical professionals should not exhibit lack of expertise to patients. If the terminals were placed close to the patient's bedside the nurses would be obliged to display their unfamiliarity with the computer system, at least while learning to use it. Thus, they requested that the terminals be placed away from the patient's immediate observation.

Every system design solution involves tradeoffs. If access is restricted to only the attending physician and specified nurses, the loss of flexibility could be catastrophic. In an emergency the staff would have to act without a patient's basic data. The integration of information that is possible with the MAGIC System would be largely defeated.

For professional staff, the MAGIC System relies on retrospective audits of computer access to monitor security. Attending physicians can request the computer to provide a list of all access events to each chart. Busy doctors, however, do not regard themselves as police and typically do not wish to spend time examining unauthorized access to their charts. Equally important is the *soft* nature of the control mechanism embodied in the audit of access events. The need for immediate access to information precludes the type of hard controls used in most financial or business settings where access is restricted electronically and/or mechanically.

The process of balancing the needs of different groups in the hospital is a political process. The control and the usual perceived neutrality of the Information Services Department, once the exclusive mantel of technological expertise (it is their system and they know it best) is being eroded by an increasingly knowledgeable hospital staff. As others become familiar with the system's functions and possibilities, the control and putative neutrality of the Information Services Department becomes increasingly irrelevant. Value or power conflicts involving the Information Services Department (such as who should have access to what information) cannot be hidden behind technical design specifications. Moreover, just as doctors and nurses often have differing perceptions of crucial priorities, the Legal, Accounting, Medical Records, and Information Services Departments also see the hospital and its information system in differing ways. The hospital's design committees are now focusing on the tradeoffs implicit and explicit in the design decisions. For example, staff in the software design committees began to ask directly about the tradeoffs between patient data confidentiality and hospital efficiency and about tradeoffs between patient data confidentiality and physician practice efficiencies.

The implementation of the computer system, because of the systematic and explicit nature of computer system design, often makes users aware of tradeoffs that were hidden, ignored, or avoided with previous methods of operation. This consequence (to make explicit processes that are and were often fuzzy) applies not only to competition among players but also to previous methods of operation.[9]

Concern about confidentiality of records, for example, existed before the new computer system. With the paper-based chart system, violations of confidentiality were almost always unrecorded. If unauthorized staff saw patient charts, it was unlikely that anyone would report such actions to a hospital ethics committee. If staff observed unauthorized persons reading patient charts, they would probably inquire about the reason and request that the charts be returned to their proper locations. With the electronic system, there is a 24-hour ledger (a full-audit trail) of every chart review and of all other transactions by every system user.

With the old system, medical staff undoubtedly made sincere efforts not to disclose information in patient charts and to make the charts inaccessible to unauthorized personnel, but this situation was radically different from the current one. Previously, there was only one chart for each patient and it was sequestered behind the nurses' station. Other departments, such as laboratories, pharmacies, or kitchens, were sent only specific and partial data about any patient. Staff had no way of viewing the entire patient record from any location in the hospital.

Conclusion

Road planners in urban areas envy their country colleagues who can plan highways in seemingly empty spaces. Urban road designers feel they must negotiate access to every inch of land, accommodating many existing structures, bridging over existing pathways. Even worse is the need to hack through the dense tangles of power, money, and political arrangements. Implementing an integrated computer information system in an existing organization is a task somewhat analogous to that of the urban road designer. Every organizational inch is thick with vested interests, desires to maintain or enhance skills, authority structures, and concerns about quality, professional status, and autonomy. The road building analogy continues in another way: Just as a road transforms a community it traverses and the relationships among the communities it links, computer systems change the organizations they "integrate." In our case, hospital routines are altered and relations among departments and workers are changed or brought into sharper relief; conflicts are created or exposed, power is made more clear, and even interactions are revealed that few previously acknowledged or understood.

The roadway analogy falters eventually because it fails to capture the interactive nature of computer system development. Although the planning process is open to political decisionmaking, a roadway, once built, is substantially fixed. Software, however, is more malleable throughout its life cycle. The forces within the hospital will shape it at the time of installation and throughout its existence. Of course, the power to shape the computer system depends on the power of the individual or group within the hospital and on knowledge of the system's capabilities. It also depends on who else the changes will affect as conflict arises when the system affects the authority or autonomy of another.

Software development may be a plastic process but the logical relationships and speed of the information it distributes are hard and fast. Value or power differences only implicit in prior record keeping and medical practice are made salient. Because of the systematic and explicit nature of computer system design, the implementation of the computer system often requires users to confront tradeoffs that were hidden, ignored, or avoided in previous methods of operation.

In the case of the conflict between pharmacists and the nurses about who should determine the first day's medication dose, the computer system made explicit an issue that was not confronted because the old medication ordering procedure did not directly connect the actions of the two groups. From the pharmacists' perspectives, the new system allows better control and more logical distribution of medication. From the nurses' perspectives, the new system engenders an invasion of their traditional authority and professionalism.

A similar phenomenon is observed with the conflict between the attending physicians and the resident staff. The computer system again precipitates conflict where previously it had been rare. Conflict could have occurred frequently if the attendings were willing to call or visit the hospital several times per day, but that was unlikely; the slack in the old method allowed younger doctors to practice their skills but still be guided by their more experienced advisors. Now the patient records and the residents' authority are electronically tethered to the attendings, thus generating occasions for conflict to arise.

The controversy among the doctors about "treating the patient and not the chart," demanding that doctors visit the patient to countersign all orders from remote terminals, reflects the controversy between high tech versus high touch medicine. The new computer system facilitates a kind of medical practice at a distance that some doctors chose to restrict.

St. George's Hospital purchased the integrated patient information system to meet a variety of economic, regulatory, and clinical needs. It approached system design and implementation as involving only technical issues, but other organizational issues quickly emerged. Computer software design is a human endeavor in which systems are reconfigured as they are implemented. A computer system will continue to evolve, reflecting the organizational struggles, oversight regulations, economic imperatives, stakeholder power, and, in this case, the needs of medical practice. Just as urban road systems create and are created by the social and economic forces in an area, the computer system will affect relations among groups within the hospital and will be changed by the demands of those groups.

Endnotes

1. See, for example, Kling (1986), Mumford (1983), Mirvis and Lawler (1983), and Markus and Pfeffer (1983).

2. In 1988, approximately 135 U.S. hospitals had point-of-care systems (Packer, 1988) and the figure had tripled by 1990.

3. Teaching hospitals, in addition to their general hospital activities, serve as training facilities for younger physicians and for the many other health care providers, such as physical therapists, dieticians, technicians, and nurses. Teaching hospitals also provide continuing medical education for their many practitioners and research scientists, informing them of emerging knowledge and techniques.

4. *Hospital Trends,* American Hospital Association (1992) and Dr. Joel L. Telles, Delaware Valley Hospital Council, personal communication (January 26, 1993).

5. Eventually, Koska (1989) reports, administrators convinced the physicians that cost consciousness would result in a better bottom line and they became interested in the reports.

6. Data in St. George's MAGIC System can be viewed in many ways. Data elements can be grouped for display in almost any format and combination, providing a great deal of flexibility. Persons authorized to look at the chart can view it in whatever format they find most useful. For example, doctors concerned about a patient's blood gases might request that blood gas data be displayed on their terminals before any other information on that patient is shown. Similarly, doctors examining the relationship between two clinical measures could program their terminals to display a graph comparing the patient's information on those two variables.

The system will also provide hospitalwide information from patient charts. An example is of a nursing director who may request a listing of all patients who must receive medication on the third shift. Here, the nursing director uses the system to forecast the total nursing workload. Another example is the system's capability to generate a list for a medical clinician or researcher who seeks data on all patients who have contracted a specific infection within the last 72 hours.

In other words, the MAGIC System incorporates a database management system. Physicians, nurses, and social workers, for example, can view the same record, extracting only the data elements they need. In addition to aiding clinicians, this function allows support departments, such as medical records and quality assurance, to extract data in whatever format they require.

One group of doctors, at first reluctant to learn the computer system, became captivated by desires to customize their initial menus and to reduce the number of keystrokes required to obtain certain information. Several morning meetings were spent with the physicians comparing the results of their friendly competition. Dr. A would inform the group that he was able to see the latest data on his hospitalized patients by just signing on to his terminal and typing three keystrokes. Dr. B. would counter that his screen automatically gave him the "order form" for a preselected group of patients and required only two keystrokes. St. George's Information Services staff were pleased because the doctors were learning to use the system. Even more helpful, their competition was forcing the doctors to teach themselves how to use the system, often in ways that few other hospital members were attempting.

7. The hospital has established training sessions for clerks and other employees who wish to improve their knowledge of the computer system. It is hoped the training will lead to more extensive use of the new system within the hospital. The additional training is also intended to assist clerks who wish to advance within the hospital.

8. We note that most hospitals are not teaching hospitals and, thus, do not have the same potential for conflict between attending physician and residents. Also, there are several different orientations toward the role of attending physician. Some argue that an attending should never place an order. Rather, attending physicians should give very general guidance as to diagnosis and treatment. Others, however, see them as more involved in the direct care of the patient.

9. Several nurses have commented that with the old paper system, doctors could often be found near the nurses' station or in the areas of the patient rooms while they (the doctors) were hunting for the patient charts. At such times, the nurses could ask questions of the doctors or request new or modified treatments for the patients. Thus, the inefficiencies of the old system allowed the nurses to convey information or receive guidance that otherwise would be unavailable.

7

Software Design, Social Choices, and the Workplace

Social choices characterize applications software design as much as technical engineering issues. In examining software design as a social process we have identified as important issues the tradeoffs and compromises among competing interests and objectives of users and of others in the user organization, the process by which decisions of designers are shaped by their organization, and the role of various pressures in the market. The chapters in Part I explained and justified our basic premise that the interplay of such factors would significantly influence both explicit and implicit design choices. We emphasized how software designs necessarily reflect organizational choices about objectives of different users and others in both the vendor and user organizations. Then in Part II, for each of the cases we studied, we identified a range of design influences and the specific values underlying the social shaping of particular software features and functions. This chapter considers what we have learned from our several case studies and survey. The final two chapters translate these findings into an action agenda for managers (Chapter 8) and consider the implications for research in this area (Chapter 9).

Crucial design choices about software that regulates operations of the user organization reflect social choices that may not necessarily be optimal choices. In fact, we found that for many choices there may not be an objectively optimal design; rather, the choices will favor some objectives over others with decisions shaped by organizational politics for example. Indeed, by providing greater integration within the organization, software systems lead to tighter "coupling" of structures in organizations, among different groups and between formal policies and

171

informal practices. The following discussion of the three industries, banking, field service, and hospitals, focuses on the consequences of different choices in software design. The software, as part of its substantive task (e.g., storing information), was designed to automate and control procedures by formalizing them in design, emphasizing managerial control objectives over operations objectives, as it integrated the work of functionally different groups. This emphasis can be traced to the initial choices about features and functions of the software.

An important point to recognize in analysis of these cases is that the design decisions were not "bad" in the sense of being made because of ignorance about user needs or failing to properly analyze user operations. On the contrary, we found that designers understood quite well which design decisions were important for building a successful commercial product. We also derived insights, presented at the conclusion of this chapter, into how technology is adopted by organizations and into the nature of the interplay between technology design and its use in organizations.

Banking Software

The banking cases discussed in Chapter 4 showed how certain software design specifications derived from traditional priorities of ensuring the integrity of account data, security, and reducing transaction costs. In particular, design choices reflected management's quest for reduced labor costs, increased managerial control over service delivery functions, decreased discretion of tellers, and minimized training requirements. Some of the objectives for greater managerial control were viewed as necessities in a tight labor market where tellers were likely (given the low wages banks were willing to provide) to be low skilled and have high turnover.

The design of the teller system incorporated a decision, the use of the officer card to approve irregular transactions, that traded customer service and teller efficiency in favor of security of information and money. It also reflected the formal rules and procedures of the bank. However, in practice the operating requirements of the branch required a tradeoff in which service and efficiency were more important than security for day-to-day operations. The solution developed by the branches was to readily allow tellers access to the officer card to address one specific feature of the system (the hold status on accounts accessed three or more time in one day). So doing compromised all supervisor oversight of customer security that was regulated by the system. That is, ensuring security still depended upon teller compliance and judgment to invoke supervisor oversight.

"Enforcing the rules" uniformly, an important selling feature of the system, required it to be designed at the level of lowest common denominator, that is, for the most inexperienced, least trustworthy teller. Because the teller system is an important factor structuring the teller's job, its design had a significant impact on the teller's quality of work life. Designing for the lowest common denominator may also limit the extent to which workers can perform their work in ways that rise above this minimal level.

The design of the teller system was viewed by the software engineers as a sensible response to the job characteristics of the teller. However, the set of design choices made by the software engineers also played a role in shaping new job characteristics. In this instance, if implemented as designed, the system would remove all teller discretion regarding transaction processing, treating all tellers in a consistent manner. Not only would the system enforce all rules and ensure that all work was conducted uniformly, but it also would minimize positive discretionary action by tellers, aside from their exchanging perfunctory pleasantries while processing customer transactions.

Reducing job discretion this far changes the essence of a teller's contribution to rote adherence to procedures rather than the exercise and development of judgment, skill, and discretion to respond to varying conditions of the work. Such formal working conditions minimize opportunities for development and recognition of new skills or initiative; it is not surprising in this setting that advancement is based largely on endurance (i.e., seniority). Ironically, because this system design regulated procedures too tightly, in use it became ineffective in achieving the goal of enforcing security rules.

The software design brought into conflict various arrangements, such as security versus efficiency and trust, that previously were made at a local level. The software system thus changed the basis of discretionary action. In this instance it brought informal arrangements into conflict with formal procedures by removing the buffer, through loose coupling, between formal policies and informal practice. By implementing the security provision in the software, branch management lost flexibility to modify policies in accordance with local operating requirements (of both bank activity and management-employee relationships), thereby limiting the autonomy of both branch managers and tellers. Changing the software to allow such local arrangements would have required a formal policy change at the central office of the bank, implemented by the programming department and approved at the executive level.

In principle, the bank management would not want to formally change this policy and allow this discretion. The policy was established with a tradeoff made in favor of security over efficiency. It was also established in an era when competition in banking was low and when little attention was paid to customer service. Moreover, the perspectives of central office managers were forged when noncomputerized procedures allowed flexibility and the exercise of discretion. Previously, because of the nature of noncomputerized operations, informal operational procedures allowed such accommodation without a formal policy change. However, changing the software to accommodate actual operating requirements would necessitate the software designers or branch managers to formalize this conflict between rules and regulations and office practice, between the formal and informal operational procedures.

In the BSC system an additional set of features, designed to meet the new banking objectives, was overlaid on the design features of the older systems, which were enhanced by state-of-the-art technologies. One of the software developers' objectives was to design the teller system to enforce the rules of the banks. To this end, they designed elaborate decisionmaking capabilities into the system to handle exceptional transaction situations (adding an expert system based function to address the types of problems noted in the other bank situation discussed above). For example, this function determines when to allow customers to cash checks against uncollected funds (e.g., if they have a substantial balance in another account with the bank) and other conditions that previously a teller would evaluate and then make a decision or consult a supervisor. Recall that automating all decisionmaking was a design objective for the BSC system because of two important factors: tellers were viewed as having minimal skill and intellectual capabilities and banks did not want to invest in training tellers. Accordingly, the BSC teller system functions were designed to allow the bank to increase control in an attempt to improve productivity and decrease labor costs.

At the same time, however, the BSC system was designed to respond to the new competitive market conditions of banking by introducing new types of functionality into teller stations. Analysis of each customer's account enables tellers to sell him or her new products, maintain existing products, and generally manage the customer relationship. To achieve this objective, the system is designed to be a marketing tool for the teller and a resource providing product information, such as current interest rates, that allows the teller to be knowledgeable about complex and changing products. This set of design objectives leads to features and functions that are tools for the teller rather than a means of enforcing operations objectives of management. In this role the teller is implicitly viewed as the key salesperson to a particular market segment, thus as a revenue generator rather than a labor cost.

On balance we found that software designed for the new banking objectives still carried the legacy of the traditional banking environment. It brought into conflict design of features and functions that devalued tellers' abilities with other features and functions that depended on tellers initiative for the bank to gain a competitive edge.

At one level the BSC system can be viewed as "in transition," moving from a design reflecting traditional banking and managerial objectives to a new set of market requirements that were not fully appreciated by user organizations. Both trying to follow and lead, BSC's design was an attempt to capture the existing market by designing for the requirements current management articulated and simultaneously trying to introduce its vision of design for the new competitive conditions of banking. In this respect the system was designed to fulfill selling requirements and to address serving market requirements but did not satisfy ultimate end user requirements or reflect actual operating conditions of the bank. The system design was shaped by different, and in this case conflicting, user requirements; some apparently essential requirements of banking operations were not met because they were not formally accepted within the user organization.

Field Service Software

The field service management system (FSMS) described in Chapter 5 reflected tradeoffs in design and implementation, shaped by conflicting objectives, similar to the banking cases. These cases also provide a contrast between two organizations that formulated their objectives differently: Some of the key issues concerned tradeoffs among features and functions that could be used for increased control of, and decreased autonomy for, field engineers or that could be used to improve organizational performance. They also illustrated how conflicting goals, both hierarchical and functional, shape software design in ways that create new tensions in organizations.

The FSMS application changed the way groups within both user companies interacted. This occurred for two reasons. First, the new capabilities the FSMS added to the organization created contention over whose objectives the system should serve. Second, the structure and procedures imposed on the operational tasks required that groups within the field service organization interact in new ways. Design of certain features and functions of the FSMS was shaped by political power in the user organization. The FSMS was designed to centralize control by enforcing uniform operational procedures across all field offices and by centrally determining most decisions.

The structure and discipline of coordination and control that the FSMS supports altered the entrepreneurial aspects of the local office. Job design became more specialized and narrowly focused. People did not do what was right to satisfy the customer because it needed to be done; they did what they were directed to do. The loss of autonomy and the "hard" controls, particularly in the first company, Zeno, transformed the job of the field engineers (FEs) into one of performance of instructions issued by the FSMS and the central office; lost was their primary role as diagnostician.

Interestingly, these effects were not all intentional. Because it was thought that traditional field service problems were the result of failure to follow established procedure, design of the FSMS was based on the premise that enforcing "good procedure" would ensure good outcomes. Using that system to enforce procedures changed a number discrete job characteristics and practices in varying degrees, but overall it resulted in a significant transformation of the essential qualities of the job in ways not always predictable from analysis of any one feature or function of the FSMS system. For example, the added data capabilities of the system were used by central organizations and branch managers to support their reporting objectives at the cost of field engineers' efficiency. In one organization it was further used in an attempt to monitor FE performance. FE resistance to the latter objective resulted in negating its usefulness for either purpose. Although redesign was attempted to prevent entry of inaccurate data, experience after installation of the system suggests that as long as the data were used to monitor performance the ability to ensure its quality would never surpass the ingenuity of the field engineers and their ability to "pencil whip" the data. In this way, the FSMS brought to the fore and precipitated organizational conflicts.

Hospital Software

In the hospital system described in Chapter 6 different explicit objectives drove the design, but a parallel set of issues was raised. However, different power relations and underlying philosophy about professional employees led to different types of design solutions. The capabilities of the system allowed a group of high status professionals, physicians and nurses, greater autonomy and latitude in performing their work. Even midlevel paraprofessionals, such as lab or radiology technicians, could use the system to broaden their understanding of their tasks. For example, in contrast to the earlier paper-based system, the computer system provided a considerable amount of information about the patients they treated, allowing appreciation of the larger context in which they performed their work. In this sense, the system enhanced skill utilization and development and greater integration of activities, potentially leading to better health care delivery. It also had the potential for engendering greater conflict between different groups, as in the case of the nurses and pharmacists. The tighter integration of different functional groups removed the buffer that previously existed. Differences in procedures and practices that could be ignored, or that one or both groups were ignorant of, had to be confronted with the greater integration provided by the new system.

The hospital system had the potential to expand the scope of discretion exercised by many hospital personnel and also to increase the ramifications of this greater discretion. Unlike policies that depend upon individuals and local interpretation for implementation, the software enforced established rules. Consequently, issues of informal practice must be confronted when such rules are considered for inclusion in design of the software. In the hospital, some end users had the power to confront formal policies that conflicted with informal practice.

The system design committee, for example, became concerned that the remote order capability of the system increased the possibility of physicians delegating tasks to their assistants, nurses, and secretaries and increased the potential for physicians to practice at a distance by "treating the medical chart" with decreased patient contact. This concern led one group of physicians to propose software restrictions on remote entry to enforce normative standards of good medical practice. Although the rationale of enforcing procedures could not be challenged, or at least a challenge could not be medically justified, the dislike of this design was based and justified on personal preference. Because there was no hierarchical superiority of one group and autonomy was respected as an underlying principle for this group of workers, the physicians compromised by establishing a noncomputer enforced policy of onsite verification of computer-generated orders. A set of soft controls was used to keep records of order changes and onsite verification but no restrictions were designed into the system nor was there active monitoring of the records.

Another issue confronted in the design of this system was the level of trust ascribed to various groups in the hospital. In comparison to the bank where there is a very low level of trust, hospitals (and the medical system in general) operate in a high trust environment. The unpredictability of events, the high level of training, legal and professional licensing, and the system of peer review allow the hospital to rely on trust in individuals. The contingencies that individuals at all levels may need to respond to (i.e., medical emergencies) require that enforcement of routine procedures not impede a response to such events. Unlike a bank where convenience for the customer may be sacrificed for security, the consequences for the hospital's "customer" can be lethal. This situation raised the question of enforcing access limits by hard restrictions or by soft policies. At the hospital they chose to use noncomputer enforced limits and monitor access retroactively. In principle this provided accountability but in practice it largely rested on trust (i.e., the monitor log generally would not be used unless a problem developed). It established a formal system of accountability that still allowed informal practices to continue.

Implications for Design

Procedural Compliance

The enforcement of procedures is often an important part of computer mediation of work. We have presented several examples of how software systems were designed to uniformly enforce policies and procedures. Previously, rules may have been specified by company policy, but enforcement depended on individual managers, doctors, or administrators. Flexibility in interpretation and enforcement allowed adjustment according to local conditions and latitude for individual workers to exercise judgment and skills as conditions or supervisors permitted. There was a distance between those establishing policies and procedures (e.g., central office or higher level management) and those conducting the work subject to those policies and procedures. This distance allowed those at lower levels in the organization to develop their own systems and procedures for conducting their work and organizational operations. This is an aspect of the "loose coupling" of systems in organizations and the divergence between formal policy and informal practices that may provide efficiency through flexibility.

Such flexibility was viewed negatively by upper level management in the bank and the field service organization and by some physicians in the hospital. Formal sanction of actual practices was feared as eliminating accountability and allowing abuse or unproductive activity. Uniform enforcement was viewed as a positive function of each of these new software systems. However, tradeoffs among conflicting objectives in systems design were handled differently in each of the three industries. In the banks and hospital, security of data was a fundamental concern and tradeoffs had to be made between security and access. Less restrictive access than originally designed in the software systems was needed for efficiency in the bank and in the hospital (as well as to respond to medical emergencies in the hospital). The bank systems were designed for security by decreasing individual discretion with hard enforcement of procedures (i.e., with functions that interrupted the teller's tasks). In the hospital, security was achieved through soft functions (i.e., a message and tracking of access) because of the potential for unacceptable consequences to patients from limiting access of staff to information in emergencies and because of the autonomy accorded physicians. In banks, tellers could work around the system as long as branch managers approved. In field service, by contrast, FEs could not work around the system without being noticed by the central office. The result in the field service organization was an only implicitly acknowledged battle being waged through software design.[1]

Hard Choices in Software

Formal procedures and policies are naturally considered more legitimate than informal work practices and are thus more likely to be reflected in software design. Despite official acceptance, formal procedures may not be well accepted by people who are actually performing the tasks. Automation through software systems tends to erode the flexibility for "work-arounds" and the local autonomy preserved when procedures are implemented in noncomputerized bureaucratic systems. The software, because it directly controls or regulates the work process, can then introduce dysfunctional procedures, or procedures that will be resisted by users. Through this process software can thus lead to a tight coupling of organizational systems and a narrowing of the gap between formal and informal organizational structure.

Alternatively, loose coupling allows two realities of the organization to exist, much like the formal espoused ideology of Victorian morality and the actual licentious practices of the times. Just as the dual morality of Victorian times accommodated both puritanical ideology and base human drives, so the divergence between the formal procedures and the informal practices of organizations is necessary to conduct the work and keep the organization operating smoothly.[2] As organizational systems become more tightly coupled through use of mission critical software it is harder for this divergence to coexist peacefully. How this is resolved often depends upon the particular organizational context.

As illustrated in the banking example, the system was designed, through the use of hard controls, to remove all discretion. The dysfunctional consequences of such a design resulted in users essentially disabling all the security provisions of the software. The power relations within the organization reduced the ability of system users to confront the rationality of the procedures and have the software design changed. By contrast, in the hospital the enforcement of procedures was challenged by physicians. The rationality of the procedure to be enforced (e.g., follow-up on remotely issued orders) was not challenged, and could not reasonably be done because all agreed it was "good medical practice," but its enforcement through software design was challenged (changing the design from hard to soft controls). While the more critical and nonroutine nature of medical procedures explains part of this difference, so does the relatively great power of physicians.

In field service, similar issues arose with the design of the FSMS system, resulting in a mix of hard and soft controls. The traditional autonomy of field service engineers and the local office structure allowed resistance to some of the intended effects of the design, resulting in revision of codes in favor the FEs, for example. The use of other software functions, to collect engineering data that were used for performance evaluation for example, could not "legitimately" be resisted by the FEs and were instead subverted in implementation. It is important to note that the company using the data collection function for supervision continued to use the software for evaluation based on procedural compliance. The software was redesigned in attempts to improve enforcement of data collection, despite its destructive consequences, thus undermining the value of the data for other important indirect uses, namely quality engineering and marketing.

Specific objectives for a software system (i.e., how the information will be used and how work will be controlled), can be "contested terrain" by different groups within the user organization.[3] There is a tension in software design objectives that is not unique to this specific technology, but is perhaps raised to a qualitatively higher level. In general, software may be both a means for conducting work and for controlling work processes and, in service sector work, it is distinctive as a technology that can execute intangible work (as compared to other industrial technologies such as machine tools). We have seen how the nature of execution and control of service sector work leads to divergent objectives for software design.

Another tension in software design stems from the managerial objectives of incorporating restrictive control features into the system and the potential flexibility of software to meet the unpredictable and amorphous character of intangible service production. It is the capability of software to be flexible and analyze contingencies to some degree that enables automation of this work in any significant manner.

Most organizations seek to achieve specified and predictable outcomes with high levels of efficiency, whether production of a tangible item or delivery of a service. The dominant industrial model to achieve this outcome is through centralized control of procedures to obtain predictable results. This model is built on the fundamental objectives of Taylorism to transform skilled work that could only be measured by output into a set of procedures whose performance can be measured. Output is thought to be a direct function of procedural compliance and thus the use of procedural measures rather than output measures. However, because it is difficult to measure procedural compliance, in Taylorist work systems the enforcement of procedures is often dependent upon the evaluation of output. That is, analysis of procedures is used to determine "appropriate" levels of output but, depending upon the type of process (particularly whether it is skilled and the extent to which it is routine) evaluation of the level of output is still the significant performance measure.

This distinction is important to understanding the design approaches used for software in service work. The intangibility of service sector work and the nonroutine nature of task performance lead to different types of performance measurement approaches than in manufacturing. Bureaucratically-based work is often organized on the basis of a formal rationality or enforcement of procedures and rules rather than measurement of tangible outcomes.[4]

The software design task for mission critical applications is often implicitly based on the objective of enforcing procedures to ensure performance outcomes. This approach to gaining control of tasks and outcomes is predicated upon control of procedures and thus workers because they are the means of enacting procedures. This approach to controlling workers is often used instead of controlling tasks or outcomes to ensure a rationality of worker performance. That is, the nature of the work in service industries often makes it difficult to control and assess "outcomes," particularly with software systems, but it is theoretically (or assumed to be) possible to control procedures. The disjuncture between the rationality of procedures and actual operation is generally not adequately assessed in determining software design requirements.

Consensus versus Conflict in User Requirements

Another source of software design problems is the tension among a multitude of user interests, which is increased by the expanded scope of software systems. Incorporating greater functionality into the system may increase the number of potentially conflicting objectives rather than achieving more satisfaction among a broader range of users. The greater the number of functional capabilities incorporated in software, the more tradeoffs there will be among systems features and functions serving one user group over another. The differences go beyond individual preferences of users that are reconcilable through developing user consensus. Rather, the differences affect actual costs in job performance, the nature of working conditions, and the structure of power relationships.

Tradeoffs made in system design often reflect the relative power of certain groups in the user organization. Higher level managers involved in software procurement promote the development of features and functions that seem important for their use and consistent with their objectives; this tends to constrain vendors from promoting effectiveness for users who rely on the software for more ongoing operational support and service delivery. It also fosters an orientation among designers that neglects and devalues such considerations.

We also find that traditional approaches to increasing user involvement in the software design process, while important, have inherent limitations. The problems of user involvement have been widely discussed, but usually not as a larger problem of organizational structure. The usual solutions are based on underlying assumptions that better assessment methods and better intentions by individual designers can improve software designs. Some researchers have considered these problems in an organizational context and proposed various solutions that address specific and often individual level issues (e.g., improving communication and understanding between designers and users).[5] In practice, however, structural organizational and market barriers to designing user-effective software and conflicts of interests and visions obscure and distort the tradeoffs in user requirement assessments. Design strategies based on technical, methodological improvements, and/or changing the intentions of individual designers are likely, therefore, to be of limited effectiveness in many instances.

Organizational theory suggests, and it is evident in our findings, that the multitude of interests in an organization may be arrayed along both vertical and horizontal dimensions. The structure of most organizations is based not only on a hierarchy of functions but on power as well (e.g., Pfeffer, 1981). Organizational goals may reflect the dominance of certain organizational actors rather than consensus. For example, when user groups are relied upon to develop statements of needs for software, such user groups tend to be composed of middle- to senior-level managers rather than hourly workers who are often the significant end users. The resulting design requirements may not necessarily relate to service delivery but instead to capabilities for enhanced supervision, control, access, and decisionmaking. In this respect, the "consensus" on requirements may not reflect the actual, functional importance of some needs over others but rather the hierarchical position of some users over other users.[6]

The assessment of user requirements must be conceptualized as a process of making tradeoffs among conflicting needs. Some of the conflicts in design choices may be resolved by careful consideration of the features and functions that promote the best operational performance. Other conflicts, however, are based on real and legitimate differences in values and objectives and thus defy easy solutions. Developers and users alike should recognize that choosing among different visions of what the software should do or specific features and functions can have broad ranging consequences. Rather than trying to achieve consensus, requirements analysis should include an assessment of the tradeoffs, particularly regarding the broader organizational impacts of specific software designs.

Mapping Social Influences in Design

One of our basic initial premises about understanding the values underlying any particular software design decision is that expressed preferences or requirements may reflect factors beyond the personal perceptions of individuals. A long tradition of research on organizational behavior demonstrates that people's actions and views in the workplace reflect, at least in part, the demands and perspectives of their positions, of operational requirements of the organization, and of external factors. These factors combine to create the design space within which the designer works. Individual designers may not see the social shaping of their immediate environment. To be more systematic in understanding values in the design of software, and technology in general, one should try to map the multiple factors shaping the expressed needs and preferences of the individuals involved in these decisions. Our case studies demonstrate how this can be studied. A map of the design process should reflect the full set of commercial and organizational factors that we found shapes software in its original design by vendors and, subsequently, in modifications by users. In particular, design considerations should include the interorganizational relations of user and designer organizations, how the process can be influenced by more organizationally powerful users, the tendency for organizations to assimilate new technology, and the change in informal and formal policies and procedures.

Interorganizational relations Software and most technology design is not an independent enterprise: It occurs within organizations and, especially in the case of vendors, between organizations and is mediated through market mechanisms. Consequently, it is subject to the fundamental features of organizational structure, power, and hierarchy. The result of organizational power and hierarchy is that some ideas take precedence over others and not necessarily on the basis of "need" or importance for actual operations at the service delivery level (cf. Pfeffer, 1981; Leibenstein, 1987).

Hierarchy Because the choice of technology design will be dominated by those at the higher levels of user firms who are most important in procurement decisions, their preferences are readily perceived and interpreted by marketing personnel in the vendor firm. Accordingly, many other features and functions that are favored through this process will reflect managerial over lower level preferences. On the other hand, during implementation technology may be informally redesigned in use by those at the lower levels of the organization. Depending upon the organizational context, the dual realities of an organization may be recreated with computer systems or new battles may develop as the political terrain is renegotiated.

Assimilation Software is more likely to be adopted and used in an organization if it does not present a challenge to formal organizational procedures. Designers and users should assess the fit of the technology with existing organizational structure, procedures, and technology use. They need to consider the extent to which the organization is able to change. This is a choice between assimilating technology into existing structure or accommodating, through structural change in the organization, potential new uses of the technology. It is fundamentally an organizational choice, not a choice that can be driven by the technology. Even the most radical new technology designs can be assimilated in use into existing structures. As discussed in Chapter 2, a powerful word processor may be used as just a faster typewriter or a new accounting system may be used in only a perfunctory manner while the old system is maintained for the actual financial analyses or projections.

The informal organization Software systems often formalize and implement policies and procedures of the user organization in an uncompromising manner. While these policies may be preexisting, their enforcement previously was left to local supervisors and modification was allowed within the bounds of autonomy afforded to individual workers. However, these informal and flexible systems are abridged as software systems apply abstract rules to actual operating routines. Consequently, while "good" software design is seen as accurately reflecting existing operational procedures and resulting in minimal organizational or job changes, these exemplary designs may, in fact, cause significant changes that undermine the ways in which individual workers exercise autonomy and deliver effective service in noncomputerized or partially computerized systems. In our observations we found most workers, at most times, used the latitude available to perform their job in ways that improved the quality and efficiency of service. In those instances when this was not the case, we found little evidence that hard controls in the computer system *reduced* the extent to which workers shirked their responsibilities; rather, it just increased innovative ways of subverting system controls.

In general, the limitations of standard approaches to software design are an overly technical and narrow focus on the context of software use and role of the user. In many ways improvements in technical methods will improve software design. However, particularly for software in the workplace, these methods do not address a larger set of issues. These are not issues that are generally regarded as part of design and engineering and software developers would probably prefer to focus on the technical aspects of design (naturally their primary interest is in designing technology, not the organizational aspects of work organization). Unfortunately, the reality of software use is that it is enmeshed in the tangle of workplace organization.

These observations differ from the conception of organizations in most software design literature, which rests on the premise that organizations are a marketplace of ideas and that optimal solutions will prevail, based on a consensus reflecting commonly held values and agreed upon organizational objectives. Instead, the "consensus" on requirements may be based on the reality that some players have more power or authority than others and thus are able to dominate the requirements determination process irrespective of the full range of actual operating requirements of the firm.

Conclusions About Design

Our study of applications software design has implications for practitioners and researchers. The organizational dilemmas that emerged from our study suggest that the design of effective applications software is more complex than the design of traditional hardware-dominated process technology. This is especially true when the software is designed, developed, and sold by an independent vendor.

We viewed the problems of designing effective software for multiple user applications as a special case of the development of new production technology. It was clear that, in general, technology developers and users have fundamentally different interests; the former aim at a generic product, the latter desire a specific set of process solutions. A vendor developing integrative, mission critical software is caught in a special double bind: Not only must the software product be effective in a variety of different customer environments, it also must be designed to serve the multiple users within any one customer's organization with their various vertical and horizontal relationships.

When Mirvis and Lawler (1983) analyzed the failure of information systems to take into account the organizational environment in which those systems were to be used, they argued that "systems are not solutions." Our research sheds additional light on this perspective. We conclude that even for a single user organization one cannot expect to derive a set of software design requirements by compiling a list of functional needs and incorporating them into a comprehensive "solution." This approach might be expected to lead to consensus only in very limited applications where an organization was simply automating an existing service delivery operation and there was general agreement on the related information processing problems.

As documented in our research, options in the design of specific features and functions of a software package will exert differing influences on the scope of jobs, the nature of working conditions, and the structure of power in the user organization.[7] The assessment of user requirements for software must be conceptualized as a process of making tradeoffs among conflicting needs and different visions. For a potential user of a mission critical software system, considerable attention, participation, inquiry and reflection would be required from a wide range of internal personnel.

Our findings suggest that we go beyond design remedies that focus on individual designers as independent agents rather than as mediators, at least in part, of other forces in the social world. In addition, we believe that a tendency to cast tensions between designers and other involved groups (e.g., marketing) as idiosyncratic personality mismatches and individual level conflicts generally misses the structural dynamics that typically prevail. Ineffective software or features and functions that are detrimental to the quality of worklife are not the result of some errant programmer or a culture with a perverse set of values.

Effective software design cannot be accomplished without

confronting the larger issues that are raised in some form in our guidelines. At the same time, particularly for the vendor, it can be a no-win situation: Make the buyer happy, design software that is consonant with power and politics in the organization, *and* displease the end user *and* perhaps impede the effectiveness of the software. Conversely, focus on the end user, resist capitulation to managerial preferences that those at the bottom of the organization find unpleasant, and the result may be a very effective, and virtuous, museum piece. As we have argued in the beginning, the latitude for individual designers is limited and the outcome fairly well circumscribed. At the same time, we also see the opportunity for changes in software design as part of a larger coalescing of change at a number of different levels in organizations and the economy.

What, Then, Is To Be Done?

"Explanations which focus on structural variables...provide no easy palliatives and imply a need for much more fundamental change in terms of affecting decision outcomes." observes Jeffery Pfeffer (1981, p. 13) in his analysis of power in organizations. In general, Pfeffer has argued, the structure of the organization and power relations in the organization are mutually reinforcing. In the case of vendor-developed applications software, we have shown how structural variables within the vendor organization combine with variables within the user organization, as well as the dynamics between the two organizations, to explain the lack of adequate attention to effective design choices. Thus, to the extent that software design is shaped by the structure and dynamics we outlined, a fundamental change in the software design process is a prerequisite for improving its effectiveness. For such an effort to be made, however, incentives must exist for the vendor organization and for the user organizations.

For an external vendor to conduct such an analysis, or even to assess the design tradeoffs if they were well posed by the user, would be all but impossible. Furthermore, it is unlikely that a software vendor would want to, or could successfully renegotiate the politics of the user organization. It is no wonder, then, that we found that independent software vendors, faced with such complexity and variety, have resorted to traditional modes of industrial product development in which marketing specialists try to ascertain the functional attributes that would best promote the sale of their next product offering. For those involved in design, particularly marketing staff, thinking more of a sale than about effective application and orienting themselves to an influential buyer rather than to a network of hands-on users are convenient shortcuts; the cognitive and political swamp of conflicting strategic and operational interests within a customer's organization would be daunting territory for an outsider to traverse. Indeed, to the extent that vendors' marketing personnel appear limited in technical knowledge of software and in extensive familiarity with the business and operations of their various customers, this shortcut may be as necessary as it is convenient.

Unfortunately, taking this shortcut avoids the central issues of software design in the early stage of specifying user needs. By default, technical product development staff in the vendor organization must make a series of critical design decisions that were not even on the agenda of the marketing person working with their customers' buyers. Furthermore, to the extent that the buyers may have a bias toward features and functions of interest to managers, vendors tend to get a very incomplete view of the needs of users who rely on the software for ongoing operational support and service delivery. This may not bode well for the customer in the short term and for the vendor in the long term.

One can envision a scenario in which greater pressure is felt by both software vendors and user organizations to consider user effectiveness at the service delivery level and to recognize the high cost of some types of design tradeoffs. The competitive nature of most industry market segments, coupled with the increased application of software technologies to organizational operations, will favor designs that promote greater market flexibility rather than cost reduction and labor-restrictive software features and functions. Features and functions that allow an organization to increase revenues by changing rapidly and expanding service delivery will become more valued than those that attempt to reduce operational costs primarily by restricting worker skills and discretion. At this point some of the dilemmas we identified could become much more tractable.

In the U.S. service sector, organizations are facing increasing competition. Pressures for such service-oriented companies to become more reliable, more responsive, more flexible, and more accountable are forcing changes of several types, including an increased dependency on new complex forms cf mission critical software. Correspondingly, as segments of the software industry mature, dominant functional designs may emerge and the rate of innovation of features and functions may lessen. These conditions could combine to stimulate competition in the vendor community on the basis of software effectiveness. Restrictive designs will result in dysfunctional features, functions, and systems that will be less successful in the marketplace (or in the workplace and thus will have marketplace effects for the user organization).

While this may be the dominant tendency, restrictive designs will not necessarily disappear or be completely dysfunctional. Contradictory elements in systems will continue to be designed and some organizations will attempt to implement them, with varying degrees of success. Moreover, the relative advantage of a less restrictive design over a more restrictive design may not have dramatic marketplace effects, particularly in the short run. While we are relatively sanguine about future directions of technology design, we do not believe designs that allow greater flexibility, promote development of worker skills and responsible autonomy for performance, and accommodate loose organizational coupling will occur automatically, at a brisk pace, or to as great an extent as we suggest is desirable.

Though perhaps limited in their ultimate impact, we propose four general principles for software design. A first step is that designs should be evaluated for their impact on users. (In this we reiterate the findings from numerous other studies.) In part the success of this approach depends upon a new philosophy of design that is based on the new conditions of competition in many industries. Software should be designed to provide resources for assuring the rationality of outcomes rather than for controlling the formal rationality of procedures. Not only does this serve the intrinsic end of creating jobs that encompasses the human-centered dimensions of work, it also serves an instrumental benefit—profit—for organizations that operate in highly competitive and dynamic environments.

Second, it is necessary to have more explicit acknowledgment of the conflicting value perspectives in organizations and the bias in definition of user "needs" and design requirements due to the dynamics of power in organizations. For example, the design process should explicitly assess the tradeoffs between utilizing workers to pursue organizational effectiveness through responsible autonomy versus the need for accountability and managerial control.

Third, reconceptualization of technology design in general, and software development in particular, is necessary to allow consciously guided, explicit social choices in design. Although our findings suggest that designers have limited impact on determining the shape of technology, an awareness of the implications of their work and desire to change can help in the articulation of new design objectives and add to the cumulative pressures leading to changing technology design. A well-articulated vision of new design principles by designers might even lead the development of these new design objectives, pushing such changes at a slightly faster pace. But this will not be enough.

Our fourth principle, which can have a significant impact in combination with these other changes, is that the process of change also depends in part on changes in the vendor organization's environment. Looking outside the vendor organization may provide leverage to change the design process. An important part of the software designer's environment is the user organization and specifically the approach taken to procuring software. Accordingly, in the next chapter we turn to prescriptions for improving the management of software procurement.

Endnotes

1. It was clear in these examples that the implications for users' skills and autonomy were not considered in terms of their intrinsic importance, only instrumentally as they affected organizational requirements. In the bank, for example, the BSC design features that assisted tellers in selling various products functioned as tools for the teller, supporting his or her increased learning and skills. The impetus for these design features was the increased competition resulting from deregulation. There was neither concern about the relationship between the technology design and working conditions nor an overall assessment of how to utilize worker skills and capabilities to achieve operational objectives.

2. See Weltz (1991) for discussion of this analogy and concept in terms of information systems. See Scott (1987, Chapters 2 and 10) for review and discussion of these concepts in terms of organizational design, as well as a seminal article on this issue, Meyer and Rowan (1991). See Marcus (1966) for analysis of Victorian morality.

3. For example, see Edwards (1979), Pfeffer (1978, 1981), Becker, Windeler, and Ortmann (1989).

4. This distinction between the enforcement of procedures rather than evaluation of outcomes as a means of control and performance evaluation in bureaucracies has been discussed extensively (e.g., see Gordon, Edwards, Reich, 1982; Edwards, 1979).

5. Studies that take a broader or organizational view of problems in software development have identified different structural aspects of the problem (for example, see Danziger and Kraemer, 1986; Franz and Robey, 1984; Robey and Markus, 1984; Grudin, 1991a, 1991b). Some are prescriptive in their suggested remedies, addressing some of the microlevel issues that can be improved through deliberate action by managers, designers, and users. However, by the very nature of the problems identified (i.e., beyond individual motivation or action), such solutions are probably limited as some of these researchers note.

6. See Robey and Markus (1984) for discussion of the political aspects of design and the ritual rationalization of information requirements analysis. They identify the political dynamics of organizations and design and, to increase system design effectiveness, suggest that designers have greater awareness of the political aspects of design. However, it is not clear how designers should negotiate this political terrain.

7. For related findings, see Koppel, Appelbaum, and Albin (1988).

III

IMPLICATIONS FOR MANAGEMENT AND FOR FURTHER RESEARCH ON TECHNOLOGY DESIGN

III

Implications for Management and Further Research

In Part II we showed how software design involves significant social choices and how they are embedded in features and functions of mission critical software. We also examined some of the implications for the users of these systems. Our concluding two chapters draw implications for two different audiences: Chapter 8 examines issues relevant for managers who can influence the purchase and implementation of technology for the workplace and Chapter 9 focuses on issues that we find important in future research on workplace technology and software in particular. Chapter 8 translates our findings into prescriptions for managers of service delivery organizatrions. It focuses on the crucial decision of how and when to procure a new software system for mission critical applications. Chapter 9 develops some general propositions about the social shaping of technology and the specific implications of software design for the workplace.

8

Understanding and Managing Software Acquisition

In today's service-oriented economy, information systems are becoming the lifeblood of many organizations. As part of this trend, applications software is an increasingly important and little understood type of process technology. In this chapter we synthesize many of our findings and explore their implications for procuring software in organizations that deliver services.[1] We will argue that it is during the procurement of software and in the planning processes that precede procurement that managers with insight about software design have the most to offer.

This book has provided several extended examples of how mission critical software is used in service organizations by operational personnel to assist them in service delivery and by management for monitoring and control purposes. We have shown how service delivery becomes redefined in terms of the combined capability of workers and the integrative functionality designed into mission critical software. We have also shown how software may affect the structure of a service organization and the scope of individual jobs within it. Mission critical software thus serves important integrative functions, such as job restructuring and service redefinition, for the service delivery organization.

Although vital to any company's production capability, process technology is often viewed as an ancillary concern of top management when it comes to purchasing it. Procurement is thought to be best left to technicians who have both the time and inclination to preoccupy themselves with comparison shopping. Many managers are uncomfortable with technological decisions. In large organizations, decisions about new technology tend to be delegated to groups far removed from senior management. Only when procurement costs rise above a certain threshold will the level for such decisions be escalated in the organization. By then, assessments are usually reduced to some sort of financial payback calculation and the substantive issues associated with the proposed technology become submerged.

The crucial shortcoming of this approach is that technology acquisition is an important strategic issue, not just a technical matter. By shaping the capabilities of the organization's production function, process technologies, can dramatically affect productivity, quality, and the range of possibilities for making goods or delivering services. Management literature has emphasized how strategic dimensions of these benefits can be missed if top management is overly preoccupied with traditional quantitative return-on-investment calculations. What is less generally recognized is the significance of the procurement process in determining the desired design and capabilities of new process technology. One of the major managerial implications of this book is that there can be significant risk in leaving crucial technology procurement actions to the purchasing department (or, for software, specialists in information technology) for reasons that are discussed below.

Lessons about the Design of Mission Critical Software

Software is as much a process technology in service organizations as robots, machine tools or conveyors are in the world of manufacturing. What makes software particularly complex compared to these other process technologies is that its range of operational implications is less readily specified as different design options are being considered. These peculiarities of software as a process technology, coupled with the changing requirements of service delivery applications, create serious risk for those who are charged with its acquisition.

Because software systems integrate the work of people throughout an organization, a technical failure in one aspect of service delivery can easily cause considerable chaos or error elsewhere. Unfortunately, the term integration as applied to manufacturing or service delivery operations is often characterized as "a desirable technological capability that everyone should strive for." However, examples of integrated systems gone awry, such as the Three Mile Island nuclear power plant disaster or General Motors Corporation's early experience with computer integrated manufacturing (where improperly programmed robots were found to be spray painting each other rather than the new automobiles), should remind us that there are hazards as well as glory to be gained from the pursuit of integrated operations.

We have already seen how the design of effective software is fraught with subtle complexity. Seemingly "technical" decisions about the information to be contained on a screen, the sequence of screens, access controls, and the types and forms of data entry can fundamentally influence the interaction of the worker and customer. Furthermore, the scope and structure of a mission critical software package can force changes in operational models of service delivery in ways that are not obvious to the software engineers who specify the software design.

Senior management cannot afford to assume that others understand either the strategic significance of different software design options or the ways in which software affect operational jobs and organizational relationships and, therefore, service delivery. Furthermore, managers who appreciate the kinds of risk that are inherent in the design and procurement of mission critical software are in a better position to help others conduct an effective procurement process.

Central questions in procurement are: Who should attend to what kinds of design questions? Who should make strategic decisions that influence software design? What criteria should be adopted as a basis for the procurement of such software? Who will be affected by the implementation of the new software and in what ways? Our findings and analysis suggest the following guidelines to address these questions.

First Assess the Service Mission and Changing Directions

Our findings from three different industry case studies suggest that one cannot evaluate the design of mission critical software without first reflecting on the mission itself. Before investing in a major new software system management needs to assess the extent of change that is likely to occur in the kind of service currently being delivered. Where the perceived strategic need for change is low, software design priorities will center on questions of assimilation. For example: What software features and functions will facilitate the execution of current service delivery activities? What types of automated information processing are compatible with existing skills and organizational responsibilities? Managers who raise such diagnostic questions will stimulate operating units to distinguish software products that readily can be assimilated from those that cannot. However, these questions may tend to bias the software selection process toward less operational change than might be most effective.

Many service delivery organizations, in contrast to the above situation, are in the midst of radical, rather than incremental, change. We use the term "radical" to refer to the development of new types and forms of service products as distinguished from modifications of traditional service offerings. In retail banking, for example, we saw how an improved system for transaction reporting might constitute an incremental change while a system for implementing "relationship banking," in which packages of financial products are offered to customers, would be a more radical change.

As market requirements shift and competition responds with new forms of service and heightened performance criteria, service deliverers need to reconceptualize their mission. New mission statements lead to changes in the service delivery system itself. This includes jobs, skills, organizational structures, and operating procedures as well as the introduction of new software systems (or other technology).

Under this scenario of change, application software options must be assessed in terms of accommodation concerns. Managerial attention must focus on such questions as: What features and functions of a software package will facilitate the kinds of service delivery changes that are of strategic importance? How can we use the design of software to enhance the effectiveness of our response to customer needs and thereby achieve marketplace innovations? Such questions of accommodation lead to very different software specifications from those that emerge from assumptions of assimilation.

Identify the Key Operational Objectives of the New Software

One conclusion from the case studies presented in this book is that management must try to understand what it means, from a particular operational viewpoint, to have an effective software package. To gain this appreciation, managers need to explore in more depth important aspects of their service operations, not just the organization's strategic mission. One of the common traps is that managers often view themselves, rather than those with ongoing direct service delivery responsibilities, as the primary beneficiary of the software package.

Because senior management is a consumer of information, it may set a high priority on software that satisfies needs that they can readily understand, such as the extent and variety of management reports that can be produced. If the primary purpose of the software is to enhance the managerial control over service delivery, then such a criterion might be a leading consideration because management might be the primary user of the software. However, the primary objective of many software applications is to facilitate the delivery of a service rather than to report on what has been accomplished. For this very broad class of applications, managers must learn to put their own needs for information into proper perspective along with other objectives that may be less apparent to them. This requires assessing the costs and benefits associated with software designs that enhance management control functions at the expense of service delivery functions.

In contrast to mission critical software for service delivery, the procurement of new manufacturing technology tends naturally to be more effective. Senior manufacturing managers are not likely to assume that they intuitively understand the crucial aspects of new process technology. They know that the primary users of the new equipment are factory workers and that equipment requirements are best understood by operations personnel and process engineers. Accordingly, manufacturing managers are more likely than service delivery managers to draw on operating personnel to identify crucial performance specifications for new technology and to select from among the existing options that which is most cost-effective.

Avoid the "Bells and Whistles" Mentality when Dealing with Suppliers

Mission critical software products are increasingly being designed and developed by external suppliers rather than internal MIS groups. In Chapter 3 we described how the existence of an independent software supplier complicates the dynamics of strategic planning and operational thinking that is so essential to successful software design. Vendors who are in the business of designing and developing generic software packages cannot afford to tailor their product to the specific operational needs of any one user. Even as they try, through their own marketing experts, to understand the needs of a major customer, they generally lack the necessary detailed operational knowledge of their customers' industry and way of doing business. Finally, a customer's sense of the software design requirements is likely to develop slowly over time (even after the software has been installed) and is therefore not easily transportable to the vendor at a point at which it might make a considerable difference.[2]

In this situation the supplier rather than the user is likely to become a catalyst for innovation, with the basic idea for the software innovation coming from the marketing arm of the software company. Following this sequence, operating management in potential customer organizations is likely to be confronted by alternative software packages before having an opportunity either to articulate the future mission of the organization or to decide on the relative amount of operational change the company is willing to endure.[3]

Lacking such advance planning, software buyers are in a difficult position. They would like to comparison shop but they have not yet developed a coherent shopping list of their own. As a result, an outside software supplier may end up exerting too much influence on the resulting analysis. Simple comparisons of the number and variety of features and functions offered by competing software products are likely. It is especially easy to miss important but subtle issues of software design and performance. For example, readily apparent extra reporting features in one system, even though their need is questionable, may become more highly valued than a less apparent quicker terminal response time in another. Under these circumstances, the software supplier with the longest list of features often will win the sale.

However, this need not be the case. If buyers truly understand the significance of different design choices for their own operations, they will be better equipped to select a system that fits their needs. The existence or absence of a single feature (or even the configuration of that feature) could easily be more important than a host of other possible features that would turn out to be merely "bells and whistles." A wide range of options for executing a particular data entry function could be either valuable or extraneous, depending on the kinds of operating situations that might arise. Similarly, the provision in the software design of choices for the sequence of screens to be presented to an operator might provide effective shortcuts for handling the mix of events that arise; alternatively, this feature might present an unwanted complexity with little operational advantage.

Expect Operational Users to Have Limited and Perhaps Conflicting Perspectives

Senior management must try to have their service delivery organizations consider such questions before calling in the software industry. Operating personnel and first line supervisors must be taught to appreciate that their job responsibilities include being aware of the potential value of new software aids. Unfortunately, many operating personnel may find this surprisingly difficult because it requires a different mindset than typically expected from those who perform routine transactions. Our research suggests that such personnel may be ill-equipped to conduct more than a perfunctory review of their software needs.

The most natural trap for operating personnel is to consider new software options only within the constraints posed by existing service delivery operations rather than within a strategic context. Obtaining strategic considerations from service sector personnel is by no means impossible, however. Some manufacturing managers have successfully empowered factory workers to suggest significant process improvements. The pursuit of Total Quality Management by manufacturers and service organizations provides approaches and techniques for identifying needed operational improvements through systems redesign. Managers need to experiment with ways of encouraging workers to think creatively about options for service delivery with specific reference to what information could make their dreams for improvement a reality. The best incentive for such activity is probably the shared belief that through new appropriate software systems, service jobs could be made more interesting and that individual workers would be in a better position to provide effective service to their customers.

Another complication is the integrative nature of many software packages being developed for service organizations. Such applications software is designed to require connections among various operational and management groups and thus calls for more extensive planning than more incremental software applications. Involving all affected groups is one important step. However, as illustrated in our analysis of the field service system described in Chapter 5, special precautions must be taken to appreciate the interactions among the work activity of individuals who are linked through the software system.

Senior management must strive to lead their organizations in a more proactive direction when it comes to software procurement. Because software designed by vendors trying to produce a generic product for widespread application may or may not lead to effective use in particular contexts, the customer should avoid premature procurement decisions. Because procuring the wrong software product can easily hinder the type of progress that is most important for the organization, a crucial criterion for assessing a new software product is the loss of potential operational capabilities in service delivery. Senior management has a role to play in helping to avoid common traps.

Senior managers should also aggressively encourage the early identification of how behaviors will have to change as information systems serve to bridge the work of people performing different but related operational functions. Admittedly, it can be hard to specify in advance which potential software capabilities are most likely to facilitate improved coordination across departmental lines or the particular features and functions that will best accommodate such coordination. Nevertheless, the need for training programs can be identified and resources can be allocated in advance with the expectation that the content of the programs will be defined as soon as the specific operational issues become clear.

Learn to Deal with Complexity without Overreliance on "Experts"

Managers instinctively turn to MIS staff when faced with new software acquisition just as they are accustomed to looking to process engineers for expert advice on manufacturing technology. Management has generally been slow to appreciate the new strategic importance of computer-based technologies. While internal MIS staff are often experts on traditional questions of systems compatibility, database consistency, or hardware requirements, they are not as likely to provide the most effective decisions on the acquisition of mission critical software.

First, MIS staff are not likely to be sufficiently acquainted with either current or future service delivery operations or plans to be experts on software requirements from the users' point of view. Competent MIS staff ought to be able to assess the constraints that certain features or functions of the software impose on the user (data input, modes of interaction, limits on number of terminals). Such staff usually are more interested in the technical side of software performance than in its functionality. However, the payoff in service delivery terms will be more dependent upon specific features and functions of the software than upon traditional engineering criteria. MIS staff are not in the best position to assess the operational implications of software capabilities and constraints. Neither can they be expected to articulate the benefits in service delivery terms (rather than in measures of computer access or capacity) of adding more enhanced features or functions to new software designs.

Managers also ought to anticipate that their MIS staff are likely to consider outside software vendors as their competitors in supplying information technology to the operating units of the company. Accordingly, there may well be a conflict of interest (implicit if not explicit) in asking these internal specialists to assess the software designs of external suppliers. Even if MIS staff had a reasonable familiarity with the operational requirements for mission critical software, they might be inclined to design the software differently than an outside vendor would because of their own technological preferences (hardware, software language, database) or resource limitations (skills, existing workload).

For these reasons, senior managers must resist the temptation to delegate the software development and procurement decision to the MIS group, be it corporate or division. Certainly such professional staff ought to play a role in the procurement process, but it is senior management's responsibility to ensure that the process is effective and, in particular, that it deals with the full range of operational objectives and complexities. A variety of operational perspectives must be involved if this process is to succeed.

Appreciate Differences between Software and Hardware Procurement

Much has been written about the ways in which computer-based technology is different from other forms of technology but specific distinctions between computer software and other process technologies have generally been ignored. A manager who wants to help the company to procure and use software effectively must have a sense of these differences.

Process technology embodied in hardware can be described in terms of meaningful technical specifications (capacity, cycle time, access speed, compatible interfaces, suitable operating environments such as heat, or cleanliness). When hardware is designed by an experienced and reputable supplier, its essential limitations are known in advance. Machine tool suppliers, for example, can tell their customers the types of materials that the latest tool can cut and the tolerances to which this can be performed with the expectation that this customer will understand the effects for manufacturing existing and planned parts.

Those procuring hardware can, therefore, review standard lists of performance specifications and translate them into capabilities of importance to a company's employees or to customers. Managers may expect to get some sort of reasonable answer to questions such as these: What types of production situations are likely to require this hardware feature? What are the chances that we will find ourselves faced with this type of production demand in the next few years? What training is necessary to facilitate workers' effective and efficient use of this hardware capability?

In contrast, those who design mission critical software are likely to have more trouble anticipating how their users' employees and customers may be affected. The compounded intangibility of the software and the service system in which it is embedded, compared to the relative concreteness of a piece of equipment in a manufacturing setting, raises the risk of acquiring unsuitable software. Assessing software features and functions in terms of the company's strategic service mission is itself a difficult task. Relating them to impacts on ongoing service operations is yet an order of magnitude more complex. This is especially true considering that the adoption of mission critical software potentially yields a more integrated delivery system with complex interrelationships among the multiple specialized users of the software and its associated databases.

While new software features, accurately developed and implemented with the requisite training, can dramatically improve a service delivery system, this result is far from automatic. Mission critical software typically does more than automate formerly manual processing activities. It can provide new information that facilitates operational decisions, enhances the scope of services that can be provided to a customer, or signals the need for corrective action. In these ways, software can significantly alter the work of operations personnel and fundamentally modify the service that the customer perceives. The problem is that software designers rarely have prior work experience in the job settings of the intended users of their software.

Furthermore, those who sell a software product are different from the people who design and develop it. Selling is done in terms of a generalized set of "solutions" provided by the black box of software. Even to the potential user, software of the mission critical variety contains features and functions whose particular operational implications are not readily apparent. Sales people can recite the features and functions of their products but are not usually fluent about how the software actually works. Even when a software product is demonstrated to a potential buyer, its capabilities and limitations are presented in a strictly mechanical sense, through simplified examples, simulated situations, and artificial operating contexts. What the potential user cannot easily learn is the constraints and opportunities that are embedded in the software design and the implication of technical design choices for the user.

Concluding Comments

In summary, our research has identified two dilemmas confronting any company procuring a reasonably complex package of mission critical software. First, the software appears as a black box to its users. It is difficult for a potential user organization to establish in advance what the software will do in a particular operating context and what the associated implications will be for organizational effectiveness and the quality of worklife. Second, the user organization appears as a black box to the software supplier. Consequently, the transaction through which software products are bought and sold is based, to some fundamental extent, on mutual misunderstanding.

Be Realistic about "Flexible" Software

Software suppliers have a high incentive to design products adaptable to a wide range of organizations. Vendors commonly claim that they are selling "solutions" to a standard class of information processing tasks. They believe, despite the fact that initially they may not be familiar with a customer's business requirements or organizational realities, that the software nevertheless will be effective in a variety of organizational contexts. Moreover, they try to design software that can be used under situations of growth and shifting business orientations.

To software designers, flexibility is usually a technical concept different from and narrower than the notion of responsive service delivery. From this limited technical perspective, flexibility means that the user can set parameters to control the actual functioning of the software. A package for handling transactions of a bank teller, for example, lets the bank management decide the conditions under which a supervisor must to deal with a potentially difficult customer account situation. A package to handle field service dispatching is written so that the user can decide how many different levels of "urgency" are employed for categorizing incoming calls for service.

Flexibility features of this sort will help sell software because they lessen the chances that a software designer has forced potential customers into a problem formulation that is unnatural or inappropriate for their particular operating situation. Nevertheless, there is no software that is infinitely flexible. Every feature and function has some built-in limitations. Potential users have to be able to distinguish superficial indications of flexibility (highly visible but inconsequential features that can be easily modified by the user) from those that are more central to the primary purpose of the software. They must also be alert to (often implicit) constraints in the core set of features and functions.

Identifying such limits to flexibility may be very difficult, in part because the software developer is not likely to be of much help. As mentioned above, part of the reason is that software marketers sell features that are incorporated in a package; they do not publicize those which were intentionally not included (for reasons of limited market appeal, high development cost or technological complexity). A more basic difficulty is that some crucial limits to flexibility are simply not known by the software firm. This occurs when the software designers fail to recognize that for some users a particular technical formulation will not work over a sufficiently broad range of possible operational situations.

Senior managers have an important role to play in guiding their operational and technical staff to critically evaluate any and all claims for "flexible software." The cases described in earlier chapters suggest that questions such as the following should be asked and answered: flexible for what purpose? flexible for whom? at what cost to whom?

Unfortunately, the biggest and most significant challenge is to be able to understand, before procuring a software package, those attributes that are not flexible and how crucial this could be for ongoing service operations. Some outcomes will be unknowable because those in charge of operations cannot adequately appreciate how the software will fit current modes of service delivery. It will be even harder to take a dynamic rather than static view of service delivery and to imagine how a particular software design could raise obstacles to handling future service delivery requirements under changing conditions.

One way senior management can help to provide a vision or forecast of emerging service requirements and service delivery strategies is by assembling a task force of employees who are particularly close to market trends and competitive industry dynamics. An examination of data on industry trends may offer needed clues. Another approach is to commission a study by a consultant group with special skills in "futures" studies. Forecasting techniques, such as the Delphi approach, may prove valuable. Alternatively, executives could plan a special brainstorming retreat on this topic. Although dealing with scenarios about the future is risky, one or more of these approaches is likely to identify a few priority capabilities for new mission critical software.

For Software, Implementation Requires Additional Design

To the extent that interactive, mission critical software continues to follow the trend toward flexibility, a new burden for software design has to be passed from the software developer to the customer. The software user, in effect, customizes the software by selecting the many parameters that will drive the data processing features of the purchased product. Such customization is not a technical task to be handed to the users' MIS staff as a one-time installation activity. Instead, it involves the selection of operating limits, categories, conditions and trigger points, all of which require decisions and continuing review by those close to service operations.

The implication of this type of customization is that the user must take part of the responsibility for achieving an effective software package. A perfectly appropriate piece of software can produce significant operational problems, in the service delivery sense, if the technical flexibility inherent in the software is inappropriately implemented. Buried in the selection of software parameters are policy decisions. Operations managers must be cautioned against delegating such "technical" matters to either staff specialists or lower level operating personnel. Instead, managers must actively strive to involve representatives of all groups involved with actual service delivery. What service providers get from a software package is no longer a simple matter of what they purchase. In a fundamental sense it is also what they, the users, have created after customizing a flexible package. This customization may affect both the quality of worklife and the effectiveness of service delivery more than constraints imposed by the original software developers.

Summary

Senior managers in service organizations can no longer afford to view software procurement as simply another kind of capital investment decision. Mission critical software is a fundamental process technology for service providers, perhaps more strategically important than an individual piece of machinery or equipment is to a manufacturing company. Implementation of any new process technology, applications software included, requires attention to matters of job design, training, methods and procedures. Choices on the extent of change to be attempted through the procurement of new software systems deserve careful identification and analysis. To this traditional list we have now added the implementation task that drives everything else: the completion of the software design as part of the user's installation responsibility, above and beyond the more straightforward delivery and installation responsibilities of the vendor.

Regardless of whether a company's primary concern is productivity or customer satisfaction, senior management can expect a significant payoff from involvement in procuring mission critical software. Getting all levels of "users" involved, especially those providing direct service delivery functions, is particularly important. The payoff increases if the same managers stay involved well past the point of selecting and approving the purchase of a package to ensure that the design choices made during software implementation are also thoroughly considered from a broad set of operational and strategic viewpoints.

We have outlined ways in which management can facilitate the procurement of software that improves the performance of their service delivery systems. These recommendations derive from our findings on the nature of software design and the ways in which design choices can shape the workplace. Unfortunately, this agenda defies general cookbook procedures because the sociotechnical systems many service companies are trying to develop are complicated and the competitive dynamics in their industries are inherently complex. Armed with the perspectives outlined above, however, management can identify particular actions to increase the likelihood that new software will contribute to more effective service delivery.

Endnotes

1. This chapter is a modified version of an article "Hard Choices about Software: The Pitfalls of Procurement," by Stephen R. Rosenthal and Harold Salzman, that appeared in the *Sloan Management Review*, Summer 1990, pp. 81-91.

2. See Rosenthal and Salzman (1990) for elaboration of this central point.

3. A counter-example to this tendency was identified in our research of the field service industry (summarized in Chapter 5 and presented as a case in the Appendix). A company that had a prior disappointing experience in hiring a small software company willing to work with it enhancing an existing software package subsequently hired a computer firm to help survey the company's requirements before considering the purchase of another software system to support field service operations. About 130 interviews were conducted with the company's employees and customers. Over 600 problems were identified and this became the basis for assessing six of the leading software products currently on the market.

9

Social Dimensions of Software Design: Challenges of Effective Design for the Workplace

Software design is enmeshed in the social world of organizations. Software embodies characteristics of the organizations within which and for which it is created. This book has dealt with both of these dimensions; first, the social dimensions of the software design process and, second, the nature of work organizations that the user inhabits and the implications for software design. In this final chapter we develop some general propositions about social dimensions of software design and the implications of software adoption for organizational change. First we draw some concluding observations about two processes. Our research, coupled with related work of others, suggests that crucial to understanding software design (and technology design in general) are the role of history in the long life cycle of software design, especially the redesign of technology by its users, and the politics of software design.

The Software Life Cycle and Technology History

Technology design is a process with a life cycle of its own. During this process, design changes occur from the initial stage of determining user requirements through the design and development of the software and then continues during its implementation and use. In retrospect, it is possible to show how different aspects of any particular technology were established at various stages. However, it is not possible to deduce all the attributes of the technology without following the design process through implementation and ultimate use.

Understanding the constraints that a technology will impose on the users' (and the organization's) "action space" thus requires an examination of the social as well as the technical history of its development. Organizational politics are crucial in the early phases of technology development and provide opportunities for those in positions of power in the user organization to exercise the most explicit influence. Furthermore, past technology and organizational choices form patterns that are institutionalized and form the structure shaping current technology choices (cf. Kling, 1987, 1993; Thomas, 1993).[1] Thus, the initial stages of technology definition provide partial constraints on the action of users when the technology is implemented. The late life cycle stages of design are the result of a continual process of actors interpreting and negotiating the technology design and use within structural bounds of hierarchical power, resources, authority and autonomy. Thus, one must also examine the subsequent interpretative or subjective construction of the technology by the user, although that, alone, is not sufficient.

While technology structures an organization, organizations and their environments also shape technology. Our case studies illustrate how the organization/technology division artificially separates this ongoing and recursive process. (For example, our banking case showed how the system influences or shapes the job of the tellers but the system was designed as a result of the organization of banking and definition of teller jobs.) We see "technology" as thus representing a particular moment in history during which the technology as artifact takes form. The same technology is reinterpreted and redesigned at later stages reflecting changes in its environment of use. This occurs as a seamless dynamic process, with less separation of stages in the life cycle than appears in a formal retrospective analysis.

The Politics of Software Design

The politics of the design process involve the politics of the user organization and directly affect the content of technology design. In their study of the way software systems requirements are determined, Robey and Markus (1984, p. 9) advance this political perspective of technology design. They find that "systems development activities may well serve purposes beyond the rational goals of system quality and user acceptance." Our case studies illustrate how a software system has multiple users who have conflicting interests and differing concepts of what the system should accomplish. A consensus about the purpose of new software systems may not be possible. Because a single software design is required, there is often a bias in requirements analysis reflecting the interests of those with the greatest power. Thus, there is an inherent tendency for "new" software design to maintain existing arrangements in opposition to significant change.[2]

The political nature the software design process is often not apparent. Robey and Markus (1984, p. 12), for example, show how the design of software follows certain rituals such as the formal procedures of information requirements analysis or user groups to show rationality in the process, to provide at least the appearance of objectivity:

> The rituals of systems development perpetuate the prevailing ideology of rationality and provide an acceptable cover for unexpressible political motives in the dealings between users and designers. Overt conflict and manipulation are thereby controlled, lending stability and order to systems development. In effect, the rituals of systems development enable participants to act in their self-interests without discrediting the organization's rational ideology.[3]

We have illustrated in our cases how those in power often have conflicting goals vis-à-vis their subordinates in the organization. Rituals or formal reality come to bear not only during the designing of software but also in governing the environment in which the software is procured and then used.

The important point in this analysis of software design is not only that it is a political process, but that the politics of software (or technology) design tend to have certain systematic outcomes. Our analysis of the software design process (Chapter 3) shows that the objectives and interests of some groups will prevail over the objectives and interests of other groups, as reflected in design specifications. This is not a politics of pluralism in which different groups all vie for power by mobilizing control of resources and authority and which will shift, for example, as organizational needs or requirements change. It is not freely contested terrain in which all comers are on equal footing.[4] Thomas (1993, Chapter 1) also proposes that the politics of technology are important to understanding technological choice and use, arguing that we should:

> conceive of the relationship between technology and organization as *mediated by the exercise of power*, i.e., by a system of authority and domination that asserts the primacy of one understanding of the physical world, one prescription for social organization, over others...[it is] the opportunity...for different categories of organizational actors to try and put in place their own unique world views about the "proper" way to organize work [emphasis in original].

In earlier studies of engineering and technology design, Perrow (1983, 1986, p. 151) similarly concluded that "in general equipment and technology are chosen to require and reinforce centralized authority structures, even where decentralized ones would be more appropriate." Thus, we argue, software design should be viewed as a political process in which the interests of the existing power structure will dominate. This does not, however, determine the final impact of the technology because of changes that occur later in the design life cycle and because of how the technology interacts with characteristics of the organization.

Dilemmas of Software Design

The Dual Reality of Organizations

Technology designers must work largely within the constraints shaped by the user organization. Particularly for mission critical software, issues of work organizations are embedded in the more obvious issues of software design. Organizations generally function according to a dual set of realities: the formally prescribed procedures and policies and the actual practices its members use to conduct their work. These two realities are important and have implications for the effective design of software (see Weltz, 1991, on implications for software implementation).

The formal reality of organizations has been characterized as

"Myth and Ceremony" by Meyer and Rowan (1991). Organizations have practices and procedures (the myths) that represent prevailing concepts of rationality but those in organizations do not actually follow them except "ceremonially." Organizations maintain this formal reality as a means of increasing "their legitimacy and their survival prospects, independent of the immediate efficacy of the acquired practices and procedures" (Meyer and Rowan, 1991, p. 41).

Formal structures of organizations develop in accordance with traditionally accepted principles of bureaucratic functioning such as a very detailed division of labor, formalized standard operating procedures that specify every allowable contingency, rigid and hierarchical lines of authority and responsibility, and objectives of minimizing necessary skills at the lowest levels of the organization.[5] As Meyer and Rowan (1991, p. 45) explain, the operating procedures for organizations

> are prefabricated formulas available for use by any given organization...Similarly, technologies are institutionalized and become myths binding on organizations. Technical procedures of production, accounting, personnel selection, or data processing become taken-for-granted means to accomplish organizational ends.[6]

Generally, powerful actors in the organization believe these principles are the proper if not most efficient way to run and control the organization and they provide a patina of legitimacy to the organization to others (e.g., stockholders, board of directors, the public). There is an expectation by those inside and outside the organization that there will be suitable mechanisms for accountability and means of dealing with uncertainty.

The formal rules that are of significant consequence for software design are those that tend to be developed as highly proscribed procedures for dealing with every contingency and providing little discretion at the lowest levels of the organization. These rules for accountability often require not only specification of procedures for operation but also procedures that conform to accepted, generally quantifiable/measurable types of criteria.

A bank, for example, might have trouble justifying a policy of providing tellers a great deal of latitude in decisionmaking. Many both within and without the organization (e.g., customers, stockholders) might look askance at a bank that allowed, as policy, its lowest level employees, tellers, to have significant decisionmaking authority. Instead, sets of strict procedures and oversight provide demonstrable accountability and responsibility to those who might review the bank's operation. It might be possible for the bank to justify decisionmaking responsibility by tellers if it were very selective in its hiring and provided substantial training to its tellers. This, however, generally is seen as a less legitimate means to run this type of organization and requires more resources (for salary and training) than the bank might be able to justify, that is, given the norms within the organization and throughout the industry. In prevailing organizational norms there tends to be greater legitimacy for technology investments, particularly if they promise to enforce procedures and increase productivity according to traditional quantifiable measures (versus, for example, quality and flexibility).[7]

In this regard, the thrust of formal policies and thus principles of technology design may be characterized as trying to remove control from those workers at the lowest levels who are responsible for actually producing a good or delivering a service. The goal of engineering is to embed mechanisms for control over the worker and the process in the technology. In this approach there tends to be a devaluation of people and their potential contribution to the work process. David Noble (1984) observed that engineers traditionally express a "a delight in remote control and an enchantment with the notion of machines without men...a general devaluation of human skills and a distrust of human workers and an ongoing effort to eliminate both." As in bureaucratic procedures, in technology design there is a belief that all contingencies can be anticipated and processes can be completely and continually controlled through specified procedures.[8]

The technology use or design approach in service sector work and in software design is similar to that found in research on engineering of manufacturing technology.[9] Work organization in services is often being pushed to become more like factory work, to develop an assembly line for bureaucracies. In bureaucratic organization of service work, formal policies are developed based on the goal of eliminating discretionary action. It is assumed not just that there are known methods for achieving the goals of the organization, but that nearly all the necessary methods, situations, and actions can be anticipated and specified. Control over individual discretion is part of the accepted means of ensuring fairness, legitimacy, and uniformity of outcomes.

Despite grand and ever-present promises, the theoretical possibilities of engineering fully automated technology controlled systems are somewhat elusive in the day-to-day reality of work. The problem is that actual operating conditions, whether a piece of physical material to be machined or a person requesting a service, regularly deviate from the specified and anticipated procedures. Even in basic manufacturing processes it is difficult to operate a fully automatic process: Metal may vary in its properties (e.g., hardness, purity) and machine tools wear or operate with some variability. Moreover, new technology as well as changes in the organization's environment can lead to changes in the organization and/or its processes, such as new products, new services, new methods of conducting business. These changes can introduce new conditions that were not anticipated in the technology design and may require adaptation by the people using the technology. A highly integrated, fully automated system may inhibit innovation.[10]

The nature of most service sector work makes this problem even more complicated. People's actual and perceived situations, and thus their service needs, are almost infinitely variable and thus quite frequently fall outside normal operating procedures. The ability to anticipate and plan for every contingency is limited, and dealing with it efficiently requires a response that may not be in accord with the specified procedures. As Brunsson (1985, p. 4) has observed in *The Irrational Organization*: "Efficiency seldom goes hand in hand with flexibility. Coordinating different people's actions also means reducing the range of actions available to each one of them. And while the reduction in variety may increase efficiency, it also tends to undermine the ability to promote new values, to perform new tasks or to handle new situations."

The solution to this problem in many organizations has been found in "decoupling" the formal policies and the informal procedures or in designing loose integration of automated systems.[11] The demand for legitimacy and control, however, places limits on the degree of loose coupling usually permitted in organizations. One approach is found in professional occupations where norms are established but individual practitioners are expected to exercise judgment to achieve a given outcome. Education, training, and certification of workers provides legitimacy to their procedures without requirements for strict procedural observance or monitoring. In our hospital case (Chapter 6), the prevailing ethos of professionalism was used to justify soft controls in the system that allowed for decoupling, that is, of *not* taking advantage of the potential of software to enforce agreed upon procedures. In the field service cases (Chapter 5) there were two different approaches. One company did not use the system to enforce procedures because it viewed the field engineers as skilled workers who would use their best judgment and skills to perform their work properly. Assessment of the field engineers' performance was based on the final outcomes of their work (e.g., customer satisfaction) rather than adherence to detailed procedures. In contrast, the other field service company tried to use the software to enforce detailed procedures regulating the work process. The bank similarly designed the software to enforce their formal procedures. However, the *implementation* of the system differed in the second field service firm and the bank: When the field engineers subverted the system, the field service management and system designers responded by trying to tighten the controls to ensure compliance. In the bank, branch managers decoupled the system by allowing tellers to work around and subvert the controls designed into the system.

When legitimacy and accountability are not achieved through professionalism, the formal and informal procedures tend to be decoupled in a nonsanctioned way. People who perform the actual production or service delivery tasks are then permitted to do what is necessary only by their immediate supervisors or are able to do so surreptitiously. Just as religious ceremonies are observed with varying degrees of orthodoxy, so too the ceremony of the formal organization is followed in varying degrees. Some in the organization religiously try to enforce the procedures while others require only perfunctory observance.

Software systems are designed, however, according to the formal procedures and policies of the organization. In part this is done because the software, like the organization, gains in credibility and legitimacy if it appears to operate according to the formal policies. Mission critical software exacerbates the uneasy tension between those who enable decoupling within the organization and those trying to constrain or restrict it. Current approaches to software design increase that tension even further. Changes in software design and the organization present a formidable challenge.

Assimilation, Accommodation, and the Prospects for Change

Our study of software design suggests that there is no "correct" design. Software designs ought to be evaluated in terms of their contribution to the effectiveness of the user organization and their impact on end users. Our findings in this regard suggest a model for thinking about technology and the prospects for change.

Technology designs may be characterized in terms of the degree of technical change as compared to previous technologies. Consider, for example, the development of word processors in which there were significantly different design approaches taken in the early models. The dedicated word processors tried to replicate the features of typing on a typewriter. The system was designed to make typing faster and easier without changes in previous routines or concepts of the tasks. This made it easier for the transition from typewriters to word processors. The technology itself might be considered an incremental advance over typewriters. In our banking case the design of the teller system was similarly oriented to appear as an incremental advance over previous systems by replicating the design of existing screens even though they were considered inefficient. In one instance the account numbers were entered as two fields, as they had been in the previous system because of limitations in the technology. The designers originally developed the system to take account numbers as one field which they saw as overcoming a limitation of the earlier systems. Users insisted that the system be redesigned to have two fields because that was the way they were accustomed to entering the account numbers. One designer characterized the request of users to have two-part account numbers as "limitations turned features." It was an effort to assimilate technology into existing work routines, to make the technology reflect existing practices and gain high user acceptance.

In contrast, the development of modern word processing systems on standalone personal computers can be seen as radical advances in technology when compared to the earlier systems. These systems do not try to preserve "typing" but rather transform the task into document composition. Documents appear to scroll continuously rather than be formatted page-by-page.

Additional text is entered and footnotes added or deleted without any page adjustments by the user. The attributes of the technology could be characterized as a radical advance over typewriters by embodying a vision of the work task as document composition rather than typing.

The characterization of the technology on a continuum between incremental and radical represents attributes of the technology as the designers constructed it. "User requirements" are identified and interpreted through the filter of the organization of user and vendor firms and their environments and embodied as particular physical and functional characteristics of the technology. The technology, in short, reflects an interpretation or vision that was shaped by the structure of the design process. User organization attributes and system requirements are first expressed and then interpreted through the structure of the user organization, the market, and the vendor organization. These attributes and requirements are then interpreted by the designers, within additional constraints of the design space, as they develop the technology.

When the technology is adopted by an organization, it becomes a constraining, though not determining, structure that in part shapes the action space of its user. The technology in the user organization interacts with other organization features. Technology implementation and use is a process of reinterpretation and redesign according to organizational characteristics. Here, the technology as designed confronts the requirements of the informal organization and the conflicting, often irresolvable interests of different users, and brings to existing routines new technological possibilities and constraints that, in part, redefine the action space of the user. This leads to a reinterpretation of the potential of the technology, in effect a change from its intended design. Technology is not received by an organization as it was originally defined in part because of the inherent differences between the process of defining and of using technology.

What does it mean to "adopt" a new technology? On the one hand the user organization might assimilate the technology to fit into existing structures and modes of operation. Alternatively, it might change its work processes to accommodate new features and functionality of the technology. Which of these two situations actually dominates will be influenced by the attributes

of the technology in combination with an organization's characteristics such as its general approach to organizing the work
process.

Using the example of a word processor, we can construct a
matrix of technology attributes and implementation and use
characteristics (see Figure 9.1). For this example, the word
processor can be designed as an incremental change over a
typewriter or as a radical change. Each can be assimilated by the
user organization or lead to reorganization of the work process
as an organizational accommodation of the technology. The
early word processors could be assimilated to replace typewriters and both the work task and organization of work might
remain largely unchanged. However, the higher cost of word
processors might lead some organizations to increase their utilization through creation of word processing pools with specialized word processing secretaries. The latter reorganization
would be an accommodation of a technology that was designed
to be only an incremental change over typewriters.

A technology designed to be a radical innovation, such as a
personal computer for word processing, could also be implemented and used by the organization through assimilation or
accommodation. The organization assimilating it might use the
computer as just a faster typewriter and not substantially change

Fig. 9.1. Attributes of Technology Design and Implementation.

| Implementation and Use | Technology Attributes | |
	Incremental	Radical
Assimilation	Dedicated word processing replacing manual typewriter	PC used as faster typewriter (no change in work process or flow)
Accommodation	Dedicated word processor leading to creation of typing pools	PC used for document composition; more typing done by document author; secretary does new applications

the work process in terms of the substance of the work or responsibilities or skills of the users. (Its lower cost than the original dedicated minicomputer word processors might allow greater assimilation because the organization could afford to replace typewriters on every desk.) An organizational accommodation might change the substance of the work, perhaps having the authors of letters and documents type the first drafts and assigning more sophisticated graphics, spreadsheet, and document formatting tasks to secretaries. In an even more radical change in the organization, as occurred in one large computer company, secretaries no longer did *any* typing for others as everyone was given a personal computer and printer and expected to do all his or her own typing.

Something new *can* be assimilated in ways that shore up existing routines and power arrangements, but it can also be assimilated in ways that provide openings for change if inconsistencies and contradictions develop. Piaget (1967) has shown how a child will assimilate and ignore contradictory evidence until developmentally ready to develop a new schema or structure. In our model, it is through a social process (rather than biological or developmental) that a combination of factors— technology, organization, market environment, or the nature of particular people within the organization—strain the existing structures (cf. Kuhn's [1970] analysis of paradigm shifts). A failure to assimilate fully new conditions and technology will strain the existing structures. It can be incremental and continuous or radical and discontinuous. Often stasis can be maintained for long periods, with the organization resisting change even in the face of continued problems, until some traumatic event becomes a crisis and unfreezes existing structures, allowing change to occur.

Software is a technology that potentially can precipitate such crises by imposing formal procedures and changing the collection and uses of information. This kind of technology therefore becomes increasingly difficult to assimilate into existing structures. In this way, the expansive power of new computer technologies can lead, in unintended ways, to organizational changes that, in turn, allow for better design and use of the technology. The model presented here may help to clarify the choices facing those who seek new software in the cause of enhancing organizational performance.

The Coming Challenge of Design

As the medium through which work tasks are performed, software provides the means to implement and regulate procedures to a degree not possible in noncomputerized bureaucracies. When user requirements are defined only as the formal policies of the organization, there is little latitude for the informal practices to be sanctioned by those designing the software. Under such constraints, systems that were designed to embody informal work practices would lack legitimacy. Thus, if software that reflects the formal policies is implemented as designed, it will collapse the divergence between the formal and informal realities of the organization. That is, because software mediates the actual execution of work, because it operates as a tangible technology, there is much less negotiation possible than when formal policies of the organization are embodied as operating procedures that depend upon people for their implementation. There is less space or latitude for the informal realities of the organization to coexist with the formal structures of the organization *if the software system is implemented as designed.* Thus, we can see a source of dysfunctionality of software as coming from structural or inherent features of organizations rather than from an inadequate technical process of user requirements determination.

We have noted the design solution to use "soft" controls in the software (recall the hospital case). This design option often depends upon the legitimacy of the users as autonomous decisionmakers and their power to resist encroachment on their territory (as the physicians had in that hospital case). Soft controls in software are generally possible only in organizations with intentional explicit loose coupling and accountability through professional norms. In most other cases, however, software that does not reflect formal policies and procedures may be difficult to sell to user organizations. As we discussed in Chapter 3 and our cases illustrated, the "buyer" and those in upper levels of management, who generally endorse the formal organization, exert the most influence in defining the systems and in procurement decisions.

Incorporating traditional types of controls in the software design often leads users to subvert aspects of its intended functionality. In our bank example, tellers and their supervisors found ways to defeat the security provisions built into the system. In our field service case, the field engineers devised ways to "pencil whip" the data to make the monitoring function ineffective. Sometimes these software functions are just regarded as poor design features or as a burden to endure, as a ritual that the organization requires and to which workers need to pay homage. If any thought is given to these features or functions of the software, they may be seen as serving a legitimating function for the organization (e.g., providing data for tracking productivity, however suspect the data may be, or providing at least appearances of having approved procedures that regulate the work process). Others, however, will believe in enforcing the prescribed procedures and work to increase the hard controls in the system and devise ways to identify users who do not conform. Much like battles over Victorian morality, there are the true believers who fear the dissolution of society without at least formal observance of prevailing norms and there are those who appear to capitulate by dutifully agreeing yet follow their desires into unsanctioned behavior.

When software systems are designed in accordance with the formal reality of organizations with hierarchical decisionmaking and authority, the outcome is generally a system that must be subverted to restore flexibility to end users or that leads to an organization that hobbles along with a dysfunctional system. In some environments firms can survive quite well, or at least survive for long periods of time, with systems that do not provide the necessary flexibility to end users. In dynamic environments, with high pressure for efficiency and competitiveness, there is less latitude for organizations to continue with dysfunctional operations. As we show in our cases and discuss in more detail in Chapter 7, changes in the competitive environment of banks, the field service industry, and hospitals increase the tension in organizations trying to implement formal policies and procedures through software.

The issue we have identified is not solved simply through improved methods for identifying user requirements. Instead it calls for a more complex process of generating fundamentally new operating alternatives within the user organization. Alternative forms of work organization, for example, allow for developing new means of accountability. Some firms are experimenting with new forms of work organization that expand the role of frontline or shopfloor workers. The alternative scenarios require the simultaneous and deliberative restructuring of software design *and* the user organization in ways that are mutually compatible and reinforcing. The vendor alone cannot create new technology, as we have shown in our case analyses. There needs to be a redefinition of the design space and the user space. This involves changes at a number of levels. It requires changes in the cognitive maps of designers but they must be sustained, or motivated, by larger changes in the organization norms and the external environment such as market demand. Market changes involve the user organization which similarly must change at a number of levels. This includes not only management philosophy but often control over resources and power in the organization. In Chapter 8 we suggested how this might happen in software procurement. However, a more thoroughgoing change requires systemic and ongoing restructuring. There generally needs to be a more sustained and extensive pressure on the user organization to change. The success of new technology, such as new software designs, requires changes in the user organization to accommodate it rather than assimilate it into existing patterns or operating procedures.

Ironically, technology is often an object of contention *because* it can provide an opportunity or catalyst for change and thus, in practice, its potential to spark change is likely to be muted. Traditional user requirements analysis will tend to be dominated by those in the organization with more power who will generally define the "objective requirements" as those that maintain the status quo and specifically their own position. However, in the scenario we just outlined, the software, because it implements the formal reality of the organization in an uncompromising way, may lead people in the organization to confront the conflict in the dual reality of the organization and, through this confrontation, provide an opportunity for change. If this opportunity is taken, the outcome can lead to new ways of maintaining organization legitimacy through, for example, a professional model of responsibility and accountability for frontline service workers. However, the change opportunity must be broader than merely designing new types of technology because the software designer alone cannot reconcile the user organization's formal and informal visions of needed functionality.

Ultimately, the solution to this aspect of the problem of software design is to be found in the solution to the problems of how the work process is organized. Depending on an organization's particular service mission, customer satisfaction requires a blend of consistency and responsiveness in the process of service delivery. Accordingly, to realize the full potential of mission critical software, organizations must avoid becoming so entrenched in maintaining the façade of formal policies and procedures that they lose the ability for effective, flexible work performance. In this regard, one important change in the user organization that has implications for software design is acceptance of soft controls rather than trying to use the theoretical potential of software to implement polices completely through hard controls. Taking this step requires reconceptualizing the role of the worker in the work process as a knowledgeable, responsible, and skilled person and of the workplace as best operating with some degree of discretion. It also requires changes in the traditional conceptions of technology and giving up on the engineer's common dream of full automation. In short, it means looking for effective organizational solutions rather than narrow technology fixes. It means that software becomes more a tool for the user than a means for control.

We have argued that software necessarily reflects the objectives and sanctioned procedures of the user organization and those who hold power in the organization. The software designer, as technology supplier, thus faces a fundamental dilemma in trying to reconcile existing gaps between formal and informal ways of achieving effective organizational performance. Ultimately, those who shape the policies and practices of user organizations must step forward with concomitant changes of their own. Software design alone cannot address the full problem of high performance service delivery. But will organizations learn to use those skilled in software design as more effective partners in shaping the high performance workplaces of the future?

Endnotes

1. Structuration theory offers some important possibilities for a new model of analysis of technology and organizations that, we find, is most important in viewing this dynamic technology-organization relationship. We have found such theory generally useful in our analysis of service delivery cases involving new software. Thomas' (1993) research addresses similar issues in the manufacturing environment. Thomas (1993, Chapter 6) adds some additional elements

to structuration theory to develop what he refers to as the "power-process" approach. He finds consideration of "purpose" lacking in structuration theory and argues that:

> in order to understand how and why exogenous developments come to be recognized or how and why strategic choices come to be made, it is essential to understand who or what segments of an organization have the power with which to define the parameters of search for problems and solutions, the criteria with which alternatives are evaluated, and the manner in which a choice once made is implemented. Of necessity, the power-process perspective accords a central role to power relations in the organization.

We agree with Thomas' emphasis on these particular theoretical elaborations.

2. Organizations attempting to "empower" the workforce, a common theme in U.S. management in the 1990s, are not immune to this constraint. Empowerment, typically seen as a way of seeking incremental improvement in organizational performance, frequently stops short of playing a key role in the design of new technology. See Chapter 2 for further discussion of this point.

3. Robey and Markus (1984, p. 12) show how defining system requirements is a political process, at least in part, and how information requirements analysis is distorted, serves legitimating functions, and is conservative of the status quo:

> Regardless of whether it actually produces rational outcomes or not, systems development must *symbolize* rationality and *signify* that the actions taken are not arbitrary, but rather acceptable within the organizations's ideology. As such, rituals help provide meaning to the actions taken within an organization [emphasis in original].

While showing the ritual/political part of systems development, they stop short of analyzing any systematic tendencies or content issues versus process at the individual level. They do not discuss implications for design beyond "beware of what is really going on" (p. 13) in the process.

4. The implications for software design can be seen in the example of design choices for implementing controls (e.g., hard versus soft controls). Robey and Markus (1984) and other analyses on software design locate the locus of change with the designers, as we discussed in Chapter 2. This is limited because designers have limited latitude in which to maneuver. Those designing the technology do not, and cannot, act with great freedom from their social environment. Their design space is constrained by factors beyond their own perceptions and perspectives. Thus, the focus of design changes needs to be much broader than the attitudes, personalities, and education of engineers. We need to view their constraints as also related to an environment of organizations, markets, and industrial culture of the society. The term industrial culture is used to denote the nontechnical factors that shape technology and that can be examined as related to specific societies. That is, thinking in terms of industrial culture suggests how different industrial countries deal with issues of technology design and production organization. Rauner and Ruth (1990, p. 121) list important dimensions of industrial culture as "national traditions and societal

institutions; organizational preferences; social institutions and government policies; educational institutions; social (and individual) psychology."

5. In Chapter 3 we noted how such longstanding principles of organization have their intellectual legacy in the works of Adam Smith, Max Weber, and Frederick Taylor and their practical roots in the factories of Henry Ford.

6. Meyer and Rowan (1991, p. 45) also note that "Quite apart from their possible efficiency, such institutionalized techniques establish an organization as appropriate, rational, and modern. Their use displays responsibility and avoids claims of negligence." Not only, for example, do formal accounting procedures and economic analysis provide legitimacy and rationale for a decision, "such analyses can also provide rational accountings after failures occur: managers whose plans have failed can demonstrate to investors, stockholders, and superiors that procedures were prudent and that decisions were by rational means" (Meyer and Rowan, 1991, p. 51).

7. This point has been made by many researchers and was found to be an important part of technology justification in studies of manufacturing technology design (e.g., Salzman and Lund, 1993; Lund, et al, 1993), and was explored in detail by Thomas' (1993, Chapter 6) study of manufacturing technology where he found that "the idea of technology—and, more specifically, the idea of automation as a labor-saving device—can itself become institutionalized...the presumed benefits of automation have become so taken-for-granted that in the absence of overwhelming proof that other alternatives are possible, automation becomes the default option." It is not only the value of technology solutions as an ideology but also the means of justification that support this ideology: "...the subordination of process to product helps explain why manufacturing managers and engineers would adhere to traditional return on investment metrics. In most cases, those metrics provided a functional substitute for an explicit manufacturing strategy." When there was uncertainty,

> ...the default option [i.e., traditional return on investment metrics] was also the safest: to restrict the search for both problems and solutions that fit with traditional measures—even when doing so might produce deleterious consequences (e.g., increases in the volume of indirect labor). On those few occasions when managers and engineers chose to go out on a limb, they ardently resisted arguing for alternative measures because 'having the numbers'—even numbers that they might have ridiculed in private—enabled them to argue that their choices were legitimate. The numbers were legitimate because they had been screened through a *procedure* that was deemed to be legitimate and defensible.

8. Similar findings are reported in Perrow (1983) and in Thomas (1993). This perspective in engineering was found in our survey of software design and engineering textbooks and reflected in other interviews with engineering managers (see findings as reported in Salzman, 1992; and Lund, et al., 1993). As we noted in this review, although management theory has evolved during the post-war period, design principles do not appear to have undergone a similar development. Our review of design textbooks indicated that engineering proceeds with the same basic understanding of the human role in production as first articulated at the beginning of the twentieth century.

9. Although much of the software design literature is more advanced in its recognition of the cognitive dimension of humans and the role of users in design, it does not depart substantially from a basic engineering paradigm, as discussed in Chapter 3. The cognitive psychology models used in systems design, for example, have been criticized for being mechanistic and deterministic models of human functions (Coulter, 1979, 1983; Dreyfus, 1979). We addressed the limits of user involvement for overcoming this problem in Chapter 3 and the case studies.

10. These problems and the general problem of automation in manufacturing are discussed in general by Noble (1984) and in the case of attempted automation of printed circuit boards using Computer-Aided Design in Salzman (1989), flexible manufacturing systems in Graham and Rosenthal (1986), and in other manufacturing cases in Lund, et al. (1993) and Salzman and Lund (1993).

11. Several studies of decoupling in organizations and in manufacturing systems are Meyer and Rowan (1978), Perrow (1984), Hirschhorn (1984). Accounts of actual shopfloor activity and their divergence from formal polices and procedures are described in Burawoy (1979) and in Hampers (1992).

APPENDIX A

Outline of the
Research Project

Outline of the Research Project

The first stage of research was a survey of software vendors, involving a lengthy semi-structured interview with the president or chairman of 23 software companies and additional interviews with vice presidents of marketing, vice presidents of development, and lead developers in five of the firms. In-depth case studies were subsequently conducted spanning three types of industries, including two software companies and four user organizations.

The survey included 23 Massachusetts software companies ranging from small start-up firms to large, long-established vendors. They were selected from the Massachusetts Software Council membership list (150 companies) to represent a range of sizes and applications. Seven of the firms employed 49 or fewer employees, eight firms had 50 to 100 employees, and eight employed over 100 people. The product areas included financial and legal services, manufacturing, and general business software (see Figure A.1). In these interviews we examined the internal structure of software companies, the organization of development and design processes, the involvement of software users, programming procedures used, how tradeoffs were made among competing design choices, and how software companies conceptualized their design and development goals. The interview schedule was developed through consultation with several experts in the information systems field, discussions and reviews of preliminary instruments with software industry executives, managers, and programmers, followed by pilot testing. Our telephone interviews were open-ended, letting the respondents define and discuss the important issues in each of the topic areas we queried. Respondents discussed these issues for up to 1 $\frac{1}{2}$ hours, well beyond our original expectation of a 30 minute interview.

Two vendor case studies were selected from among the 23 vendors, one in banking applications, the other in field service. In both of these instances we examined the process and criteria used by the software vendors to define user requirements and as a basis for software systems design. We also identified several case studies in user firms in the three

---

23 Software Firms

Product Areas:*
- 10 Financial and Legal Services
- 3 Manufacturing
- 12 General Business Software

Number of Employees
- 7 with 49 or fewer employees
- 8 with 50 to 100 employees
- 8 with over 100 employees

* Totals to 25 because two companies had more than one product.

Figure A.1. Companies Interviewed.

industries of interest: banking, field service, and hospitals. Here we examined the design changes made by users and the impact of specific software features and functions on the worklife and effectiveness of users. In banking, the selected user firm was a large commercial bank and the vendor firm was a large vendor producing software to support all banking operations for midsized banks. In field service, the user firms were two major electronics equipment manufacturers and the vendor firm was a leading developer of integrated software packages to support all business functions associated with handling field service calls and associated logistics. The hospital system was for storage and retrieval of all patient information, handling of all medical orders, and computerizing information transfer among all departments in a midsized hospital[1] (Figure A.2 outlines the case study types, orientations, and coverage). These case study sites provided an interesting group of recently developed mission critical software applications in diverse industries within the service sector. The diversity of sites was more appropriate than a large random sample, given the exploratory rather than hypothesis-testing nature of our research.

The case studies of the user firms involved interviews with the "hands-on" users, their supervisors, trainers, and managers, and in the software firms with people from all departments involved in the development, production, and sale of the product. We interviewed at all levels of these organizations; top management, middle management/supervisors, technical staff, and users. Our subjects included: programmers, managers, sales representatives, marketing managers, product managers, vice presidents of development and of marketing, and the presidents and chairmen of the companies. In the banking vendor case the most extensive interviews were conducted with technical staff directly involved in the development of the product; background exposure included our attendance at sales meetings and demonstrations of the product. In all cases there was extensive observation of the product in use. For example, in the banking case we went to four

Figure A.2. Case Study Sites, Products, and Subjects.

Industry/Product	Focus of Case	Interviews & Observations

Banking/Teller System	User Organization	Central Office:
		  Systems Analyst
		  Training Supervisor
		  Systems Manager
		
		Branch Office
		  Branch Manager
		  Tellers
		  Customer Service Reps.

Banking/Integrated Operations (teller, back office accounting, reporting, analysis, etc.)	Vendor	Management
		  President
		  Vice Presidents
		
		Marketing Staff
		
		Development
		  Managers
		  Analysts/Programmers

Field Service/Integrated Operations (dispatch, logistics, accounting, etc.)	Vendor	President Dir. of Product Development Development Staff

	User Organizations (2)	Central Office:
		  Management
		  Dispatchers
		
		Field Offices:
		  Management/Supervisors
		  Field Engineers

Hospital/Patient Chart and Orders	User Organization	Direct Care Personnel
		  Physicians
		  Nurses
		  Physical Therapists
		  Social Workers
		
		Support/Technical Personnel:
		  Secretaries
		  Laboratory Technicians
		
		Designers:
		  MIS Staff
		  System Selection Committee

bank branches (spanning large and small, urban and suburban, business district and inner city); we each spent at least two hours in each of the four offices standing behind the teller line and in the customer service area. When we observed the software system in use, we were also able to query users to understand the job requirements and actual operating conditions of software usage.

Endnote

1. The field service case study was conducted with Fred VanBennekom; the hospital case study was conducted by Ross Koppel, Albert Crawford, and Robert Cort as part of this study.

APPENDIX B

Teaching Cases on Software Design and Use

Teaching Cases on Software Design and Use

This appendix consists of four case studies in three industries: Banking, Field Service, and Hospitals. These cases are based on the research conducted for this book. They provide more detail on design decisions and implementation issues than discussed in the book and are written for use as teaching cases in courses that cover issues in the design of workplace technology. These cases can be used for courses in management, engineering, or information systems and for examining issues about technology in general or software in particular. Our intention is that the instructor using these cases would provide students with assignment questions that would encourage them to think through the kinds of issues examined in this book. The case discussions can then provide an opportunity to cover some of the analysis presented in this book. The cases are intended to be used independently of the case study chapters and thus there is some common descriptive passages in both the teaching cases and earlier chapters of the book.

Branch Office Automation in Banking: A Case in the Design and Use of Software Systems*

Introduction

"Big Bank" (a pseudonym) is a very successful institution. It has a long and profitable history and has been particularly outstanding in the commercial banking field. As a retail banker it has been well established throughout its geographical region and there is a strong commitment to maintain profitable operations that serve a broad customer base. The bank's customer service code demands courtesy, responsiveness, and professionalism at all times.

Big Bank has continued to upgrade its computer systems capabilities and has implemented two major systems for use by branch personnel: the Teller system and the Administration system. Big Bank has a corporate systems group dedicated to branch office automation. This group currently has nine professionals, eight of whom program in COBOL and one in FCL (a special financial control language) programmer. It is generally acknowledged that among the many priority areas for infrastructure development at the bank, branch office automation does not rank near the top. Cost-benefit justifications are required for new systems developments including major expansions of existing systems. The cost side is estimated by the project leader from the systems development group, while benefits are estimated (often qualitatively) by the central User Liaison Group for branch operations.

* This case was developed by Stephen R. Rosenthal and Harold Salzman. It was prepared as the basis for class discussion rather than to illustrate either effective or ineffective systems development, implementation or management practices. This material is based upon research supported by the Ethics and Values Section of the National Science Foundation, under Grant No. BBS-8619534.

Retail Banking Activities and Structure

Organizational Goals

Four organizational goals, common in banking, set the stage for the branch automation systems: accuracy, efficiency, security and customer service. The relative importance of each of the goals depends upon the nature of the relevant activity, and tradeoffs among goals may be necessary (e.g., accommodating some customer requests may compromise security or accuracy). Each of these goals needs to be appreciated in terms of the kinds of requirements that it sets for the design of software-based systems.

Accuracy Accuracy is non-negotiable in retail banking. All accounts must be correct and kept fully up-to-date. Transactions must be verifiable. A considerable amount of cash is handled at each teller window and regular or significant discrepancies in cash balances cannot be tolerated. Periodic cash tabulations and reconciliations are necessary. The bank must also keep accurate information on the names, addresses, social security numbers, and other items for every account held by each of its customers.

Efficiency Retail banking is highly competitive and there is strong pressure to reduce unnecessary costs, particularly as deregulation has resulted in intensified competition. Efficient transaction processing is, therefore, important and is facilitated through automation of teller functions. The speed with which data can be entered into the computer-based system and inquiries made through it depends on both the response time of the technology and the skill of the tellers who use it. To the extent that the system is designed for ease-of-use, some skill requirements can be reduced. Nevertheless, with turnover in the teller ranks being common, training is an important prerequisite for achieving efficiency through automation.

Security Tellers deal with money and information about money. Both of these dimensions call for measures of security. Someone must be made accountable for the security of the cash that flows in and out of retail banks. When there are questions about the legitimacy of customer requests for withdrawals, someone must be authorized to approve or deny special requests. Account information needs to be available to tellers and to customers but not to unauthorized parties.

Customer Service In branch banking, service to the customer includes the ability to execute requested transactions in a smooth and courteous manner, provide account information as needed, and to have the flexibility to respond to contingencies as they arise without unduly inconveniencing the customer.

These multiple and sometimes conflicting goals of branch banking provide a basis for assessing the possible benefits or drawbacks of particular features and functions of automation systems.

Organizational Structure

To understand the function of computer systems for branch automation, one must first have some appreciation for the division of responsibility between the "back room" operations (conducted in a central location) and the positions and functions within the bank's branch offices.

The Branch Office

A branch office typically has a manager, a number of Customer Service Representatives (CSRs), a head teller, and a number of tellers. The CSRs handle account openings and closings, sell various services (e.g., premium rate accounts, certificates of deposit, etc.) or handle special customer requests. CSRs also have the authority to approve or disapprove special transactions that tellers are not allowed to process. CSRs are referred to as people on the "platform," and are considered to be "officers." Tellers process customer transactions at the window and the automatic teller machines (ATM) (they unload and process the ATM transactions twice a day). There is a head teller who typically has more experience than the other tellers and has responsibility for overseeing the teller line, authorizing a first level of special transactions and customer problems, and conducting monthly audits of each teller's cash drawer.

Bank tellers conduct highly "programmed" transactions while in direct face-to-face contact with retail banking customers. As the number and variety of demand deposit accounts and other services have grown, tellers have been called upon to handle a greater variety of transactions and services. Fundamentally, however, their jobs have remained very similar over recent decades. As branch banking has become increasingly automated, following back office automation in the 1960s, the teller's job has become dependent on the functioning of computer-based systems for recording and monitoring customer transactions. One must recognize, however, that processing these kinds of transactions is but a part (maybe one-half on average) of what tellers spend their time doing. Providing other services such as issuing money orders or travelers checks, dispensing large quantities of coins to business customers, and counting and transferring cash are other aspects of the teller's job.

An "experienced" teller has come to mean (in recent years) one who has been on the job for a full year because turnover normally occurs more frequently. Senior tellers, who have supervisory responsibilities, are selected from among the best of those tellers who have demonstrated proficiency and reliability on the job. They have a number of routine administrative tasks, such as keeping attendance records for the group of tellers. Senior tellers are also charged with providing guidance and supervision to the tellers throughout the day.

The Back Office

Many of the retail banking functions are only "handled" at the branch office but processing of transactions are completed in a central office. Two of the important back office functions of this sort are proof and transit and records control. Tellers are responsible for maintaining accurate records on cash balances at their window and for ensuring that customers making withdrawals have sufficient funds in their account. Before a customer's account is actually updated, transactions must be processed and verified through centralized groups and systems, including proof and transit, in the evening shift. Similarly, not all functions initiated in branch offices by CSRs are automated, so much updating of customer accounts and information is accomplished through the flow of paper to the central records control group. The activities and responsibilities of back office and branch office positions has changed, and continues to change, with the introduction of new or enhanced computer systems.

Automation

The Teller System

Big Bank is no exception to the trend toward increased automation at the tellers' windows. In the mid-1970s, the bank acquired an IBM system for recording a wide range of payment, withdrawal, and deposit transactions. The terminal, specially designed for these banking functions, has separate keys for indicating each of the different kinds of transactions. The software and communications network allows tellers to view certain account information. The system was designed to be triggered by plastic identification cards that are issued to tellers and their supervisors.

Big Bank provides training to all new tellers which includes hands-on exposure to this system. To be a teller, one must be conversant with the features and functions of this system, as well as having other proficiencies such as the counting and handling of cash.

While each minute aspect of the teller system has some effect on each teller, most are likely to be imperceptible since they quickly become perceived as "the way the job is done." After all, the use of the terminal and the software that processes the transactions do not fundamentally change the job activity or level of responsibility or skill of the teller. Furthermore, the teller system has remained basically the same since its introduction at the bank over a decade ago. Some branches have an older terminal, while a updated model has been installed in others.

Routine Use of the Teller System

Typical actions, aside from entering the transactions themselves, that are required by the system include:
- teller signs on at beginning of the day using his or her plastic identification card.
- using the teller card to override "hold" status messages.
- "settlement" of the daily transactions at each teller's window, which requires "batching out" work according to several standard categories (cash in, checks in, savings deposits in, cash out).
- verifying the cash balance at the teller's window at the end of the day (teller counts cash, then compares it with the amount that the computer has tallied from the day's starting balance, inflows and outflows.

More specialized use of the system includes activities such as: account inquiries, correcting a transaction previously recorded, the frequency with which various types of inflows (cash, checks, savings deposits) are "batched out." (Note that on the old systems only, due to the printing mechanism and size of paper used to send information to the centralized proof and transit unit of the bank, the batch size is limited to a maximum of 35 items.)

Tellers report that the system is very reliable and it also seems easy to use. No troublesome operating errors have been detected. When the host system is down, withdrawal transactions cannot be verified for adequate funds through this online connection with the centralized account database. Tellers continue to process transactions on the teller terminals thereby generating receipts for customers. (There are plans to implement, at some future date, a "store and forward" systems capability to allow transactions to be entered even when the host computer is down and then automatically transmitted when the host is again functioning.)

When, on very rare occasions, the controller system is down, the terminals cannot function and tellers must conduct transactions manually (customers do not get a computer-generated receipt) and later enter all of those transactions when the system service is restored and time permits.

An experienced teller can use the system to complete the end of day "settling" function in as little as five minutes by monitoring cash early and "batching" throughout the day (tricks of the trade). Less experienced tellers take up to a half-hour or more to settle.

Non-Routine Uses of the System

Cash audits of each teller are conducted unannounced every month. The head teller may use any of the terminals to audit a teller's balances at any time. Certain types of audits (e.g., a teller's use of the "correct deposit from savings account" feature) could signal possible irregularities.

The teller system was designed to provide a certain amount of allocation of responsibility between tellers and their supervisors. Under a prespecified set of exceptional situations (defined by management at the bank through the setting of software parameters) the teller's terminal will freeze with a message about an account on the screen. At this point, the requested transaction can be completed only if an authorized plastic "officer's" card (as distinguished from the "teller's" card) is passed through a reader on the terminal. The purpose of this procedure is clear. When, for example, an account shows an exceptional amount of activity on a single day, or a "stop order" condition is already on an account, a deliberate decision should be made by a responsible employee before more withdrawals are executed on an account. A flashing message appears on the screen whenever a withdrawal over $50 is being entered for a new account (less than six months old). If a withdrawal is being attempted for over $50, an override using the officer's card is required. For a larger attempted withdrawal on a new account, a CSR should check the activity on the account before an override is attempted.

Branch managers have the authority, within reason, to define the procedures under which the branch functions. Officer cards are officially (i.e., by central office policy) assigned to CSRs and branch managers, but the branch manager usually provides the head teller with an officer card as well. Today, at the bank, one would typically find that when the officers card is needed for most exceptional situations that the teller would borrow the card assigned to the head teller to override the troublesome condition, rather than standing by (as the customer also waits) until a customer service representative is available to personally check the situation at the teller's window. Tellers explain their decision on whether to call the CSR in terms of their own personal knowledge of the particular customer and the underlying condition. Branch managers tend to explain it in terms of how busy their branch can get and how they trust the judgment of the tellers to know when to insist on help from a superior.

Software Modifications to the Teller System

The systems group at Big Bank has instituted many changes to the original software package purchased from IBM, but these seem to be in the spirit of incremental changes to a basically stable set of system functions. Changes during the past ten years were made by at least six different programmers from the systems group plus three different outside contractors. Although the tellers' system has not received much programming attention in recent years, the list of modifications in place or planned includes the following:

- The capability to correct a transaction previously recorded.
- The ability to enter multiple transactions for a single customer (rather than having to repeat the entry of key initial information as if it were a completely new transaction.
- Better integration of loan payment transactions with the back office mainframe system that actually credits such payments to charge card accounts (thereby reducing the lag from accepting a payment to crediting it from five days to two days).
- Alterations in the number of categories of transactions handled by the system. The more categories, the more work for tellers in "settlement" of each category. More categories handled by the tellers, however, makes subsequent back office processing easier.
- Flashing message on the screen to remind a teller to fill out the necessary Currency Transaction Form for the IRS whenever a cash transaction exceeding $10,000 is handled.

Modifications to the teller system are generally attempts either to make the system more compatible with the operating function of the teller or to facilitate the integration of the teller system with other related information systems. A very small fraction of such modifications were initiated by the tellers or their management, as distinguished from the central systems liaison group. The roots of the design of the teller system seem to emphasize the efficient flow of back office operations.

Customer Impacts

Retail banking is a service and all aspects of automation, including the teller system, must be assessed in terms of possible customer impacts.

In the case of the teller system, impacts on the customer are minimal compared to having no automation at all. In either case, the customer gets a receipt for the completed payment or deposit. With regard to the time of transaction, assuming the system is functioning properly, processing time depends more on the exchange of paper and currency between the teller and the customer than the time to key in the transaction itself.

One area that might affect the customer is the system's ability to signal to the teller any of a series of special status items on an account. Some examples are: the customer is the holder of a "premium account" (signalling more courteous service), the existence of a "holds exceeded" condition (when the customer has used a single account more than a specified number of times in a day), or the occurrence of a "stop payment" condition on a previously written check. The actions that a teller (or supervisor) might take to any of such special status items could directly affect the customer. Note that features of this sort can be introduced or deleted by the internal systems group with approval of operating management. Thus the system's impact on the customer is a shifting phenomenon within a basically stable service domain.

The Administrative System: "ADMIN"

Customer service representatives are the branch employees who work at a desk rather than behind the teller's counter. They assist customers in a number of ways, such as handling problems with existing accounts, opening new accounts, providing information on new products, etc. As with the tellers, customer service representatives (CSRs) deal face-to-face with customers, although the CSRs can also be reached by telephone and use the telephone to get information from central sources at the bank. The job of the CSR has evolved through the years as retail banking has become more competitive and the range of products and services has grown. In 1982 the bank introduced a computer-based system to assist the CSRs with some of their administrative functions. Dubbed the "Admin system," its capabilities have grown to the point where, in 1988, this tool has become an indispensable part of CSR operations.

Functions of the Admin System

One of the newer features of the Admin system is the ability of a CSR to give a printed transaction history for the past month to a customer who has come in with a problem in reconciling a particular account. (The amount of history that can be made available is limited by available disk space. Earlier data can be acquired by the CSR by telephoning a central support staff group.) This listing contains transaction codes that must be translated for the customer. Some branches have begun to charge customers a nominal amount for this service while others have not.

Customers can open new accounts through the Admin system. A customer desiring to open a new account sits next to a CSR who enters the information (provided orally by the customer) directly into the system.

The system has certain features designed to help the CSR to accurately set up a new account. For example, if the customer already has an account of some type with the bank, the CSR can enter an existing account number (if the customer has it handy) and thereby avoid ending up with "duplicate customers" on the Customer Information File (CIF). Typically, a CSR will try to avoid such a duplication by accessing the CIF using the customers name and a screen will appear with a directory (by name, in alphabetical order) which can be used to gather all basic data (address, social security number, etc.) from the existing account file rather than entering them once again on the keyboard. How easy it is to use this capability depends, in part, on how unusual or common the customer's name happens to be. It also depends on how motivated the CSR is to go through the process of checking this directory (that is, for a customer with a very common name, such as Robert Smith, it is easier to enter the new account information without checking the many screens of name listings).*

Development and Modification of the Admin System

The Admin system was originally developed by an outside software firm. Its installation at the bank was conducted under the direction of the bank's internal systems group. As originally conceived, the system was developed in stages, the first being to provide passive access to the central host computer of the bank for online inquiry of account status. In the second stage of development, the Admin system was provided with data entry capabilities to handle transactions that modify account status. In the third and current stage, the system has been extended to

---

*These checks cannot be done automatically because name and address matches are not reliable if, for example, Robert Smith uses a middle initial on one account but not another, or leaves "Jr." off one account has moved but not updated an old account, or has one account with his wife's social security number and another with his son's social security number. It is only by asking the customer about each similar account and name that duplicates can be verified.

accommodate the opening of new accounts. The host computer continues to maintain the same retail database that was originally developed
20 years ago.

In Stage 2, Big Bank used its User Liaison Group (directed by a central
office manager with staff who had prior branch operations experience)
to identify the desired data entry functions. This group asked for 17
different data entry functions and this list was pared to a top priority list
of seven items to be developed and installed in an initial period.
Included on this list of seven were items such as the initiation or closing
of stop payment orders and the issuing and reissuing of banking cards.
Several criteria were applied in selecting the items for this "short list":
complexity of the logic necessary to implement the feature, the systems
development time that would likely be required, and the training
requirements that would be imposed on the CSRs if a particular feature
were to be included in the Admin system.

In Stage 3, the implementation of an account opening capability,
systems development required the inclusion of many internal edit
functions to assure accuracy and to avoid undesirable duplication.

In general, features and functions for the Admin system were derived from an understanding of existing operational activities of the
branch offices, coupled with requirements of other centralized groups,
such as product management, whose work has implications for the
branches. The content and format of existing bank forms were considered in the design of new computer screens. Considerable attention
was placed on editing incoming data to check for obvious errors (e.g.,
birth dates before 1890 or after the current year).

Use of the Admin System

A CSR can "sign on" to the Admin system at any time by entering his
or her user ID code and password on the terminal on his or her desk. If
the system, once "signed on", is not used after a specified period of
time, it will sign itself off. This is a precautionary measure to discourage
nonauthorized users from trying to use the system from an unattended
work station.

Before CSRs had an automated Admin system to work with, all of
their account inquiries had to be performed on the telephone with staff
support personal from the central office. They had no choice but to trust
the accuracy of the information that was being passed on to them. Now,
using the Admin system, they are in direct touch with the original
account data and they have found both accuracy and detail of information much better than that previously provided by telephone. When the
system is down or when they seek information that is not available on
it (e.g., account transactions older than a specified number of days) they

must once again trust their telephone sources. Some CSRs are less comfortable than they used to be when having to rely on this second-hand source of information.

By placing a terminal on every CSR's desk, customers sitting at the desk can have visual access to their account information. CSRs who turn their screen to face the customer report that occasionally the customer will spot an error (e.g., spelling of a name or an address). They also report that when the customer sees the data on an account in question, he or she is drawn into the service transaction in an active way. This facilitates the job of the CSR who may have to report a problem to a customer but, with the Admin system being shared by the two of them, there is less of a chance that defensiveness or arguments will ensue. In short, the computer system lets the CSR feel that he or she (through the technology) is providing a service to the customer, rather than simply being a nonproductive link between the customer and the downtown back office.

The Admin system was designed with flexibility and ease-of-use in mind. For example, if a customer does not know his or her account number, the CSR can enter the customer's name and address and get a list of all existing account numbers with that registration. Each type of transaction has both a letter code and a number code, leaving the CSR free to use whichever is most convenient. An effort was made not to provide an excessive amount of information on any one screen.

Despite the emphasis on ease-of-use, designers of the Admin system included certain constraints aimed at ensuring the accuracy of account registrations. For example, back office management insisted that some new account information (e.g., customer name) cannot be updated online by the CSR after it has been entered and transmitted. Such modifications must be sent via written documents to the central records group for subsequent modification of the computerized file. The same used to be true of change of address modifications, although in a recent revision of the Admin system such online changes are now accepted. One current system limitation is that if a customer has multiple accounts which happen to be registered in slightly different ways (e.g., full first name on one and initials only on another), there may be an advantage for both the customer and the bank to modify the records so that they are consistent and then can be grouped together on a single report or screen. At present, in the interest of ensuring the accuracy of the Customer Information File the CSR is not authorized to make (and the Admin system will not accept) online changes of this sort; they must be written and sent to the back office for processing. Providing this online update capability on the Admin system would probably involve careful negotiation between front and back office personnel, involving turf issues and how to share responsibility and accountability for accuracy and account integrity.

Another type of system constraint involves limitations on what is presented to the CSR. Currently, a CSR can only view a customer's accounts one at a time. While this is usually adequate, occasionally the CSR will be trying to help a customer to remedy a problem involving more than one of his or her accounts. At these times, it would be useful to be able to access both accounts simultaneously. A different kind of limitation is the lack of access to data that might be important to the CSR. For example, outstanding loan balances can be accessed online but loan payment histories cannot. Most system constraints can be eliminated by establishing what the preferred solution would be and by assigning a programmer from the bank's systems group to develop the desired modification or extension. Whether or not this is done in any particular situation depends on existing systems group priorities and the perceived benefits of the new feature in comparison with the effort required to implement the change.

Customer Impacts

Customers seem generally pleased with the Admin system because it allows them to get immediate information and enhanced service from their local branch personnel. Some customers have grown quite dependent on the transaction histories that CSRs can print out for them. It is a good way, for example, to help balance a checkbook. However, the virtues of this system can generate other problems. For example, in its current form the Admin system cannot provide online access to credit card files. Customers who get information at electronic speed regarding their checking or savings accounts are sometimes puzzled and somewhat concerned that the bank cannot provide the same speedy service to them for their credit card accounts. Similarly, with all this technology at the fingertips of the CSR, it can seem strange to a customer that branches only have access to the signature cards of accounts opened at that branch. Neither by microfiche nor by computer can a CSR check the signature of a customer who wishes to withdraw funds but does not have an authorized identification card and whose account was originally opened at another branch. Such inquiries, however, can be attempted by phone if the CSR calls the branch where the signature card is filed and hears a description of the original signature on file.

Concluding Observations

Using automated systems is now an essential aspect of branch office operations, be it at the teller counter or at the CSR platform. Customers have clearly grown accustomed to their service providers using computer technology to get the job done. The considerable acceptance of automated teller machines by many urban retail banking customers has allowed customers themselves to interact with such technologies so there is no reason for them to be concerned about bank employees taking advantage of what the technology has to offer. However, studies have shown that a substantial subset of the retail banking population (up to 70 percent in some areas) is still hesitant to use ATMs to their fullest capability. Assuming this is likely to remain true for at least the near future, there will continue to be demand for traditional teller and CSR functions in branch offices.

As systems like the ones described above are enhanced and even replaced, managers of retail banking will continue to be confronted by issues of how much to automate and what features and functions to provide to the workforce through these systems. Such decisions contain inherent tradeoffs. At a broad level there are issues of cost versus benefits. At a more refined level there are tradeoffs between the efficiency and effectiveness of particular system "solutions." Moreover, effectiveness depends on one's point of view. Employees might disagree among themselves about choices between alternative system capabilities or the value of some new feature. Customers might well have similar differences of opinion among themselves. Finally, there are likely to be different perceptions between employees (tellers, CSRs) and customers regarding the value of these computer-based systems in general and particular features and functions in particular.

With respect to the teller system and the Admin system in their current forms, the bank's employees appreciate the benefits they provide. Their main source of irritation is when overload conditions seem to slow the system's response time. Very few tellers or CSRs readily articulate other, more subtle, difficulties in using these systems. Branch managers tend to assume the systems are fine unless they hear particular complaints from their front line employees.

Expansion of branch automation at the bank appears to require a delicate balance. For the most part it seems to be characterized by user demand rather than technology push. User needs are almost exclusively voiced by a central user liaison group rather than by individual branch managers. Knowing that a problem exists with the existing version of a software system is often a challenge for the systems development group. Learning enough about day-to-day operations as a basis for suggesting system changes is a challenge to all who are not working in branch offices. And even for a branch manager, anticipating the value of potential system improvements (not to mention identifying what sorts of improvements ought to be considered) is no mean feat.

In addition, there is a need to appreciate systems requirements that come from outside the branch office environment. For example, the batching operation described above for the teller system, is driven essentially by the back office needs of the proof and transit division which must conduct and complete its processing functions (for all branch activity in that day) between 4:00 p.m. and midnight. Finally, one must acknowledge that there is often a strong interaction between systems solutions and training solutions. When a systems programmer includes an override option (say to avoid a limitation in the method for automatically updating a savings passbook), someone must identify the training requirement to show a teller how to "work around the system" to handle special situations that arise occasionally. One must never forget that there are practical constraints on training possibilities in retail banking today. Considerable turnover in tellers (due to low entry wages and limited promotion possibilities) means that training must be simple and effective.

Hard Choices About Software: Design Decisions for the New Banking Environment*

Background

Banking is becoming increasingly dependent upon "mission critical" software systems for operations. These mission critical systems provide support for the ongoing operations of the bank, analysis of operations for management and marketing, and are the medium through which bank branch tellers and customer service representatives conduct their work. Designing mission critical packaged software by a vendor (rather than the bank's internal MIS department or contracting for a custom system) requires a broad perspective inclusive of the many factors which shape the user's application needs and the role of software in influencing the user firm's operations and job design.

In the late 1970s, the banking industry began undergoing significant changes. Deregulation and high inflation and interest rates created a highly volatile environment and a more competitive environment for banks. Banks restructured, offered new services and products to attract customers, and suffered the consequences of increased competition. By the late 1980s, the changing environment coupled with poor investment decisions, resulted in a postwar record of bank failures, numbering 1,319 from 1981 to 1991, and savings and loans failures in the same period numbered 1,022. To compete more effectively, many executives

*This case was developed by Harold Salzman. It was prepared as the basis for class discussion rather than to illustrate either effective or ineffective systems development, implementation, or management practices. This material is based on research supported by the Ethics and Values Section of the National Science Foundation under Grant No. BBS-8619534.

began to look toward technology to gain a competitive edge and software was often the centerpiece of a technology strategy. Designing software for this market, consequently, became a different type of enterprise, changing the types of criteria important for a system to be effective.

The Banking System Corporation (BSC, a pseudonym), a software vendor developing banking systems for midsized banks, was faced with crucial choices about designing its new system. To be competitive, BSC had to develop software to support banking functions in an environment with many unforeseeable conditions and that would provide their clients with a competitive edge over internally developed and other vendor-developed software. The longstanding criteria for designing a banking system would not result in developing a competitive system. Previously, BSC designed a system to reflect the FHA regulations for mortgage systems and banking laws for other parts of the system. Software was primarily for back office batch processing and a banking system was an assemblage of a number of different pieces. New systems, however, integrated all banking operations, providing online transaction processing crucial to the central banking mission of processing transactions, providing management information and support, and more generally regulating operations of the bank.

The design task BSC faced was more complex than any system either it, or its competitors, had ever faced. The environment of banking was changing rapidly, moving into uncharted waters with little certain bearing on direction; the technology was changing even more rapidly with the lower cost and higher power of minicomputers allowing smaller banks and savings and loans to purchase mission critical systems. As the medium though which most operational banking tasks were conducted, the software played a central role in defining how those tasks would be structured, how jobs within the bank would be defined, and the responsibility required of different users in the bank. The system had to improve the competitive position of banks using the system for these smaller banks to survive and, for BSC, their system had to provide clear competitive advantage over other vendors' systems and over systems designed by a bank's internal MIS department. In addition, the BSC had to consider that its vision of cutting edge technology might be beyond the range of change the current staid bank managements, who were used to a stable environment, might want in their organizations and in their comfortable banking procedures. A system that had clear technological superiority would not necessarily succeed if it could not be sold to current bank managements.

A radical departure from previous generations of systems, BSC's system had all the features and functionality necessary to provide banks with the tools to be competitive in the new environment. However, after three years of development (a year and a half beyond the planned development schedule) BSC still had not delivered a system. The protracted development schedule resulted from the many unforeseen problems that typically plague most software projects, but BSC also ran into problems in the fundamental design of the system. Thus, after three years of development, BSC was reevaluating the direction of its system design and faced making significant design choices. These design choices concerned:

- How much flexibility to put in the system?
- For whom is flexibility to be designed?
- What should the system do?
- Who is the user?
- Which user needs prevail?
- What is the role of the designer in defining the best banking practices through software functionality?
- What is the impact of software design, and thus the designer, in shaping user firms' operations?
- What is the role of the designer in making choices about the way banks conduct their business and how users perform their jobs?
- How much should designers respond to expressed user needs and how much should they anticipate future needs?

These choices would be influenced by the history of BSC, the markets it was targeting, the types of resources it had, and its overall approach to system design.

History of BSC

The Banking Systems Corporation started in 1974 when the three principals, James Simpson, George Billings, and Robert Waterman, left a large bank to sell a general ledger system they had developed. James had an MBA and George and Robert had degrees in computer science from a leading university. In the early 1970s they were working for Memorial Bank developing a general ledger system to run on IBM 360 mainframe computers. Before it was completed, the system was sold to the Finance Management Corporation which then decided not to finish development. James, George, and Robert, now out of a job but still having faith in the merits of their system, negotiated with Finance Management Corporation to buy the system. They started BSC, finished development of the system and, between 1974 and 1978, made significant penetration in the banking industry.

The systems for banks were based on 1960s technology and the IBM 360 environment in particular. Banks had been early and large commercial users of computers. In the 1950s and 1960s large mainframe systems were installed to process back room operations to process checks and update account balances. Several vendors dominated the market for large commercial bank systems, designs were well established, and system modifications were focused on incremental improvements of existing functions. The combination of the limitations of older hardware and software with highly regulated and static operations resulted in minimal demand for flexibility and change in computer systems. Arnie White, the lead systems analyst who had worked in banking for 20 years, said "banking automation is pretty archaic; most of the software for banking systems even today is at least ten years old, and that was true ten years ago. In 1978 the principle system in use was built in 1966."

Although BSC was selling a system that was better than most of the competition, it was still based on the requirements of a traditional banking environment. In this environment, mortgage rates were all fixed, banks and savings and loans were each limited in the types of loans they could offer; the types of investments banks could make and types of products they could offer were tightly regulated, with little variation. As James Simpson described it, "one bank looked pretty much like another bank because of the regulatory requirements. Banks were spreading their costs, assets, liabilities, and living off the spread. We made a lot of money in our product line by selling something called spread management as part of our back office general ledger system. It helped banks manage the spread, which was a major source of revenue for the banks."

The success of their initial product provided BSC with strong revenues but, James explained, "what we learned about the banking industry was much more important. We used to go out with consultants and used to consult to presidents of banks on how to best manage their cash flow, how to manage their spread, how to merge with another bank. These are the things we would send people out to see management about that would lead them to think there was God at BSC when it came to people who knew about banking. We had one hell of a reputation." The exposure to many segments of the banking industry gave them a broad perspective about emerging changes in the industry and their solid reputation would later aid them in obtaining financial support for the development of a new system.

In 1978 they hired Arnie to lead the development of a real time transaction processing system for mortgage loan accounting, based on a DEC PDP11 minicomputer. They felt a new technology was needed to support banking operations and the essential features were a real time system, flexibility, and providing mission critical functions. It was the first step in developing mission critical systems. The system was installed in two banks and supported until 1981, but it did not work well enough to be a commercial success. The PDP was not adequate to support the demands of a large system and BSC discovered that building and supporting mission critical systems was very different than the old banking systems. In retrospect, Arnie felt they had "confused the management end of the banking industry with the operation end of the banking industry." The focus was on providing information to improve decisions about mortgage loans and the management of these loans. However, they did not realize the commitment it would take to make the system effective as a real time, mission critical system. Arnie explained:

> We were not fully ready to accept the real time sensitive commitments of a mission critical system. The way we built the system was such that when there was a problem, you couldn't just say to the client, "I don't know what it is, I'll get back to you," and then call in the morning and start working on it. You had to stay and work on it immediately. We were not prepared for that commitment; no one got sleep, but we got an education out of it.

This learning experience provided them an appreciation of the technical requirements for the types of systems they wanted to build. Although the software requirements they established were beyond the state of the art in hardware technology, they decided to take a radical step forward in software design with the expectation that the hardware technology would advance when they were ready to deliver the new system. James, George, and Robert, with key technical staff such as Arnie and marketing staff, began to develop the requirements for a new system that would be truly mission critical, integrate many banking functions, and introduce a new technology into banking. This new system was part of a long-term plan, it was going to be a financial drain and a large commitment that had to be done carefully.

As Arnie described it, they wanted to:

> get into the business with a system that had something more than anybody else did; to redefine the product [i.e., banking systems] at a fundamental level. We wanted to open up the possibilities to the bank to do whatever it wanted to do. We didn't know what that was going to be, but we had some ideas. We knew interest rate flexibility was going to be important. James predicted that fee-based banking was going to be significant. It wasn't at the time—banks were saying, "No, don't charge customers or they will leave!" —but he thought eventually banks would be making a lot of money on fees. So, we also had to have a flexible fee structure. Regulation was changing, but we didn't know what to expect, so we had to have some heavy flexibility in recording so we could adapt to whatever requirements came along. Also, it was important to have flexibility of data entry, to define your own

status and maintenance screens, and to do business the way you [i.e., the bank] want it done. There was also a lot of untapped potential in the area of marketing by banks.

They began the project in early 1982 with an 18-month target date for delivery of the first system. The new programming group moved to new offices because "we did not want to be viewed with the bad habits of the old crew; we wanted to have a fresh start." They hired new staff in addition to the three programmers from within BSC, eventually growing to 89 people. They had an enthusiastic development group and got a quick start. This group, Arnie explained:

> had a lot of experience. My boss was good technically, with a lot of background in this area, I had done two large projects before, and other people had good backgrounds. We knew what we needed to know, or thought we did. We started building and then found that we didn't really know the requirements. We were faced with, "How do you get requirements when you don't have any clients? How do you define industry requirements when you expect everything to change?" So we put in everything, parameterized everything. We built a report writer without knowing what it had to produce, with complete flexibility.
>
> In the previous system we were able to put everything in because application is in low volume. But with a mission critical system there are a lot more constraints: 60, 100, 200,000 accounts; lines of tellers, etc. Performance had to be topnotch and we ran into a performance versus flexibility tradeoff: Would we have less flexibility to protect performance?

The system kept growing in size as new features and functions were added and each was designed to have complete flexibility. A market analyst was hired to help with requirements definition, but the group had no patience with her. The technical people had a concept of a system that was tool-driven, not built for a fixed set of requirements. When the market analyst wanted to set parameters, the development group resisted. A focus group was formed, but it did not contribute requirements the development group thought were compatible with the type of system they wanted to develop.

The first deadline was missed, then the second deadline was missed in the middle of 1984. At the end of 1984 there was a major shakeup and the manager of the project was replaced. The entire development group stopped work for two weeks to review the project and list all the things the group thought necessary and then built a project plan. They brought in a leading business consulting firm to audit the project and help set priorities on tasks according to risk. They set a new deadline for the end of summer 1985. Again, they missed their deadline and had to reconsider design choices they had made. Some of the decisions were technical, about specific development methods for example, but many of the choices concerned the fundamental definition of the system, about what it should do in the bank. As a mission critical system, they began to realize they were making choices about how the bank would conduct its business and how people working in the bank would perform their jobs. Following are some of the choices they had to consider.

Flexibility or Standardization: What Should be Built into the System?

Some of the people within the marketing group, BSC's major investors, and even a few within the development group thought complete flexibility was an overly ambitious and impractical goal. The system was becoming too unwieldy; there was no critical evaluation of flexibility; for which features was it important and for which features would fixed parameters be adequate? This group claimed that the flexibility and tool concepts were being taken to an extreme, that the direction of development was being driven to fulfill these concepts for their intrinsic value rather than critically evaluated for their importance to bank operations. One marketing representative said, "many of the functions the development group wants to parameterize are not used; some flexibility is just not relevant in practice." One of the systems analysts agreed, saying, "We spend a lot of time putting features into our system that the customer may use as criteria for buying the system, but we find they never actually implement them or use them in practice."

At a more practical level, the management argued that BSC had to deliver a system. Several clients had canceled commitments to install the system and BSC was low on cash flow. At the same time they had been working closely with one bank they had planned to use for a beta test site. They could meet the requirements of this one bank if they sacrificed some of the flexibility and "hardwired" some of the functions with the parameters and features this bank needed. By building the system for this bank they would be able to complete it and deliver it quickly. This would give them a demonstrable product, some desperately needed cash, and increase the faith of their investors, as well as improve the morale of the development group who were discouraged at not being able to deliver a system. Flexibility could then be added in later releases, this group argued.

"We can't sell a system with limitations," argued Arnie White. As a vendor, he thought BSC had to make a system that was generic, that could be sold for many different types of banking environments, and that was best achieved through complete customization. James Simpson agreed: with the increasingly volatile banking environment, it was imperative that nothing be hardwired into the system. "Client-customizable" was one of the essential selling features of the system. He argued that the initial costs and delay would, over the long term, be more profitable than hardwiring some features now and then repro-gramming the system later. James recounted the reasons for being client-customizable. First, a large portion of the company's target market was smaller banks that would not be able to pay for either customization or for an expensive system (redesigning and reprogram-ming the system would raise the selling price of the system). It was the price, comprehensiveness, and flexibility of the system that gave BSC a competitive advantage over internal MIS departments and custom software houses. One marketing representative added that "it may be true that some of the flexibility is never used in practice, but it is an important selling feature of the system, particularly if it gives our system an advantage over other systems, then it is worth doing. Remember, you have to sell the system to get any of it used."

Second, he recalled the experience of a company that, in the early 1970s, built a system where the interest rate was stored with the product and allowed only a single digit for the interest rate (interest rates had always been fixed rates (e.g., mortgage rates) and never reached 10 percent during the entire 25-year postwar period). In the mid-1970s when variable rates became widespread and interest rates were higher than 10 percent, this system became obsolete. The system did not survive, although it was only five years old, when the software vendor closed the division building that system. The old banking mentality was "this is the way banking systems are today and that's the way they will always be," and the system was built with many features that had fixed parameters. Arnie explained, "they might have fixed some of these problems, but the basic architecture of the system was based on fixed parameters and made it difficult and expensive to modify every-thing." The lesson they learned from watching the rapid changes in the banking industry, James said, was to keep everything completely open; tomorrow's banking system won't look anything like today's system. The only way to have a long product life in a rapidly changing environment is to make all parameters flexible because you do not know which parameter will need to be changed in the future.

Third, as one of the dissenting marketing staff pointed out, the competitive advantage of technology by one bank over another will be through the bank's customization of the software. Because most banks will have software systems, the advantage will come from the adapta-tions a bank makes to the software. Moreover, there is a lot of untapped potential in bank marketing of services which requires more analysis of customer characteristics and services. This analysis also requires system flexibility for data analysis and reports.

Finally, both James and Arnie argued, "hardwiring the system now might be expedient, but damaging to our system. You can't hardwire a tool driven system." They thought the "repairs" to the system to make it flexible again for future sales would have greater costs than the benefits of early delivery of a specialized system.

What Should the System Do?

"The hard part is defining, not building, the system" said George Sapolsky, the marketing manager. It is the responsibility of marketing, George maintained, to lead development by establishing product requirements that make the system competitive. The competitiveness of a system is, in part, its appeal to users. Thus, an axiom of software development is that the system should do what the user needs it to do and the task of the developer is to determine the specifications of those user requirements.

Going beyond the these general principles and platitudes of software development required a number of difficult choices and tradeoffs. For example, for BSC, user requirements were not just the operational needs of the bank, but also the "selling requirements." The success of the system, for a vendor, depends first on its saleablity and, second, on its performance. When the development team and marketing mangers met to discuss user requirements, the important requirements were those that would attract users to purchase their system rather than a competitor's system or to use an internal MIS department or a custom software house. Much of the discussion centered on functionality: What features and functions did users want and what features and functions would make this a competitive system?

Marketing sought to discover what the user wanted, but first had to decide whom to ask. Because the company had no current client base, there was no natural constituency to survey. Second, which level in the bank would be targeted as the user? The system was designed to serve the operational needs of nearly all levels of staff, from teller to senior bank managers. The marketing managers quickly pointed out to the development group that their first consideration had to be the needs of those people in the bank who would be making the purchase decision, i.e., the buyers. In the small to midsize banks they were targeting as their market niche, the BSC system would be a substantial investment made by senior level managers. Thus, senior managers, as buyers, were the important users for purposes of requirements definition.

Mitch O'Keefe, the lead analyst in one of the development groups argued that, although the buyers made the initial purchase decision, they were not the most important users. They were really secondary users who depended upon information from the system but would not be actively or directly using the system. Addressing only the needs of this group of users might lead to developing systems that would sell but not have the performance or features and functions needed by lower level, but direct users, such as tellers. Mitch realized that these types of tradeoffs were necessary, but he observed that:

We spend a lot time putting features into our system that the customers use to make their buying decision but that I never see implemented in actual use of the system. It's always a struggle between installation and marketing concerns, between what to put in as marketing code versus installable code. Marketing code is code that makes the buyer continue to talk to you whereas installation code is that which the customer will likely want to install. There are different programming issues with each. If I know that some code has very little likelihood of ever being installed, I don't believe it is a sin to make the wrong program worse.

As a vendor we have different pressures than an internal MIS department. An MIS department in a firm knows exactly what to deliver and you have some control over what your end user will take. In our case, we have a bunch of people who aren't technical, and they show up at the bank and they want to know, "Is it zippy?" "Does it paint the screen quickly?" all sorts of things that should have no bearing on the criteria for making a purchase decision.

Mitch's responsibility was to make BSC's system a technologically leading edge system. He looked at the latest developments in universities and private laboratories and determined what could be "reduced to practice, what is practical to apply to the banking marketplace." The problem, he explained:

Is that we have a customer who doesn't understand all the technological issues. Moreover, their own industry is evolving and they haven't realized the impact on their way of doing business. Banks are organizations that are designed to keep overhead low, labor costs low, which means they hire people at the lowest pay levels. As a result, they don't have people with a lot of expertise, they need things kept very simple, very straightforward, and very much the same.

The marketing group was providing the development group with requirements of current banking operations and predictions about future developments. However, the marketing manager asked George and Arnie to identify state-of-the-art technology that would provide them with a competitive edge over their competitors and that would make their product vastly superior to any system a bank's internal MIS department could develop. Mitch studied the latest technology and current banking systems. He observed:

> The classic systems in the U.S. are all built on third-generation languages, that is, the systems that are out there, going to be touched by thousands of people in a day. The fourth-generation software still has some fundamental problems, and the fifth-generation software is too expensive for common applications. You're not going to get them to invest in $100,000 teller stations. Some of the research computer scientists say that anything less then the right thing is the wrong thing, but they don't pay the bills.

> So, for this round of our system I decided I wanted to look at the problems that could be solved with advanced technologies that were not solvable or delivered by our competitors, and the ones that can give BSC the marketing advantage, something we could use to sell them. The kinds of things we've done are [to] put in a strong help system and a natural language system that lets them ask for things from the system without knowing specific commands. It lets you sort of wave your arms out and it will try to figure out what you want to do. If a CEO wants to, say, put $100 in Jones' account, he will get his system to obey him, [a feature] which is just not available in any other system. Now, this natural language system is a selling point, but in practice [it is] almost never used. It's a very expensive, very difficult technology to employ for very limited use.

George, the marketing manager, who once said that development people don't understand the selling issues, was at once supportive of Mitch's ideas. A natural language system would enable senior vice presidents of the bank to make inquiries of the database without learning specialized commands. George saw this as a feature he could easily sell to those making the purchase decision and that would get the support of senior management in the banks. Mitch also liked adding this to the system specifications because it would be a development challenge; he would assemble his best and brightest programmers to develop this feature and integrate it into the system.

The Teller Station

An important module of the system is the Teller Workstation. This module contains the tools for and the means of control over the operations of bank tellers. The Teller system has several significant design features and functions. First, the software for the screens, unlike the existing fixed screen teller stations, allows the screen format to be largely custom designed by each individual bank. Thus, screens can be setup to meet each bank's requirements. Second, the teller station can be integrated with many different computers. Thus, the teller station can operate across different systems without changing its features or functionality.

Third, "intelligent capabilities" are being built to provide better and more flexible decisionmaking options. This allows for the system to handle more contingencies without requiring either a teller decision or the need for a supervisor judgment. The tellers' stations are linked to supervisor stations so tellers can consult electronically about an account problem. Instead of requiring the supervisor to physically come to the teller station and discuss the situation, the teller can send the question and account information electronically to the supervisor's terminal for his or her decision. This increases the ability or requirement that tellers consult with a supervisor about transaction problems and makes the consultation invisible to the customer.

The intelligence is also being developed to do analyses of the customer's account for sales purposes. For example, while the teller is processing the customer's transaction (e.g., a deposit) the system will analyze the account characteristics for products the teller might be able to sell to the customer. If the customer has had $10,000 in a low interest savings account for six months, the system might prompt the teller to give the customer a brochure on certificates of deposit or a money market fund. To aid tellers in selling these products, they will be able to access a database on product information such as interest rates and terms.

Design History

The design of the Teller Workstation was done by a small group within BSC, outside of the usual design process. When the project was first proposed, the company had decided not to fund it. However, the chief scientist and one of his programmers went ahead and spent several weekends building a prototype. The prototype impressed the president of the company who then decided to approve and fund the development.

The chief scientist and one programmer designed and built most of the teller system with the assistance of another programmer in designing interfaces with the company's other systems. The three of them worked over a period of 18 months, writing hundreds of lines of code. They designed "the underlying software to be as flexible as the state of the art would allow," incorporating the latest cutting edge technology. They had a high degree of autonomy because they were outside the established programming groups. They reported to the president of the company periodically, but otherwise worked independently of other groups in the company. When the basic functionality was established, a product manager reviewed the designs for compatibility with banking operations and emulation of existing systems.

What to Tell the Teller?

The teller station development group had three guiding design goals: first, to utilize the increased power of both computers and new programming languages to improve the use of computers in achieving traditional banking objectives of efficiency, accuracy, security, and customer service; second, to support the "new" banking objectives of responding to the competition, responding to environmental changes, offering innovate new products, marketing and selling new products, and managing the customer relationship with the bank; and third, to preserve their customers' investment in existing equipment and training by designing the new system to integrate existing systems and emulate the teller stations being replaced.

The first set of objectives led to the design of features and functions that would allow banks to utilize the teller station to "enforce the rules as its primary objective." The significance of this objective, particularly as a selling point, was shaped by the view of the attributes, experience, and training of tellers. There is a very high turnover rate among tellers, with more than one year of tenure considered a long term. Banks generally do not invest significant resources or time in training tellers. The tellers tend to be young, "mostly kids," with high school educations. There is a view that tellers are "stupid, have little interest in the job, are careless, error prone, and not trustworthy, and thus a security risk."

The teller's only interest, according to the teller station designers, is to dispose of the customer as quickly as possible and not be burdened with unnecessary information. Tellers also do not like to restrict customer transactions, if a customer is overdrawn or missed a loan payment for example, because customers will become angry at the teller. Thus a system should be designed to have the teller refer the customer to a supervisor without knowing the nature of the problem. The designers also find that bank management does not want the teller to become involved with customer problems. Tellers will be "kept in the dark because they are not trained in human relations that are necessary to interact with the customer; you can't afford to do that because of the high turnover. And tellers are just not that discrete."

The system design must primarily satisfy those who make the purchasing decision. As one designer said, "You're going to deliver this to the teller, so you want to make it nice for the teller, but more importantly I have the guy who's making the purchasing decision and I have a board of directors who have a set of criteria that they want to run their bank as profitably as possible. This means they want their policies enforced, they want their costs minimized. I want to deliver them tools that will enforce their policy better than the competition can, and I've got to stay no more expensive than the competition." Eventually, they hope to achieve these objectives by designing systems that allow little, if any, discretion by the teller.

The tellers express to the developers dissatisfaction with this aspect of the design. "The tellers complain that they don't like to have to tell the customer that they can't handle the transaction; they don't like the fact that the only information they get is that there is a problem with this account that can only be handled by a supervisor over there." The tellers say that they want to be able to handle a wide range of transactions and have the information and authority to serve the customer without being required to consult with a supervisor. "The first thing tellers ask for is the override function [so] that they can make the thing override complaints if they don't think they happen to need a supervisor."

Features and functions to aid the teller are not considered the highest priority by systems designers because, "very far down on the list of goals of the board of directors [of the bank] is teller satisfaction. The banks take a stab at making sure someone from the teller line — after the head teller, who is someone who has been away from actual teller operations for maybe five years — is involved in the process [of establishing system definition]. It's very clear that the management, board of directors, and tellers have two completely separate agendas. The board of directors likes it when they find out our system will stop `bad' transactions" that pose risks to security.

When deciding which information to make accessible to the teller, the designers note that "the first guideline is that banks purposely and deliberately keep tellers, and others in the branch, ignorant of what the bank is trying to do. Banks believe that their greatest protection is in having the teller, including the branch managers, being [kept] purposely ignorant. The less your people seem to know about the actual reasons behind the actual policies and details about how you are operating your institution, the better off they seem to think they are." When the users within an organization have differences about how the system should be designed, "The guy who signs the check wins. That's the bottom line."

All decisionmaking was to be built into the teller station software so that no discretion would be left to the teller and there would be few instances when consultation with a supervisor would be necessary. In previous systems, there were limitations in the types of nonstandard transactions that the system could evaluate and little flexibility to respond uniquely to an individual situation. This resulted in need for regular supervisor intervention or increased decisionmaking autonomy by tellers. Because this was viewed as a negative condition, this new system was developed to evaluate a much broader range of conditions and to allow for more flexibility.

Parameters for decisionmaking can be set according to each bank's policy and multiple factors can be used to evaluate an individual situation. If a customer tried to cash a check for an amount greater than the balance of his or her account, the computer can check for funds in other products, such as CDs, so that it can permit the transaction to proceed. The system is also designed to monitor all of the customer's "relationships" with the bank, such as loans and credit card accounts. Depending upon the bank's specifications, the system could require the teller to refer a routine transaction to a supervisor if there was a problem, such as a missed payment, with one of the customer's accounts.

The system was designed with the potential for extensive capabilities to assess nonstandard transactions and individual situations, rather than just display information for the teller or supervisor. This is intended to simplify the teller's task, eliminate discretion, and increase security. The system was built to give the teller three responses for a transaction: one, "proceed with the transaction"; two, "do not proceed with the transaction"; or, three, "call a human," for those few situations outside of the system's decisionmaking capability.

The interest of management in reducing costs and increasing profit traditionally focused on reducing labor costs and increasing security. More recently, profit also may be increased by gaining a competitive advantage over other banks and by increasing the customer's amount of funds and types of products he or she maintains with the bank. The teller system's functionality to meet the new objectives of banking include analysis of the customer's accounts while a routine transaction, such as a deposit, is being conducted. The system will prompt the teller to provide the customer with a brochure on a particular product, suggest a new service, or inform the customer about the status of his or her funds, such as the need to rollover a CD.

There is an interest in reaching the low-end customer whose usual contact with the bank is only with the teller or ATM. The teller system is designed to change the teller from a cost to a revenue generator. Instead of trying to minimize the time of each transaction, the teller system provides the analysis and information necessary for the teller to sell new products to the customer.

The third objective required of technical development is to build a system that will emulate a competitor's existing technology and allow for gradual replacement with the new system. Most bank's existing systems are built on 1970s technology. Banks want to replace these systems but complete immediate replacement of an entire network is cost prohibitive for many banks. The teller station, by emulating the old system and having compatible interfaces allows for gradual replacement and minimal retraining. It also allows integration of incompatible systems. The mergers allowed by deregulation have resulted in large banks buying a number of smaller independent banks. Each of the banks often had its own computer system. The workstation allowed banks with incompatible local computers to be integrated into a central network.

Concluding Remarks

Designing an integrated banking system to sell as a standard product created a significant challenge to BSC. There was a great deal of uncertainty about what the product requirements were and how complex the system should be. Moreover, BSC had to be responsive to the market and its own viability as a company.

    The final design of the system reflected tradeoffs and critical design choices that were the result of a dynamic interaction among different people and in response to many different factors. Significant design choices were seldom simple decisions. The decisions that were made have outcomes crucial to BSC's success, the success of the banks that purchase the software, and the work lives of the users.

Keeping the Customer Satisfied: Field Service and the Art of Automation*

Part I: WHAT IS FIELD SERVICE?

The business role of field service organizations is to repair and maintain capital goods after the sale of the product to a customer. While a service aftermarket exists for many products, for example, automobile repair service, the essential distinction for the field service aftermarket is that this service is provided at the customer or equipment site, that is, "in the field." Certain characteristics of the item, for example, its physical configuration, make bringing the service provider to it the logical method for delivering service as opposed to bringing the item to a service center. Although the tangible task of field service is to fix broken equipment, the overriding goal of the operation is to fulfill customer service requirements and satisfy the customer, thus leveraging future service contracts and possibly future hardware sales for the vendor.

Field service is not a new concept (the Maytag repairman has been with us for some time) but the growth of the electronics and computer industries since the 1950s has spawned a corresponding growth and development of field services for its products. Essentially, the steps to fix a washing machine and a computer are the same: diagnose the problem, fix, then verify. The particular nature, business purpose, reliability, and customer service requirements of electronic goods led to

* This case was developed by Stephen R. Rosenthal and Frederick Van Bennekom. This case consists of four parts: an industry note, a design case, and two user cases. It was prepared as the basis for class discussion rather than to illustrate either effective or ineffective systems development, implementation, or management practice. This material is based upon research supported by the Ethics and Values Section of the National Science Foundation, under Grant No. BBS-8619534.

a more complex, demanding mission for the electronics field service
industry.

Advent of Electronics Industry Field Service

Electronic equipment often cannot be transported easily and safely.
The size of such goods and the various electronic connections make
service at the customer site a typical requirement. Although each
generation of electronic products becomes smaller and thus more easily
transportable, the diagnosis of an operational problem frequently
requires accessing the equipment while it is connected to the network
in its environment of normal use.

Further demands are placed upon the field service providers because for many customers these electronic goods support crucial business functions. Such equipment has become part of the operational
infrastructure of the organization. Manufacturing process controls,
airline reservation systems, and bank funds processing are examples of
operations which are highly reliant upon electronic technologies.
Prompt, dependable, quality service is crucial to these customers. The
requirements for field service, however, vary among the customers for
any particular kind of equipment. Different customers' particular
service requirements will be reflected in the contents of their service
contract.

Equipment manufacturers established field service organizations
when their product complexity necessitated that they take responsibility for its installation and that they offer warranty coverage, bundled
into the purchase price, for the customer. Once the core of a service
organization had been established, most equipment manufacturers
naturally decided to sell similar service after the warranty period had
expired. Initially, field service was provided only by the original
hardware vendor, known as first party maintenance (FPM) vendors.
The field service organization was treated as ancillary to the company's
overall mission even though it operated with high profit margins and
generated a considerable cash flow. A typical annual service contract
averaged 10 percent of the original hardware price, margins were 35
percent or higher, and return on investment has been shown to be
significantly high.

The nature of field service logistics led to the common strategy of
placing field technicians in offices dispersed throughout the country.
Customers would call the local or regional offices and technicians
would be dispatched to the site. The reactive unstructured nature of the
operation where technicians performed their work remotely from the
office required that first and second level managers spend a good deal
of time exercising operational control. During the 1960s and 1970s,

locally devised manual dispatch systems were developed to aid in handling the logging service requests and monitoring the operation. Eventually, some manual systems were sold as products to be used by other than their originators.

As the dispersement of field technicians throughout the country became a common practice, the appropriate level of decentralization (in terms of operational effectiveness and efficiency) began to be debated. Of particular concern was the handling of staff who provide high levels technical support to the field service business. These are the gurus who would be called in to handle situations where extended outages had already occurred despite routine attempts to fix them. Should such people be located in every office or be concentrated at headquarters, or somewhere in between? Different companies may have different answers to this question based upon the nature of the hardware being supported, the servicing task, and the competitive thrust of the company.

Other Industry Players

The profitability of the field service businesses of the FPM vendors was soon recognized by others and two new sets of players emerged in the industry. The first group was customers who took responsibility for their own maintenance. They were the second party maintenance (SPM) vendors. These companies typically possessed some degree of technical sophistication or had some unique service capabilities which they felt could not be met by others. The other group that entered the industry was independent service providers, the third party maintenance (TPM) vendors. These companies compete with the FPM vendors on the basis of price and convenience in that they will service all the different makes of equipment a customer might have on site. (The FPM vendors typically service equipment only of their own manufacture). There are two categories of TPM vendors. One group, competing on a large scale, typically consists of divisions of large companies with adequate resources to provide field services over a large geographic area. The second TPM group, niche players, are smaller organizations that compete within a more constrained geographic area by providing field services for a limited range of products. Many TPMs have been started by a technician from an FPM vendor who left to service a former account independently.

Changes Affecting the Field Service Industry

The environment for field service organizations has been changing significantly during the late 1970s and 1980s. To understand the operational and organizational tasks that field service companies face today, and thus the requirements that they place on their crucial business support systems, several key environmental forces must be appreciated.

The field service industry experienced such enormous growth rates that management's objective for its operation generally was to manage growth while maintaining a dependable level of quality service. The measures of quality that customers emphasized were response time and down time. The related questions asked, respectively, were: How quickly does a field engineer arrive on site after the request is phoned in? How long does the outage situation last? Operating profit margins were high enough that excess capacity in the form of large inventories of replacement parts and extra field engineers (FEs) were tolerated to meet service objectives. This was especially true because such resources eventually would be needed due to the continuous growth in this service business. This growth also meant that the TPM vendors served a useful purpose. They picked up the slack that could not be handled by the FPM vendors, who in turn made money by selling them replacements parts.

At present, however, the industry's environment has changed. The highly competitive electronics industry is characterized by constant product innovation with an unyielding trend toward more advanced technology. Since the newer products have more power and a higher degree of reliability, contract revenue from field service, especially in relation to the original selling price, has declined drastically. In fact, the prognosis for the industry is that by 1992 total industry revenue from repair services will peak and then decline. Whereas management's task had been simply to manage the extraordinary growth rate while delivering quality service, cost effectiveness while maintaining or improving quality is now a key objective.

In addition, new product technologies are allowing for or requiring new servicing technologies. These more sophisticated products have different technical architectures. The difficulty of each stage in the diagnose-repair-verify sequence of servicing has shifted. Repair is becoming simple board swapping, while diagnosis now requires more sophisticated techniques. The result of these trends for service firms is that their operational strategy and the composition of their own core technology, people and assets, is shifting.

Finally, the increasing rate of new product introductions with shorter product life cycles requires that field service organizations have the operational capabilities to service these new products. This is different from the previous volume-based (as contrasted with variety-based) growth because the new products require service businesses to have correspondingly new (not just more) assets in the form of replacement parts and trained personnel. A further complication for service providers is that electronic equipment, no longer functioning individually and in isolation at the customer site, has become increasingly integrated with other equipment creating a network of functionality. Related to this is the increasingly blurred distinction between hardware and software. Whereas separate service organizations typically handled each of these, that operational strategy is no longer as feasible. Servicing in this networked integrated environment is a more complicated task, demanding a greater breadth of ever-increasing knowledge.

Customers have increasingly become more sophisticated about the technologies they are employing. Large nationwide customers have been demanding consistent standardized service for their entire installed base of equipment regardless of where it is located geographically. They also are frequently looking for a single vendor to deliver or coordinate service on their various equipment.

As all of these factors have affected the field service industry, some participants have been affected more than others. In general, however, the need for more effective control of the service delivery operation has been recognized. A variety of software applications to service this need has emerged to the point where this type of applications software development is itself a growing field.

Service Delivery Operations and Planning and Control Software

The fundamental task of the field service organization is to provide service for equipment at the customer site. An operation to fulfill this task will include people, equipment, a process, and a supporting infrastructure. Companies providing field service may organize their operations along different lines, depending upon their customers' service requirements and their own service delivery strategies.

Field Service Obligations

A field service company usually has a service relationship with a set base of customers. The service contracts sold to these customers define the requirements of each party. The specific pieces of equipment to be serviced and the priority to be received when corrective problems arise are specified in the contract. Contracts usually have a set annual fee that covers all labor and materials (i.e., replacement parts); the amount of the charge will be related to the amount of risk that the service vendor is reducing for the customer and to the cost to provide that level of service.

Data regarding the service contract and associated obligations need to be stored so as to be accessible when service is requested. The amount of detail stored in the system can vary. Sometimes a detailed listing of the configuration of the customer equipment with special conditions will be included. Other services beyond corrective action also may be specified in the contract. For example, preventive maintenance may be required at specified time intervals and installation of field change orders (FCOs) may be part of the contractual obligation of the vendor. A contract may even contain an uptime guarantee where the service vendor guarantees that the system will be available for use (i.e., operating) for a percentage of time, otherwise a financial penalty will be applied. More complicated contract structures will require more flexibility in the way in which contract information is stored in the system.

Operational Design of Field Service Delivery

Due to environmental factors, the focus of field service is shifting away from the corrective remedial task although this is still the primary focus of the operation. The method of handling service calls is discussed below.

In addition to the proper handling of all types of service calls, there are other important supporting business functions common to most field service organizations. These are: logistics management, operational control, management control, planning, and billing. Whether the operation is supported by an automated system or is purely manual, these essential tasks remain.

Human Resources in the Field Service Operation

Field engineers (FEs) perform the fundamental service delivery task of the organization. Typically, the field engineers are dispersed across the geographical service territory and operate out of a local office. There may be many different skill levels among the engineers and they may have specific areas of technical specialization.

While the field engineer is the one who performs the fundamental task, the first point of contact with the customer is usually a telephone receptionist who records the information. An additional function is supplied to the dispatcher, who assigns the service request to a specific engineer.

These two functions, receiving a call and handling and dispatching it, are keys because they interact with both the customer and the field engineer. Sometimes these two functions are combined, i.e., the same person will answer the phones, record information, and dispatch. These functions may be centrally located or they may be dispersed throughout the service territory, possibly even in the offices from which the field engineers work. Deciding where to locate these functions will depend on management's business strategy and on the opportunities or limitations provided by the existing management information system.

Management is also part of the field service process. First-level managers monitor the status of the operation and exercise operational control, especially when expediting problem situations. They also spend a good deal of time visiting with customers to get feedback and to manage the customers' perception of service, thereby increasing the likelihood of contract renewals.

Managers higher in the organization will perform the planning functions to respond to growth or changes in the field service business with reassigned, enhanced, or new resources. Inputs to the planning process will come from industry trends and data about the internal operation. Management may also become involved in customer situations where an extended problem has hurt customer relations or where a major new account is being pursued.

Other Resources in Field Service

Replacement parts are necessary to a remedial service operation and parts will be stored in warehouses dispersed to some degree across the service geography. The value of the parts and their frequency of use are factors in determining the stocking strategy of the firm. These parts are usually stored in kits for each equipment type. Generally, each local office will stock some parts from which the field engineer will secure those parts necessary for a specific call or series of calls. Possibly, each field engineer will stock low value or frequently used parts in his van.

Defective parts removed from customer equipment frequently can be refurbished for reuse. Thus, all parts must be tracked and accounted for. An information system to handle these latter functions, special ordering of parts, and overall inventory management will be necessary. Such a system may interact with the call handling system.

The service delivery operation often uses diagnostic and test equipment. The field engineer usually will have some test equipment, but the firm also may have invested in highly sophisticated remote diagnostic equipment which can diagnose the problem in the customer's equipment via telephone lines. In the latter case, the complexity of the overall process is increased by the need for more coordination.

Call Handling Process

Typically, the sequence of events on a service call is initiated with a customer request by telephone for service on his down equipment. Some requests for service will not be initiated by a customer directly, as when preventive maintenance service calls are required at intervals specified in the contract. (Also, in the near future, equipment will have the internal capability of identifying when a failure is about to occur and will be able to log its own call.)

When the call is first received, the telephone response person will identify the customer, the equipment, and the contractual level of service obligation. This information is maintained in the customer files. Once identified, certain information will be verified and situation-specific data will be collected over the telephone. The customer contact will be given some identification number for the service call (a log number or incident number), and possibly an estimated time of arrival (ETA) will be provided.

After the request has been logged by the service organization, some type of evaluation of the specific service request may follow. This could be nontechnical screening by the telephone response person or possibly a technical evaluation via remote diagnostics. The intent is to help identify what resources, both human skills and replacement parts, to dispatch to the customer site.

The call is then assigned to a particular field engineer. Several methods of assignment logic may be applied. Each customer account may be the responsibility of a specific FE for account management purposes (called the account representation mode of call assignment). Alternatively, if the failing device is identified from the start, then a technical specialist in that type of device may be dispatched. A different mode of assignment is for the field engineer closest to the customer site to be assigned and dispatched when he becomes available. Finally, when the service contract requires that an FE arrive at the customer site within a specified period of time, the next available warm body may be assigned and dispatched as the deadline approaches.

Upon arrival at the equipment site, the FE will diagnose the problem, perform the fix, verify the fix, and return the equipment to the customer for use. At this point the call is closed and data describing the procedures taken and the resources consumed will be recorded and collected through some medium. The FE is now available for another service call.

Problem Escalation Process

The call may not, however, proceed this simply and smoothly. The FE may be unable to correct the problem and may require assistance. Higher level technical support could be provided by telephone or if necessary by dispatching a second FE to the site. Should a replacement part be needed that the FE does not have with him, a return trip will be necessary. If the local stockroom does not have the part, it will have to be ordered from some central warehouse, possibly with priority shipment procedures. As the customer outage situation lengthens in time, escalation procedures are typically implemented to help resolve the process and to bring the matter to management attention for customer relation purposes.

Thus, multiple visits by multiple persons may be involved in a service call and all these events need to be coordinated. All this happens under the watchful eye of the customer whose perception of the quality of service will be determined in part by the efficacy with which these situations are handled.

Software Systems for Field Service Call Handling and Dispatch

Applications software with planning and control capabilities provides a consistent structure to the call handling process and aids in monitoring and responding to field service requirements. The software is usually composed of several modules each designed to address a specific function, but the key module(s) is the one which controls the call handling process and the customer data.

How the software system is integrated into business processes is determined by the design of the service organization and by the capabilities and functions of the software itself. The telephone receptionist will likely log the initial data into the system. The dispatcher will also likely interact directly with the system. The FE may provide status information and call closure information to this same person over the telephone or the FE may enter the data on a handheld terminal which will then upload the data to the main system. First level managers may be directly advised of situations needing management action.

The software may be designed to be passive, that is, simply store information entered into it, or it may actively control the service process. For example, the dispatching logic may be applied solely from the brain of the dispatch person or the system may execute some programmed algorithm. Also, service delivery management may simply be notified that certain time thresholds are being approached or the system could initiate action unilaterally.

There is a passive-to-active continuum along which any particular software package can be placed. This will determine the role that the software system will play in the process. However, the more comprehensive and complex the software, the slower the system performance and the more cumbersome its likely to be. Because the system will be executing its functions while the telephone receptionists and others are using the system interactively with a customer on the phone, system performance could negatively affect customer perception of service quality.

Designers of software systems need to consider all these factors when developing their systems. The full range of field service situations must be handled, each requiring differing degrees of operational capability. The issue for software designers is how to incorporate the needed functional flexibility while maintaining simplicity and speed of use.

Part II: DESIGNING THE SYSTEM

Fred Watriss, Director of Product Planning and Designing at SMC (a pseudonym), was reviewing the existing process for enhancing and improving SERVICEMASTER. His group is responsible for planning and designing this software package which was already sold to and used by a variety of customers who offered field services for their own or others' equipment. The company's software development goal had been to meet 85 percent of the average user's needs. Now, toward the end of 1988, Watriss wondered whether that goal had been met and, more importantly, how his company's software design and development process might be improved.

SMC, Inc.

SMC, Inc., became a subsidiary of a communications company when it was purchased in 1985 as part of the company's diversification efforts. As of 1989 SMC had a total of 155 employees and about $20 million in annual sales. SMC's primary business area is the development and marketing of software products for application by companies that have a field service business. The largest group within the company produces and sells a standard software product known as SERVICEMASTER. A second but smaller part of SMC, the Professional Services Organization, writes custom software code to customer specifications.

The purpose of the SERVICEMASTER package is to facilitate the control and monitoring of service delivery operations within a field service business. The software is used in a variety of field service settings including major companies in the manufacture of medical equipment, third party maintainers of computers, other original equipment manufacturers, and communications companies. Companies from all three types of industry players (first party, second party, and third party maintenance organizations) have purchased and used SERVICEMASTER.

SERVICEMASTER is designed as an integrated set of software modules, each addressing one aspect of a field service business. The heart of the package is the Dispatch module which facilitates control of the crucial activities of a field service operation: logging service call requests, dispatching field engineers, and managing service calls in progress. While this module can operate alone, other modules can be purchased and combined to form a more comprehensive system.

SMC has three versions of its SERVICEMASTER product, each designed to function under a different operating system environment: IBM, DEC, and HP. Customers must decide which of the three versions they wish to use and which modules within that version they wish to purchase. Because SERVICEMASTER is continuously being enhanced, customers also can purchase updates of modules already purchased as well as other modules.

Customers also have the option of purchasing the source code for SERVICEMASTER. Because the source code is in COBOL (and is not encrypted) it can easily be read and edited. Consequently, purchasers have the flexibility to make customized enhancements to more closely meet their own needs. Such purchased and modified versions of SERVICEMASTER have an obvious drawback. Because they are no longer the same as the standard product, which SMC continues to enhance, these customers can no longer simply adopt SMC's subsequent versions. Instead these customers have become responsible for implementing any and all future changes or enhancements to the code purchased. If desired, these customers can contract separately with SMC's Professional Services Organization to have customized software development done for them.

In the 1980s, as the field service industry expanded dramatically and became a more complex business, the opportunity to develop software applications for this market also grew. By the beginning of 1989, there were many companies marketing software packages to aid field services management. Packages existed for virtually all operating systems and computer sizes (IBM mainframe to Macintosh). By this time SMC's SERVICEMASTER application had emerged as one of the largest selling software products of its type. Its chief competition seemed to be from potential customers considering writing their own custom application (using their internal MIS organization) rather than an offering of any other external software supplier.

Development of SERVICEMASTER

The company was founded in the late 1970s under the name of FIELDAID, Inc., originally as a data processing consulting company. In 1979 a major provider in the defense industry contracted with SMC to write a software application for its field service dispatching function to be run on Datapoint computer systems. DATA Inc. thus became an Original Equipment Manufacturer (OEM) for Datapoint. In 1980

DATA Inc. changed its name to SMC and became a pioneer in developing applications software for the field service industry.

In order to tap the potential of a broader market base, SMC rewrote the original dispatching software to run under an IBM operating system environment. One of SMC's first customers required a logistics module to track its replacement parts usage. The Logistics package was born out of that customer's specifications which were programmed by SMC.

Initially, the mission of SMC was to write field service call handling software. Maintenance of multiple versions on different hardware platforms became increasingly difficult. Furthermore, because revenues are so closely tied to the sale of programmers' time, it was hard to increase profits beyond a point. Accordingly, SMC decided to develop a standard product that could be mass marketed. This shift was possible only when the installed base had generated revenues large enough to support ongoing business operations and the next sale was no longer a survival issue. Having thus changed its business strategy, SMC was transformed from a sales-driven company to one that was product-driven.

Now SMC was faced with a series of classic design issues. What should this product look like? How should it function? No longer could one customer provide the answer to these questions. The software product had to be general enough to serve effectively in many different operational contexts while comprehensively providing information storage and processing capabilities for all the required business functions. Flexibility in the way the package could be implemented by multiple users emerged as a key criterion for SMC's resolution of many software design choices.

Having begun penetration into companies with an IBM MIS shop, SMC decided to expand its product base into users with DEC's VAX equipment. The SMC programmers had to learn to write SERVICEMASTER under VAX's VMS operating system. These programmers had no prior knowledge of VMS; they were self-taught during the project.

The VAX version of SERVICEMASTER was intended to mimic the functions of the IBM version while utilizing any inherent strengths available in the VAX information architecture. The programmer analyst working on this project saw that the software could be improved upon from both technical and business standpoints, which resulted in certain functional changes. Accordingly, the VAX version, while performing the same basic functions and following the same logical flow as the IBM version, turned out to be noticeably different in such aspects as screen formats and data entry logic.

An early customer was interested in a VAX-compatible version. Because most of this customer's service was delivered remotely by technicians via telephone rather than through on-site visits, it had a specific need for a technical assistance center (TAC) module which would handle remote service delivery. A deal was struck. At the time SMC had no VAXs of its own. The TAC module was written in exchange for timesharing use of the customer's VAXs.

The Hewlett Packard (HP) version of SERVICEMASTER was intended to be an exact duplication of the VAX version but it did not work out that way either. The HP version was written a short time after the version for DEC equipment for which business issues had already surfaced. Attempting to learn from the past, the designers of the HP version created a SERVICEMASTER product where some functions differed from the DEC version, which in turn had differed from the IBM version.

SERVICEMASTER: The Product

SERVICEMASTER is an integrated set of nine software modules designed to cover a wide spectrum of management needs. As displayed (see Figure 1) upon login on a fully configured system, these modules are:
1. Dispatch
2. Profit
3. Logistics
4. Reports
5. Voice
6. TAC (Technical Assistance Center)
7. Remote
8. RCM
9. Scheduling

Each of these modules may be acquired and used individually, but it is most common for the dispatch, billing, and logistics modules to be purchased together to provide a minimum core capability. To illustrate the way the software functions, the Dispatch module is outlined below.

The Structure of Dispatch

To implement Dispatch (as well as the additional modules), the purchasing firm must make some organizational and operational decisions. For example, a key concept of Dispatch is the service area, a logical grouping of customer sites and field engineers, usually pertaining to some geographical region. For example, New England or Greater Los Angeles or Downtown Chicago might be designated as service areas.

Welcome To

SERVICEMASTER

by

The SMC Corporation

OPTIONS

1. Dispatch
2. Billing
3. Logistics
4. Reports
5. Report–Writer

6. TAC
7. Host–Remote
8. RCM
9. Scheduling

99. Logoff System

Choice: 01

M A S T E R   M E N U
For
Dispatch Functions

01. Customer File Maintenance
02. Contract File Maintenance
03. Mass Call Generation
04. Dispatch
05. Call Tracking
06. Employee File Maintenance
07. Kit File Maintenance
08. Manual Call Close
09. Mass Change Rules File
10. Mass Sites Change
11. Message Inquiry and Update
12. Parts Master Maintenance
13. Product File Maintenance
14. Password File Maintenance
15. Code File Maintenance
16. Site File Maintenance

17. Skill File Maintenance
18. Closed Call Utilities

Selection: 04

DISPATCH MAIN MENU

Dispatcher: Dispatch Functions

1. Customer Initiated Incidents

2. Uncommitted Call Display and
   Employee Selection

3. Employee Initiated Updates

4. Message Inquiry and Update

5. In-Transit Inquiry and Update

6. Call Tracking

9. Exit from Dispatch

Selection: 0

Figure 1. Initial Screen Sequence

The firm must also decide what operational functions will be carried out at each of the levels of the organization and who is going to perform them. Will Dispatch be run centrally or will multiple applications be run in several decentralized locations? Who will assign and dispatch? What privileges on the system will each person have?

The SERVICEMASTER users' manual, prepared by SMC, explains that its audience consists of three groups of hands-on users: support staff who maintain the reference data files, system administrators who maintain the system and execute system-wide programs, and dispatchers who interact with the system to perform its service delivery control function. The dispatcher's procedural interaction with the system covers about one-fourth of the users manual while the balance is split between the other two classes of users, all of whom are employed by the companies that buy SERVICEMASTER.

Using Dispatch

When Dispatch is first invoked, the 18 functions that can be performed are listed, along with indications of the reference file maintenance, utility programs, and dispatch selections (see Figure 2). Basic data about customers, the products serviced, and the service employees are stored in these files for retrieval during service call logging and dispatching. Many of the reference files that must be maintained are accessed by additional SERVICEMASTER modules, or in other words, they serve several purposes, not just those related to call handling. Security and access limitations to the various modules and functions are ensured through the password file.

The code file is especially important in the conceptual design of the SERVICEMASTER system. This file contains various tables that each field service company builds to tailor the SERVICEMASTER application to meet the particular aspects of its operational design. At points in the execution of the software, values in these tables will be accessed to set parameters for service, for example, the particular response priority specified in the contracts sold by that service company.

The maintenance and utility functions allow for programs to be executed for large-scale updates or verifications. For example, whenever a customer contact changes, all the product records relating to that customer site can be updated automatically by executing one program. Also, the data submitted by field engineers when closing service calls can be validated against a set of parameters by executing a batch job at some convenient time; any discrepancies will be highlighted on a report.

An employee who serves as a dispatcher for the field service operation will have six selections available within the dispatch main menu.

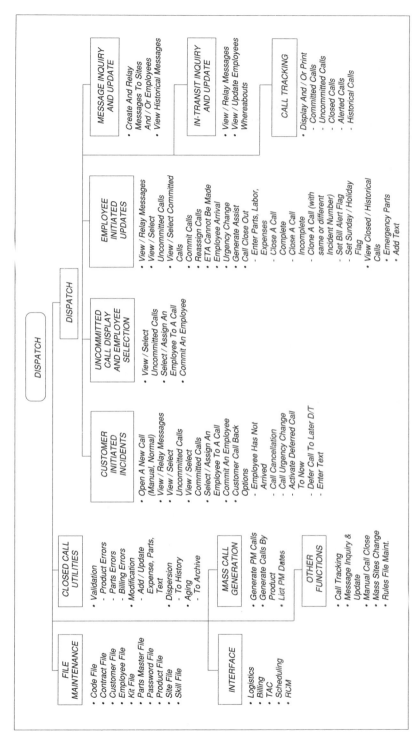

Figure 2. Dispatch.

Charts showing the operational flow of each of these are included in the exhibits. They will be described briefly.

A normal sequence in using SERVICEMASTER would begin when a customer telephones requesting service. The dispatcher would invoke the customer initiated incident selection on the dispatch main menu (see Figure 3). The first step (as with all the selections) is an identification step. Here the dispatcher accesses information about the customer and the specific equipment to be serviced by accessing the reference data files (through the use of various search capabilities). All the data for that product and site will be displayed on the dispatcher's screen. Whenever a site or product is not located in the reference files, new records can be created. A utility program will print them later for review by the proper personnel.

At this point two different flows could occur. The user can either view all service calls currently in progress at the customer site or bypass this function and move directly to logging the incident. By viewing current calls, the user can avoid duplicate logging of incidents. When the user is ready to log the incident, he or she will acquire situation-specific data over the phone from the customer, for example, the urgency of the call. Certain types of data that are accessed from the reference files are verified by phone, for example, the customer contact name and phone number. Explanatory text is then entered, describing the customer's assessment of the problem.

At this juncture Dispatch offers an option to dispatch the call (to assign and to commit a specific employee to the service call) or to cease the function which returns the dispatcher to the dispatch main menu. According to the user's manual, "whether you dispatch the call now or later may depend on situations and company policy."

Assuming dispatching is to be performed, the following sequence occurs. If a particular field engineer (FE) is to be assigned, then the dispatcher can specify that FE by entering the FE's employee number. Alternatively, a list of employees designated to the service area in which the customer site is located can be scrolled on the bottom half of the screen and a selection can be made from that list. If no assignment is made, then, by default, the employee with primary responsibility for the site, as specified in the customer product file, is assigned. This assignment may be changed prior to committing the call.

After an employee has been assigned, Dispatch offers the option of committing the call. This entails creating an estimated time of arrival (ETA) to be given to the customer over the phone. The ETA is calculated by the system based upon the contract priority contained in the reference files and the urgency code entered while talking with the customer. This calculated entry of the deadline for the FE's arrival can be overwritten by the system user currently on duty.

This dispatching sequence (assigning and committing an employee)

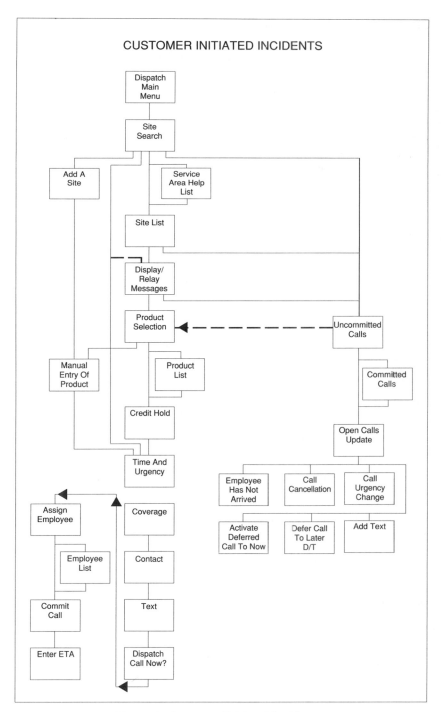

Figure 3. Customer Initiated Incidents.

can be performed within three different selections on the Dispatch main menu:

1. customer initiated incidents (as currently described);
2. uncommitted call display and employee selection; or
3. employee initiated updates.

Thus, should dispatching not be performed at the time of logging a customer-initiated incident, it can be performed at a later time through one of the other two functions. The dispatching screen sequence is identical following each of the three selections.

The uncommitted call display and employee selection option on the Dispatch main menu contains only the assignment and committing functions. The other functions found in the customer-initiated incident selection are not available through this main menu selection.

The employee-initiated updates selection from the Dispatch main menu is used to update the status of an employee or of a service call when the field employee has telephoned the dispatch center (see Figure 4). The employee may call to notify the center that he has arrived at the customer site, to order replacement parts on an emergency basis through the Logistics module, to have the history of open and closed calls on the customer site called to the screen, to request the assistance of another employee, or to reassign the service call to another employee. If he is to close the work session at the customer site, then he relates data describing the labor and materials consumed on the service call. If the incident is not resolved, the service call can be "closed incomplete" specifying the reason for work to be completed later if, for example, a part must be ordered or the work day has ended.

The message inquiry and update selection from the Dispatch main menu utilizes SERVICEMASTER as a communications device. It allows messages to be sent to a specific employee, a group of employees, a site, or a group of sites. When an employee initiates an update or a customer initiates an incident log, they are prompted that messages are on file to be read.

The in transit inquiry and update selection allows for the whereabouts of a select employee or all employees within a service area to be listed on the screen. The whereabouts entry is created during the previous employee update session.

The call tracking selection allows for service call summary or detail listings to be viewed on the screen or spooled to a printer (see Figure 5). Calls may be selected for a site, service area, or a specific call. They may also be selected based upon the status of the service call, for example, committed, uncommitted, closed, historical, or alerted (ETA deadlines have been missed). Through this function calls can only be viewed. No updates can be made.

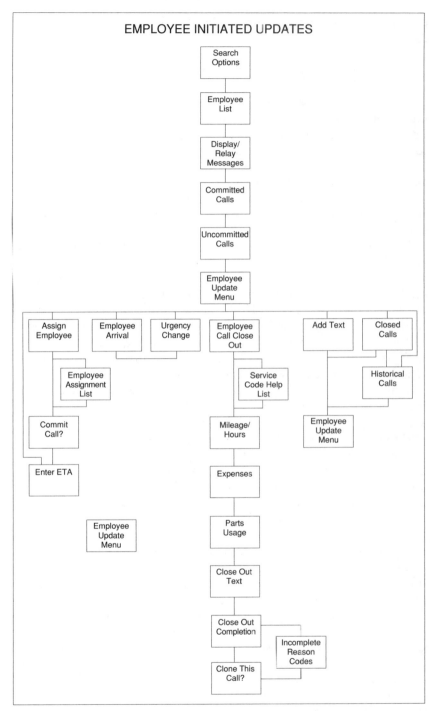

Figure 4. Employee Initiated Updates.

Designing Enhancements to SERVICEMASTER

Historically, SMC has enhanced SERVICEMASTER and extended the scope of its business functions by finding a current user or potential customer who wants the additional functionality and is willing to pay for its development. For example, a major government contractor required that the serialization of parts be retained on all records, while a soft drink company required that "Tag Number" be a secondary key to the product file, although its less sophisticated equipment did not require the more cumbersome search logic of system type and system serial number. Single customers typically have paid for custom programming to accommodate special features. Nevertheless, the intellectual property rights to this new functionality are owned by SMC and may subsequently be built into the standard SERVICEMASTER offering.

When new module or enhancement is incorporated in SERVICEMASTER, SMC's Fred Watriss recognizes that it will never be 100 percent right for all users. The customer who requested the enhancement will likely redefine or even change the functionality desired. Furthermore, due to typical problems in communication, there is usually a discrepancy between what a customer says he wants and what he really means he wants. The main objective of this approach is to satisfy a particular customer's requirement while at the same time receiving funding for the development of the standard product.

Another reality of this kind of standard product development is that SMC attempts to design a piece of software to meet 85 percent of the average user's needs. So doing results in a software package that can be marketed to a extended group of potential customers without having to bear the peril of customization. This peril arises when multiple versions of the same software product have to be supported.

SMC employs five product planning analysts whose job it is to oversee the enhancement and development of SERVICEMASTER. These people write the functional specifications documents against which programming is done, drawing upon their knowledge of the business and their understanding of the systems development process.

To facilitate the enhancement process, user groups were established to solicit input from the customer base. Three user groups exist, one for each operating system environment. Periodically (about once a year) the users are invited to come and present their requests for enhancement. Through this forum users can try to influence the development pattern of SERVICEMASTER, thereby avoiding having to get involved with custom software development whenever their requirements are designed and implemented within a standard version of SERVICEMASTER. The three user groups differ markedly in composition. The IBM user group is small, roughly 15

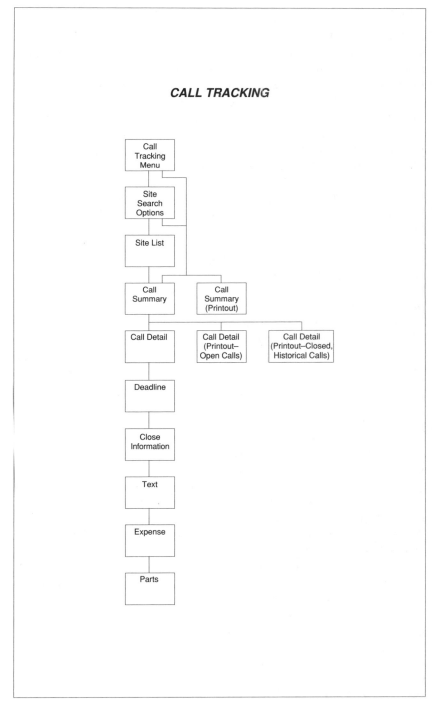

CALL TRACKING

Figure 5. Call Tracking.

users. Because companies with IBM MIS shops are typically large with internally influential MIS functions, the representative to this user group is typically someone from an MIS department who has a technical (i.e., hardware/software/database) perspective, as distinguished from that of field service operations or its management.

The DEC and HP user groups both differ from the IBM group. The DEC group is larger with about 60 users. DEC and HP products are typically installed in companies in a more distributed fashion and thus a strong, central MIS function is not as prevalent. In such an organizational context business-oriented users tend to predominate. Accordingly, the customer's representative to the SERVICEMASTER user group is more likely to have a field service delivery background, rather than that of an MIS technician. Because of the way career development has typically occurred within field service, this person probably has served as a field engineer and line manager.

Marketing SERVICEMASTER

SERVICEMASTER is marketed through a variety of media aimed at the field service community. These include brochures, trade journal advertising, industry conferences, and product seminars. A folder containing well-designed, visually appealing promotional literature has been developed which presents an overview description of the software, stressing the benefits and value of the system to those who implement it. Endorsements of the product by current customers are included in the folder. Endorsements typically come from senior managers within the respective field service organizations.

These endorsements are used heavily in various promo-tional devices to develop sales leads. They are used in the half- to full-page ads that are run monthly in the trade journals for the field service industry. These journals, read by all levels of management within the industry, are typically distributed free of charge. These journals are less likely to be subscribed to by MIS personnel.

SERVICEMASTER is also marketed at the various industry conferences in the exhibition halls. Attendees at these conferences are likely to be line managers and supporting staff persons with service delivery responsibility. SMC tries to secure a prominent location near the exhibition hall's doors for its extra large booth. The customer endorsements are displayed on the facade of the booth. All three operating system versions of SERVICEMASTER are actively demonstrated by the numerous salespersons. These salespersons typically have sales and not technical backgrounds.

At these conferences product enhancements currently in the last stages of development might be on display, for example, a graphic display of the real-time location of field engineers and service requests. Also, new product announcements might be made during breakfast sessions on an invitation basis.

SMC also sponsors frequent seminars conducted throughout the United States and in selected European locations for representatives of companies interested in learning more about SERVICEMASTER. At these seminars, the product is demonstrated in full. A current customer will be at the seminar to explain his experience with SERVICEMASTER. Also in attendance will be an industry consultant who will make a presentation of general interest about the direction of the field service industry, but no direct endorsement of the product.

Future Software Products of SMC

SMC has an advanced concepts group which is organizationally independent of groups handling its currently marketed products. This group's role is to develop a business model of field service delivery, devoid of the biases of the current versions of SERVICEMASTER. The plan is that a new generation software product will be developed around this business model. In other words, the key purpose of the advanced concepts group is to rethink the underlying architecture of the current SERVICEMASTER product and to develop and introduce new technologies to meet new requirements in the next generation of this product. New features and functions of the software might include expert systems, decision support systems, and dynamic graphic displays of real time location of field engineers.

With all these technical considerations and market realities, SMC is faced with some crucial choices. What enhancement gets written next? On what basis is that decision to be made? How can the product be developed for maximum long-term marketability in a cost-effective manner? How important is the likely effectiveness of its software in the hands of its users a guide to resolving these issues?

Part III: FIELD SERVICE AT ZENO, INC.

Zeno, Inc., makes hardware and software products that are combined into networks (typically with five to ten nodes). By mid-1988 Zeno's field service organization had used SERVICEMASTER for over one year and purchased it as a replacement of a previous automated system.

The director of customer information systems, Larry Gas, heads a small group (seven people) of data systems specialists and others who know field service and corporate MIS directions. He serves as a broker between those in field service operations and senior management. His former position was service operations manager. He has had 20 years of field service experience starting as a field engineer (tool bag carrier) and including service in sales, training, logistics, and area management.

Background on Systems for Field Service at Zeno

In 1981, Zeno delivered field service through a district organization. Field engineers answered incoming calls and then made service visits. They used a manual system whereby cards were shifted from bins to files to represent ongoing service activity.

In 1982, a committee at Zeno, comprised of the vice president of distribution and other senior field service managers, reviewed the existing proprietary software systems for assisting field service operations. They decided to implement a new system at the regional level. Zeno thus went directly from a decentralized manual system to a decentralized automated system without taking the more traditional intermediate step of implementing an automated centralized system. The committee selected a small software company that was willing to work with them to enhance an existing software product in directions that Zeno felt to be important. Zeno became the software company's primary customer and, for a while, drove the development of this package.

This package cost only a small fraction of the subsequent SERVICEMASTER software and its installation was accomplished through an effective project management approach. Nevertheless, this Field Service Management System (FSMS) system turned out not to have enough power to meet Zeno's processing requirements. Transaction processing that used to take five to 10 minutes mushroomed to 25 to 30 minutes per transaction under FSMS. (In the field the software was nicknamed Sluggo, in reference to its slow response.)

The FSMS was used for five years at Zeno, two years less than its original estimate of a seven year life. While the FSMS facilitated the desired regionalization of service delivery, it never accommodated the desired national reporting capability that was supposed to occur through an add-on feature called linkage and rollup. Due to lack of expertise at the software company and, probably, inadequate funding, this feature was never realized. Instead, regions mailed files to headquarters each month where they were converted to tape for processing.

In late 1985, Zeno brought IBM in to survey its requirements for a new software system for field service operations. A large number of interviews (130) was conducted with Zeno employees and customers. Over 600 problems were identified, including the need for new tools, improved information (both integration and accuracy), and unclear policies and procedures. The IBM survey went on to identify the state-of-the-art in field service software. A bidding process ensued and six vendors participated. From this process came the decision that Zeno would acquire SERVICEMASTER to be implemented, not surprisingly, on an IBM platform. Zeno purchased the following modules of SERVICEMASTER: Dispatch, TAC, Logistics, and they plan to add Profit (formerly called Billing). The acquisition of SERVICEMASTER was justified in a quantitative analysis that showed an extremely short payback period.

Use of SERVICEMASTER at Zeno

Zeno's field service center is currently in operation 24 hours a day, all seven days of the week, across six different geographic regions. Approximately 75,0000 calls are handled per year. Processing is done on the corporation's mainframe computer. File maintenance is done during the night due to limits on availa-bility of the centralized computer. When the mainframe is down, about once a week, field service operations revert to a manual system.

Zeno has a total of 250 customer service engineers (CSEs), some of whom are on call at night. There are 12 service coordinators who handle incoming calls during the various shifts. The telephone system has a switching capability to smooth the load on the call coordinators. Call coordinators take down information on the service request and then automatically route the call via the online system to one of the 25 service coordinators who attempt to make technical assessment and resolution of the problem on the phone. About 30 percent of these incoming calls are resolved in this manner, the remainder being dispatched for CSE visits to the customer's site.

Zeno has used its internal MIS group to develop software enhancements to SERVICEMASTER by adding related capabilities (but not changing the basic SERVICEMASTER software). One such feature is a browse capability which allows a district manager to scan the active files and select certain information to view on the screen.

Reactions to SERVICEMASTER at Zeno

Zeno is generally very pleased with its field service operations using SERVICEMASTER. Several issues, however, have emerged. SERVICEMASTER identifies a customer by a number (6-digits for Zeno). One of its most important customers complained to the Zeno president that they did not want to give a number when calling for service and that the company name and location ought to be sufficient. Clearly, good customer service requires some sort of response and Zeno is now working on new customer identification conventions. Search flexibility in the data file may prove to be a technical barrier.

Whether a customer is defined by number or name, the system designer assumes that the users have solved the problem of data integrity. This assumption may lead to unnecessary file maintenance. A search function is useful only if the users are all customers entered accurately on the master file. If a call coordinator incorrectly logs in a new site after failing to find a customer's record, duplicate records will result. Correction procedures must be executed later to eliminate the duplicate file and add its data to the original file. Zeno has established a data control group to research potential problems with the existing database.

Zeno recalls situations when the customer caller did not have immediate access to the product needing repair. Getting the caller to provide product codes and/or serial numbers may be unreasonable at times. SERVICEMASTER lacks the flexibility to search for the customer data based on an indicator, such as the local telephone number, that is readily available to the customer.

A problem with a main selling feature of SERVICEMASTER arose at Zeno. Parameter-driven financial reporting capability was a significant feature in Zeno's decision to purchase SERVICEMASTER because it was of direct interest to senior management. However, this feature was never used because the company could not meet significant requirements to keep the associated database up to date.

Zeno also anticipates a future shortcoming of SERVICEMASTER. Service Marketing is of growing strategic importance to Zeno (and elsewhere in the industry as well). Multiple types of service are being provided ranging from traditional kinds of hardware and software maintenance to upgrades and disaster recovery Accordingly, it would be valuable for a field service system to be able to accommodate more complex service product types. SERVICEMASTER allows only one level in the bill of materials. This will be a serious limitation to easily implementing a broader set of services to Zeno's customers.

Finally, although Zeno bought the source code when it acquired SERVICEMASTER, the company has not yet tried to change it. Zeno is a member of the SERVICEMASTER user group but feels that getting enhancements through this process takes too long. Zeno has not tried to push its corporate agenda through the user group. It seems clear to people at Zeno that SMC takes the basic position that SERVICEMASTER will continue to be a standardized product to meet multiple users' needs.

Part IV: FIELD SERVICE AT TRIDENT, INC.

Trident, Inc. is a young computer manufacturer specializing in powerful engineering work stations. It experienced exceptional growth (40 percent per year) in the mid-1980s. Trident's field service organization has used SERVICEMASTER for three years, having been one of the first to adopt this software package. It uses the IBM version of SERVICEMASTER. Before adopting this, system the company had a manual (noncomputerized) approach to field service operations. As an early adopter of this software, Trident was influential in affecting some of the functional capabilities of subsequent releases of SERVICEMASTER.

In 1983, Trident's field service operations were not centralized, although incoming service calls came to a single location via an 800 number phone line. Service was scheduled and conducted out of 23 branch offices grouped within five North American regions. Each region had a regional support manager with direct line responsibility over a team of systems support engineers (SEEs). A team included people at three different levels of expertise, plus a regional technical support manager who provided assistance as needed.

Trident's current organization is similar to that its earlier years, except all dispatching is done at the central assistance response center (ARC) using SERVICEMASTER. A central corporate support group acquires hardware and develops software. A SERVICEMASTER administrator is responsible for maintaining all parameter tables that are part of the system's design.

Field service is accomplished at Trident through its more than 40 branch offices where a total of about 300 SSEs are employed. SEEs are supplied with a kit with SERVICEMASTER codes and hardware part numbers to accomplish their interface with the system. SEEs learn to interact with SERVICEMASTER mostly through on-the-job experience.

Twelve coordinators handle calls at the ARC from 8:00 in the morning to 9:00 in the evening on a two-shift basis. The coordinators conduct rather routine processing functions and their average duration on the job is from 12-18 months. Coordinators are aided by a sliding hand-sized template called a field activity reference card on which all SERVICEMASTER input codes are displayed for easy use. This card was designed and developed at Trident after sufficient experience in the use of SERVICEMASTER suggested its value as an aid to both the efficiency and the effectiveness of the coordinators' actions.

Coordinators attend a two-week training program, which includes going into the field with an SSE. Coordinators are supplied with a manual which includes a call processing flow chart, a map of service regions and time zones, a list of major customers, and model numbers of Trident products. (This information is useful when a customer gives an incorrect model number during a service call.)

Background on Automating Field Service at Trident

A computer manufacturer with extensive expertise in this field, Trident's original plan for automating field service functions was that its internal software specialists would design and develop a customized system for use on its own computer hardware. This approach failed to come to fruition due to limitations of the company's hardware.

Trident then experimented with using another commercial software package (not SERVICEMASTER) on a one-month trial basis. That software was originally designed for field service applications in another industry and Trident soon ruled it out due to its limitations for its own type of application.

Finally, in 1983 Trident decided to adopt SERVICEMASTER, which had a better invoicing capability and a set of standard reports that would be useful to Trident management. Trident's objective at this time was to purchase a 75 percent complete package on a turnkey basis and then to modify the source code to satisfy its remaining requirements.

Adoption and Implementation of SERVICEMASTER

The decision to adopt SERVICEMASTER was made by a specially convened task force whose membership included the director of logistics plus two staff members, call handling managers, members of the internal MIS group, a contracts manager, and several internal users. This group met weekly during the acquisition decision period and the subsequent implementation of SERVICEMASTER modules for call handling and logistics.

Steve Morris, currently the support operations manager for field service, joined Trident before the company began the procurement process for a field service software package. He was actively involved in the selection of SERVICEMASTER and with its installation and subsequent modifications.

After implementation, systems operations was in charge of using SERVICEMASTER and for specifying its subsequent customization. A business system analyst was given the responsibility of being the primary contact with Trident's MIS group.

Trident's rationale for attempting some customization of SERVICEMASTER was that it believed that its service requirements were different from those of other computer manufacturers and from SERVICEMASTER customers in different industries. Trident felt that the people at SMC who designed SERVICEMASTER could not possibly know the service business at Trident well enough to correctly design all features and functions of the software system.

Implementation of SERVICEMASTER at Trident resulted in the creation of several new jobs and the expansion of others. First, the MIS group needed to hire a staff person well-versed in IBM technology because this was the company's first major IBM software system. Trident also needed to acquire system operators skilled in using multifunctional software. Three new systems administration jobs were created at Trident's ARC where call-handling took place. Finally, the SEEs had to be trained to capture more data on a systematic basis.

The vice president of customer services at Trident was a strong supporter of the acquisition of SERVICEMASTER. Implementing this software became a top priority for both field operations and the internal MIS group. As SERVICEMASTER was implemented region by region, network phone links had to be installed and call handling capacity had to be tested. Personnel who handled incoming service requests had to be trained to solicit the required information as efficiently as possible while being courteous in terminating such phone conversations.

Implementation and start-up of SERVICEMASTER was aggressive and smooth. The first region was put on-line in three weeks and the others followed in two-week intervals.

Trident did not want its branch managers to have to administer call handling any more than would be consistent with its decentralized delivery of field service. Accordingly, the company tailored SERVICEMASTER to its own call handling philosophy. Of the five Dispatch functions (see SERVICEMASTER Case), Create, Assign, and Page are executed by centralized call coordinators at Trident, while their SEEs in the field are responsible for Committing and Closing calls.

The five field service regions, highly decentralized, follow a franchised approach, yet it is important that they adopt consistent procedures and that they maintain a centralized SERVICEMASTER database, which requires consistent reporting.

Trident is active in the SERVICEMASTER users' group organized by SMC, its developer. Regions make priority lists of their desired enhancements. Systems operations takes these lists to Trident's customer service management committee, which is comprised of the vice president and directors of customer service. The final composite priority list of Trident is then taken to SMC, hopefully to influence SMC's aggregate priorities for subsequent SERVICEMASTER enhancements.

Trident's Reactions to SERVICEMASTER

ARC coordinators are pleased with the call handling system of SERVICEMASTER. However, others at Trident have experienced some difficulties. An early limitation for Trident was that it had to adopt the centralized IBM version of SERVICEMASTER. This decision was forced because the versions offered for use on decentralized hardware platforms (DEC, H/P) could not accommodate 35 active terminals, which Trident's local field office network would have required. Aside from imposing a centralized structure, the IBM version is characterized by screens that contain more data than are readily absorbable by users.

Another early disappointment for Trident was that the set of management reports that had been featured in SERVICEMASTER sales materials was not functioning at the time the system was purchased. Other promised features had not yet been included in subsequent releases of the software.

Flexibility and integration are two of the strengths of SERVICEMASTER, according to SMC. Trident experienced some difficulty with the notion of flexibility in that there are not enough standards to guide data entry by ARC coordinators or SEEs. In the quest for true integration of its information processing, Trident is currently writing its own conversion program to avoid manually reentering information from its product shipment file to the customer file needed by SERVICEMASTER.

Access to data has proved to be somewhat problematic. Apparently, SMC did not anticipate that an IBM SERVICEMASTER user would need to have some terminals located in regional offices. Trident decided that it would like the regional management to monitor its own local field service performance. Trident thus created a need to download SERVICEMASTER data to the various regions which requires the development of special software enhancements.

Another early shortcoming from Trident's point of view was that SERVICEMASTER tracked products only by product type and location. Trident had to urge SMC to provide the capability to track a product by its serial number. This enhancement was necessary because, in Trident's business, a customer might find it necessary to switch a failed computer from a site that had not contracted for field service to a work station that happened to be at a site that was covered by a service agreement.

A more conceptual shortcoming involves the definition of a call. Trident would prefer that a call be considered to be active from the point of an initial request until the underlying situation is remedied in the field. By contrast, SERVICEMASTER labels each SEE site visit as a call, even if this visit relates to a preexisting situation. This convention leads SERVICEMASTER to categorize as closed incomplete all intermediate incidents or events. Mr. Morris, at Trident, feels that this conceptual problem yields misleading operational statistics.

Medical Magic: Systems Design and Medical Practice in a Hospital*

Scene One: Marian Higgs, M.D., a pathologist, is working in the hospital laboratory. She reads the calcium level derived from a patient sample and wonders if the high level is a mismeasurement or if it reflects a serious change in the patient's condition. On her desk is a computer terminal that is connected to the hospitalwide information system. Dr. Higgs types in the patient's ID number and instantly views the patient's medical record, previous calcium levels and the current level just entered by the lab technician. In context, the recent levels appear understandable but worrisome. Dr. Higgs, typing in the patient's record via the computer, suggests some additional tests to the patient's physician. Then, via a different computer routine, she reorders the calcium test on that sample.

To a nearby lab technician, Dr. Higgs remarks that before the implementation of the new computer system, it would have been very difficult to see the patient's record. The record (also called the patient chart) would have been at the nurses' station near the patient's room in the other wing of the hospital and five floors down. "Often," she said, "we had little way of knowing how our analyses fitted into the treatment or outcome."

Scene Two: Dr. Sidney Dorf is in his office. On his desk is a computer terminal that is connected to the hospitalwide information system. Dr. Dorf types in the name of one of his patients and views that patient's record. He is most interested in seeing the recent calcium level, and, in fact, it has been added to the record. Based on the new results and some comments from the pathologist, Dr. Dorf changes the patient's medication and orders an additional test. His order for new medication immediately appears on the patient's chart. In addition and automatically, the new order is transmitted to the hospital pharmacy, the nurses' task list is updated with the change, and the hospital billing department is informed of the new cost. Dr. Dorf adds a note on the record to discuss the new medication with the patient.

*This case was written by Ross Koppel and is based on research by Ross Koppel, Albert Crawford, and Robert Cort. It was prepared as the basis for classroom discussion rather than to illustrate either effective or ineffective managerial or design practice. This research was supported by the Ethics and Values Section of the National Science Foundation, under Grant No. BBS-8619534.

Scene Three: Nurse Nancy Harper enters a patient's room and inserts her employee ID card (with a magnetic strip) into the bedside computer terminal's badge reader. She types in her password and, then, the name of the patient and portions of her record appear on the screen. Highlighted on the screen is a notation that the physician has altered the patient's medication. Nurse Harper also notes that the pharmacy has sent the new medication to the nurses' station (the large desk in the central alcove of the patient floor).

Nurse Harper measures the patient's blood pressure, temperature and other vital signs. She types the information into the bedside computer terminal. Also, as indicated on the computer task list for this patient, she changes a bandage. Before leaving, she adds some observations about the patient's condition and shuts off the computer.

Introduction

Hospitals are the structures to which established physicians admit their patients and in which patients are diagnosed and treated. Hospitals, in addition, engage in a broad range of mundane activities. For example, hospitals' accounting and other business systems must track expenses and invoice patients, government payers, and insurance companies. Workers and contractors must be paid regularly. Hospitals, moreover, demand both usual and unusual housekeeping and physical plant operations.

Hospitals also serve normative and social functions within their communities. Mayors and high school bands attend their openings. Important people serve on their boards or on their community committees, even if those persons are not involved with medicine or hospital financing. Last, the hospital is the flagship of the medical establishment, combining specialized knowledge, prestige, and technological innovation.

Teaching hospitals, in addition to their general hospital activities, serve as training facilities for younger physicians and for the staggering variety of other health care providers, such as physical therapists, dieticians, technicians and nurses. Teaching hospitals also provide continuing medical education for their many practitioners and research scientists, informing them of emerging knowledge and techniques.

St. George's Hospital and the Design of Its Computer System:
The Electronic Chart

Hospitals require extensive documentation of all medical plans and treatments and of patients' signs, symptoms, and diagnoses. This documentation is required because services must be provided at all hours and under extreme conditions, because of the vast numbers and types of medical and nonmedical personnel who deal with each patient, because of the complexity of medical treatment and the need to coordinate disparate elements, and because of invoicing, legal and regulatory requirements. Central to patient documentation is the *patient chart*, the record of the patient's medical history, diagnosis, treatment, and laboratory reports. It is the basic document of hospital practice and is the linchpin of the hospital's other record systems.

St. George's Hospital (a pseudonym) is a nonsectarian hospital installing a computer system to produce an electronic patient chart. The new computer system is replacing the existing system of paper records. The new system incorporates all medical orders (e.g., orders for medication and treatment), a chronicle of signs, symptoms and results (including, for example, blood pressure measurements and lab tests), and the set of practitioners' notes on diagnoses and treatments. With integration into the hospitalwide computer system, relevant data from all hospital departments and personnel are electronically and instantly inserted into the patient chart. This information may be automatically displayed, graphed, and analyzed in different formats and combinations. Also, the chart may be simultaneously viewed (and altered or added to) from the patient's room, the nurses' station, the doctor's office, or from any computer equipped with a modem.

Patient records contain much confidential information. The patient's willingness to confide in his or her health care provider requires that patient information be seen only by those with a need to know. Legal obligations of confidentiality also reinforce the need to protect such information. The electronic system, however, changes the process of viewing patient records. Soon, there will be no physical patient chart at the nurses' station, yet, confidentiality must be maintained. St. George's staff, administrators, and computer system designers are now establishing rules of access to the computer system and its records. They must determine who will have access to the system. As part of this question they must address:

- What information will be accessible and by whom.
- Where, when, and under what circumstances can this information be seen and/or altered.
- What manipulation (addition, revision, deletion) of that information will be allowed.
- How the system will track access to and alterations of records and who will oversee the ledger of activities (the audit trail).

The Hospital

St. George's decision to create an integrated computer system with electronic patient records represents the continuation of an innovative strategy and exemplifies its concern with the needs and aspirations of its medical staff. The hospital also hopes that automation and integration of information (e.g., data from patients, physicians, nurses, pharmacies, and labs) will provide clinical and economic benefits.

Economic and labor force needs have spurred sales of medical information systems. Hospitals throughout the United States are installing integrated medical information systems that allow point-of-care (bedside) data entry and retrieval.[1] Integrated medical information systems are particularly attractive to hospitals, including St. George's Hospital, because they help address many of the difficulties that have emerged in the recent decade. Hospitals are forced to become more business-like to deal with declining reimbursement from third-party payers, increasing competition, new forms of reimbursement that do not reward inefficiencies, and demands for tighter government oversight. In addition, hospitals face an aging population (thus sicker people) and a nursing shortage. We consider each of this issues in turn:
Reimbursement Government, and increasingly other medical payers, no longer pay on a cost reimbursed basis. The most common payment system now is Prospective Payment Systems (PPS) in which the hospital is given a set fee based on illness category for each patient discharged. PPS was introduced as an incentive to make care more efficient. It has succeeded in dramatically reducing the average length of stay (which has decreased nine percent in 10 years) and in shifting much of the care to outpatient services (which increased 46 percent in a decade). PPS has also lowered rates for PPS patients, shifting the cost to the comparatively few commercial insurers who pay for charges. In response, hospitals have increased their outpatient departments and have sought to expand their businesses to nontraditional hospital services, such as buying nursing homes, selling home medical equipment, and opening satellite clinics. The hospital computer system is needed to service the maze of cost-accounting systems, billing procedures, organizational links, record-keeping requirements and insurance regulations. There is, in fact, a related software industry that optimizes patient illness categories so that hospitals can bill for the highest remunerated illness categories.
Competition, Aging, and General Economic Conditions Hospitals have also come under competitive and other economic pressures. In the 1981 to 1991 period, eight percent (or 471) of the nation's community hospitals closed. The total number of beds has declined 11.8 percent and the occupancy rates have fallen 11.7 percent.[2] A significant portion of this stress stems from poverty. The percentage of poor, and those with no or inadequate medical insurance, has greatly burdened the medical system and hospitals in particular. Hospital care is the single largest category of the nation's $750 billion health expenditures, representing about 38 percent of the total. In addition, the population is aging, which results in greater illness and much greater demand for hospital

services. Some estimates indicate that 25 percent of our medical
expenditures are devoted to the last six months of life.[3] Compared to
10 years ago, hospitals are more likely to be filled with sicker and older
patients.

In response to these factors, hospitals have greatly increased their
orientation to management as business. They advertise for market
share of the insured or affluent population, engage in elaborate market
research and strategic planning, and seek allegiances with physicians
who can refer and admit insured patients. Integrated hospital computer systems give administrators crucial information on costs and on
markets. The systems allow analysis of admissions data for each
physician, geographic distribution of patients and probable patients,
and of costs and reimbursements on illness-by-illness, department-by-
department, and even doctor-by-doctor bases. In short, the computer
systems allow the temples of care and technology to understand their
operations and to market with the same fiscal tools and techniques used
by shopping malls and department stores.

Accountability The most recent decade has also seen a significant increase in demand for hospitals' technical accountability through utilization reviews, mortality reports, infection analyses, tighter audits, and
prospective fee schedules derived from a resource-based relative value
scale (RBRVS) which seeks to gauge the value of the resources required
to deliver specific services. Moreover, fear of malpractice suits is
pandemic. Hospitals regard accurate patient records as central to
oversight, documentation and legal protection. Integrated hospital
computer systems directly serve these needs.

A study of several hospital information systems found that with
computerization:[4]
- Medication errors were reduced by 34 percent.
- Patient calls were reduced by 26 percent and repeat calls by 50
  percent.
- Discharge teaching documentation was improved by 14 percent.
- Intravenous (IV) site assessment was improved by 4 percent.

More generally, the study found that computerization:
- decreased errors of omission,
- provided greater timeliness of tests and procedures, and
- improved charting.

In addition, the ability to immediately transform patient information into databases and statistics makes these systems particularly
attractive.

Nursing Shortage Last in the litany of hospitals' recent troubles is the
shortage of allied medical personnel, most especially nurses. The
problem is caused by an increase in demand, not a shortage of supply.
More nurses are entering the field, but even more are needed. Dramatic
increases in nursing salaries have gone a long way to alleviating the

shortage but the pay increases have greatly added to the cost of medical care.

Demand for nurses continues to increase and much of the new medical technologies are among the causes. Many of the new machines used in hospitals require nurses. Thus, rather than reduce the need for nurses, the new technology increases it. Hospital patient information systems, however, are a sharp contrast to the effect of most medical technology on demand for nurses. Rather than increase demand for nurses and other hospital personnel, they are designed to reduce labor input. Research by Jean Tribulski found that the systems allowed nurses to devote an average of about one-half hour per shift more to addressing patient needs and one-half hour per shift less to paperwork. Perhaps equally important, Mary Koska reports that hospital information systems improved job satisfaction among nurses.[5] Hospitals, thus, have sought computer systems to reduce nursing costs and to end their constant search for new nurses.

In sum, the past decade has been a great challenge to hospitals. Some of the difficulties reflect the successes of medical science and art. Many of the drugs and techniques that prolong life also bring lingering costs and people in need of long-term care. Many of the forces on the medical system have been external, such a poverty, insurance regulations, and government oversight. Hospitals turn to integrated computer information systems as one way of addressing the needs brought on by these forces. As we shall see, however, the computer systems also change as well as serve the organizations that install them.

Background of St. George's Hospital

During the 1970s St. George's Hospital experienced serious operational and financial problems. Although it was a prominent clinical facility with over 300 beds, it was in danger of being closed because it was the stepchild, or duplicate facility, of a larger medical school hospital. Instead of closing it, the medical school divested itself of St. George's, and a "new" St. George's was recreated as an independent institution. The new management employed a variety of techniques to reverse St. George's fortunes, so successfully that it was named by a major business publication as one of the 24 best community hospitals in the U.S. Among the managerial decisions that produced such financial and organizational success were an aggressive building program, an entrepreneurial strategy, and the recruitment of a larger, innovative medical staff. The corporate culture of St. George's administration and medical staff can still be characterized as entrepreneurial.

St. George's decision to completely automate medical records and other data is consistent with its ambitious plans and corporate culture.

The MAGIC System Implementation

To select a software development contractor to assist with the automation, St. George's assembled a task force from representatives of the medical and nursing staffs, the administration and the information systems department. The task force examined the several hospital software systems available or in advanced design stages. Consensus on selection criteria was quickly achieved; everyone wanted the state-of-the-art technology. The criteria were: electronic chart capability, bedside (or "point-of-care") data entry/retrieval, and flexibility of design and use.

St. George's signed a multimillion dollar contract with MAGIC Hospital Information Systems (a pseudonym), the vendor with the most highly developed system and with the most exultant promises. The MAGIC System is an integrated patient care system that supports almost all aspects of documentation by nurses, physicians, and ancillary department personnel. To support this on-line record keeping and automatic information transfer, St. George's installed some 500 terminals throughout the hospital, including terminals in every patient room, in all ancillary departments and other supporting areas, in physicians' offices and in clinics. Essentially, the hospital agreed to place a terminal wherever it would facilitate the work of clinical staff.

St. George's is installing a system that has been developed and tested, though never fully implemented. This case study is of late software life cycle design.

Keeping Patient Records

Most of the documentation in a medical record, either paper or electronic, falls into one of three categories: orders, results, and notes.

Orders In the conventional paper system, orders (such as directives on medication or on medical treatment) are written into the chart (really a looseleaf book) by physicians or by other health care providers. While physicians are the only ones who can order medication or other pivotal medical interventions, many clinicians, such as nurses and physical therapists, also enter orders into the chart. Moreover, students in several fields and at various levels of training also enter orders. On occasion, doctors will call in oral orders which they must countersign during their next visit to the patients' rooms.

With the MAGIC System at St. George's, orders are almost always entered (typed) directly by the clinician generating them. The order entry portion of the MAGIC System is designed to be very easy to use. Once the clinician finishes typing the order, the transaction is complete. If appropriate, a copy of the new order is also transmitted directly to the department or individual who must act on it (e.g., the pharmacy to prepare medication, the dietary department to alter the meals).

Results Results are usually defined as information that documents tests or procedures. Results range from temperature readings to extensive radiology reports. In the conventional paper system, nurses or other medical personnel wrote results directly into the chart. Laboratory reports were inserted into the chart when they arrived at the nurses' station after what occasionally appeared to be a very long and very circuitous journey.

With St. George's MAGIC System, observations and measurements derived at a patient's bedside can be immediately entered into the record, e.g., the nurse can take a temperature reading and type the number into the electronic chart. Laboratory results are entered directly from the lab where they are generated. There is no waiting and all authorized participants can immediately view the results.

To provide the most meaningful presentation of the information to the user, results are presented in many formats: numeric and textual, simple and complex. Graphic representations of numeric results, such as vital signs, are automated. The computer allows statistical manipulation and reconfiguration of numeric results; graphs and trend lines are constructed immediately on request.

Very complex graphical records, such as EKG strips (electrocardiogram graphs), however, are difficult to store on an automated record and very expensive to display as they require high resolution monitors. As a result, the MAGIC System has not yet incorporated such complex graphics. Such records are still maintained in a conventional paper chart. Also, regulatory constraints require that other forms of documentation remain in paper form. For example, patient consent forms (with signatures) must still be maintained in paper form even though they could be recorded electronically.

Notes Traditionally, with the paper system, notes and other textual material were written into the chart. Extensive comments by physicians were often dictated and later inserted. The notes functions of St. George's MAGIC System are not yet complete, but some processes are emerging in response to need and experience. It is already clear that the degree of automation of textual commentary will vary in relation to the complexity and predictability of the material.

Three types of notes software are being implemented. Each reflects differing demands and types of care:

- Menu-type choices are used to offer statements that can be expressed in a phrase or two. That is, rather than taking the time to write a note, the clinician selects a "prewritten" note from a list of options. A physician, for example, might select "S.O.B." from an on-screen menu and the notation "patient exhibits shortness of breath" would appear in the chart.
- Somewhat longer or less standard comments are just typed at the terminal by the clinician. Frequently the clinician will combine the new material with the prewritten menu choices described above. For example, a notation might read "In the early mornings `patient exhibits shortness of breath'."
- Very complex textual comments, such as discharge summaries, still rely on dictation and transcription. The transcribed notes are incorporated into the electronic record and, thus, are immediately accessible to all appropriate health care providers.[6]

Looking at the Information: The Database Management System

As indicated above, data in St. George's MAGIC System can be viewed in many ways. Data elements can be grouped for display in almost any format and combination. These features provide a great deal of flexibility in chart review; those authorized to look at the chart can view it in whatever format they find most useful. In other words, the MAGIC System incorporates a database management system. Physicians, nurses, and social workers, for example, can each have a different way of viewing the same data and extracting just those data elements that they need. In addition to aiding clinicians, this function also allows support departments, such as medical records and quality assurance, to extract data in whatever format they require.

Security and Initial Computer Screens

Basic computer system security is achieved with magnetic cards (personnel badges with a magnetic strip) and with password security codes. Every terminal has a magnetic card reader attached to it. To use the system, an employee must insert his or her badge and type in his or her password security code.

The MAGIC System computer contains a file listing every employee and his or her type of access. The initial menu screen that each employee sees upon entering the MAGIC System, thus, is specific to that employee's type of access.

Stakeholders in Computer System Design:
Hospital Functions and Access to Information

Integration of Information and Tasks

Installation of the computer system is changing the way many hospital personnel perform their work. For some employees the new system often permits a broader knowledge of their activities in relation to a patient's total care. In this important sense, the MAGIC system promotes and enables better medicine.

Integration of information is allowing many professional and paraprofessional workers to obtain more data on their tasks than was possible with the paper-based system. Lab or radiological technicians, for example, may view patient data that would have been unavailable to them when all patient information was maintained in the chart near the patient's room. Such information enables the technicians to better perform their work and/or to better understand the context of their tasks.

Similarly doctors and other medical practitioners need not wait for lab or other reports to be received by the nurses and placed in the chart. The information can be viewed from any location. Thus, their work is facilitated and enhanced by the computer system.

On the other hand, designers of the system have intentionally limited what many personnel see when they turn on their computers. That is, as noted above, the initial menu screens reflect only the authorized level of access and functional activities of each employee. In this sense, the design of the computer system reflects and extends the existing hierarchy and division of labor within the hospital. When asked about the limitations, the system's designers articulated many of the tradeoffs inherent in their decisions. They noted the several advantages and some of the disadvantages to having the initial menu reflect the pre-set limits of the user.

The advantages are:

- A simplified screen and menu increases efficiency and may reduce user confusion.
- There may be literally hundreds of users on the system at any time. Anything that reduces the amount of information presented improves computer response time.
- Clerks and other users might be frustrated by being confronted with a computer screen (menu) filled with choices and actions that they are not permitted to select.
- Staff viewing a range of forbidden choices might beseige the Information Services Department with requests for greater access

to the system. The programmers and systems analysts do not want to be in the role of approving or disapproving access requests. Access-related policies were/are determined by inter-departmental committees.

On the other hand, several disadvantages to restricting initial menus were not disputed by the Information Services Department. They are:

- By limiting the user's view of the system's possible functions, the hospital is limiting that worker's ability to find new uses for the computer system or to improve his or her understanding of the system.
- The hospital is, thus, foreclosing on productivity enhancements that might be generated by user's experimentation with the MAGIC System.
- The possible negative motivational consequences of restricting job and career development via restrictions on enhanced learning and experimentation are suffered by both the hospital and the employees.[7]

Thus, as in all systems, tradeoffs are made that involve security, task-related knowledge, productivity, confidentiality and open access.

Limiting Technology's Capabilities for Good Practice

Lower level employees are not the only ones who must endure pur-poseful limitations to MAGIC System functions. While integration of information and tasks is a key goal of the system's designers, restric-tions are often placed on the technology to ensure conformity with medical norms or with values associated with "good practice." In a key debate, one group of physicians *restricted their own use* of the computer system to ensure that they visit patients on a daily basis. The doctors were concerned that some physicians would employ the technology to neglect their actual patients and, instead, focus on their patients' laboratory and other data. That is, modern medical practice, with its myriad, high tech laboratory tests and diagnostic tools, is sometimes criticized for what is called, "treating the chart and not the patient." This phrase refers to physicians who concentrate on laboratory and other data and fail to observe or interact with the patient. Some doc-tors fear that the MAGIC System facilitates such practices. Indeed, at the extreme, physicians could conceivably avoid even visiting the patient rooms.

To address this concern, the doctors at the hospital ordered a redesign of the remote order entry procedure to restrict the practice of "treating the chart and not the patient." This redesigned procedure requires that any medical order entered into the computer system from a terminal other than the one at the patient's bedside must be countersigned (reapproved) within 24 hours at the terminal in the patient's room. Thus a remote order will be treated as the equivalent of an oral order under the old, paper record system, and must be counter-signed by the physician in the vicinity of the patient.

Placement of the Computer Terminals in the Patient's Rooms: Differing Priorities

Another example of stakeholders' values influencing what are seem-ingly technological or mechanical decisions is revealed in the place-ment of the computer terminals within the patients' rooms. After considerable debate, the bedside computer terminals, in fact, were not placed by the bedside but by the nursing server/sink cabinet at the entrance of each patient room. In each room, the computer terminal, thus, is several feet from the bed. The process of determining the computer terminal's placement is instructive.

A short medical diversion about terminals   Much of the interaction between a clinician and patient benefits from face-to-face observation. Doctors, for example, are trained to observe the way patients use their hands in pointing to sources of pain. A patient's flat palm moving generally over the belly may indicate a different sort of problem than a patient's finger pointing to a specific spot in the area. Similarly, when asking about personal activities or medical histories, a doctor or nurse would want to see the patient's facial expressions and other gestures. In terms of efficiency, also, one would expect that nurses taking blood pressure or temperature measurements would want the computer as close as possible to the bedside to allow easy typing (data entry) of the information. And, nurses are unquestionably the most frequent users of the bedside computer terminals.

Why, then, did the nurses decide to have the terminals placed away from the patients' beds? The answer, we hypothesize, is found in the medical ethos that full-fledged medical professionals do not show lack of expertise to patients. If the terminals were placed directly at the patient's bedside, the nurses would be obliged to display their unfamil-iarity with the computer system, at least while they were learning to use it. Thus, they requested that the terminals be placed away from the patient's immediate observation.

Note that the explanation of "medical professional ethos" must remain a hypothesis. The reasons for selecting the nurse server/sink cabinet area were never articulated as such. In fact, the reasons for refusing bedside placement were several and as each objection was shown to be of questionable merit, a new one was posited. The nurses' first objection was that the computer terminals would occupy too much space, preventing emergency equipment from approaching the patient.

This was dismissed with a tape measure and the offer to purchase a retractable stand (the type on which hospital TVs are placed). The second objection was that the retractable stands could not hold the weight of the terminals. This was dismissed with a scale; the computer terminals weigh less than the TVs. The third objection was that the retractable stands would be too expensive. This objection was dismissed by comparing the cost of the multimillion dollar system with the trivial cost of the retractable stands. The nurses' fourth objection was that typing is noisy. This was dismissed with surprise for hospitals are seldom quiet. Eventually, the nurses simply stated that the computers be placed by the nurse server/sink cabinet. That's were they are.

What's In A Day?: Nurses and the Pharmacy

Nurses are currently in conflict with the hospital pharmacy over the definition of "what's in a day," or, more specifically, "when to you start counting a day's worth of pills that are ordered in the middle of the day?" The conflict arises in large part from the increased integration of information generated by the MAGIC System and MAGIC System designers are being asked to help solve the problem.

Under the old system, a physician would inform the nurse that a patient was to be given a medication, for example, four times a day. The doctor would record that information in the chart, but it was the nurse who would request the medication from the pharmacy. Now, however, the pharmacy receives the request for medication directly as the doctor enters that request in the electronic patient chart. The nurse does not place the order, but only administers the medication when the pharmacy sends it up to that patient's floor.

The dispute arises because the pharmacy has a different definition of how to handle requests that are issued in the middle of the day (and very few medication orders are issued exactly at midnight). The pharmacy figures that if there are only four pills needed per day, it should send up a reduced number of pills for the first day. Thus, if the medication order was placed at 11 A.M. the pharmacy sends only two or three pills for the first day. The nurses respond that they well understand the issues and that they will do their best to space the administration of the medication. That is, the nurses say that "four pills per day is four pills per day" and that they will continue to exercise professional judgement as to distribution. The pharmacy, in contrast, points to the time and date stamp that the computer attaches to every physician order and the pharmacists claim that they are responsibly calculating the appropriate medication for the first day. The pharmacists add that the old non-computer system, wherein the nurse mediated the information, was merely inefficient and wasteful.

One other point must be included here. Nurses have often mediated information between doctors and others. And, the loss of that mediating role to the computer system has many consequences. For example, in addition to this illustration involving an uneven medication schedule on a first day of new medication, experienced nurses often question a doctor's order if they think it is ill-considered. Often the questioning is polite but firm. A nurse will ask a doctor, for example, "did you know that this patient was also taking medication `X'?" Or, "did you remember that the patient is scheduled for a `Y' procedure tomorrow?" On rare occasions, when a doctor is half-asleep or very unfamiliar with the issues of the case, an experienced nurse will refuse to carry out an order. Some observers, therefore, are concerned that the unmediated but direct and efficient transfer of information is obtained at the cost of skilled and experienced safeguards, the nurses' intervention.

Not surprisingly, there are other tradeoffs here. That is, computers do not have bad handwriting. The new system, which requires the doctor to type the medication, dosage, and schedule, is not subject to illegible handwriting. It has been estimated that up to 20 percent of prescriptions are misfilled due to doctors' illegible handwriting.

Physicians and Software Design Decisions

Dealing with Attending Physicians

St. George's Hospital, like most hospitals, has a symbiotic relationship with its attending physicians. Attending physicians are powerful organizational stakeholders over whom hospitals have only limited authority. They are the fully-credentialed practitioners who have been approved by the hospital to admit and treat patients, in contrast to residents, who are medical school graduates receiving additional training. The financial viability of the hospital depends heavily on its patient base and thus on its attending physicians' good will. The hospital must provide services to these physicians. And, now more than ever before, these services include access to sophisticated computer resources.

St. George's administration is particularly eager to maintain good relations with its attending physicians because it has an open practice plan. An open practice plan is one that allows physicians to admit patients into other hospitals. In this sense, St. George's does not have monopsony power, and must provide ongoing satisfaction to the attendings.

Doctors Dealing with Doctors

As illustrated in the short scenarios that introduced this case, different types of medical specialties have very different needs for access to the patients' charts. In the first scenario, a pathologist views a patient's previous test results. Few attending physicians would object to that sort of look at his or her patient's chart, but there are less clear-cut cases. Would the attending physician have been so happy if the pathologist reviewed the record and suggested a different course of treatment? What if it were not the pathologist but a younger doctor who just wanted to take a look at how others were dealing with their work? There are a variety of ethical, professional, and legal issues here. Not surprisingly, doctors are seeking computer system design solutions for such situations.

Every solution involves tradeoffs. If access is restricted to only the attending physician and some specified nurses, the loss of flexibility would be catastrophic. In an emergency the staff would have to act without the patient's basic data. If the nurse rotation were changed and that information were not reprogrammed, the patient would remain without care. Last, the integration of information that is made possible with the MAGIC System would be largely defeated.

One limited solution, now in use, presents few difficulties. It requires a tracking log by the computer and monitoring by the attending physician. Thus, each time an attending physician views one of his or her patient's chart, the computer provides a list of all "access events" to that chart. With this method, the attending physician performs a post hoc review function. Attending physicians, however, are not cops and seldom wish to use their time calling around the hospital to find out why an unauthorized individual viewed their charts. More importantly, if confidentiality of records was violated, the post hoc knowledge of that action is of only limited solace.

A second option, also in use, is a warning system. If a physician seeks to view the chart of patient to which he or she has not been given "programmed" authority, the computer flashes the message: "ACCESS TO THIS RECORD IS UNAUTHORIZED, A RECORD IS BEING MADE OF THIS ACCESS AND ALL ACTIONS."

A third option, also in use, involves restricting access to specific groups of professionals. Doctors and nurses, for example, are usually allowed to see all parts of the patients' charts (although a record is made of the access events). On the other hand, other groups, such as the dietary department or the physical therapists, may not access all patients' charts. Moreover, only sections of charts to which they have access will be displayed on the computer system.

Doctors and Residents

In addition to their roles as independent practitioners with control over much of the hospital's client base, attending physicians are responsible for training the residents or house staff, physicians who are in the advanced stages of specialized medical education. At St. George's Hospital, as in other teaching hospitals, there is opportunity for conflict between these two strata of physicians. The new computer system is sometimes casting the conflict into sharper relief.

The conflict springs from issues of control over the care of patients and the documentation of that care. On the one hand, house staff are supposed to be guided by the attending physicians, dutifully executing the established doctors' orders. On the other hand, house staff are also the physicians in charge of the hour-to-hour care of patients, including both routine and emergency care. Conflict often arises with regard to documentation and entry of orders. The house staff, beyond executing the attending physicians' general directives, are eager to act on their own insights and on the most recent test results. They are, similarly, eager to observe the effects of their own orders on a patient's condition. Thus, the electronic record, including both result reporting and order entry features, becomes an arena for controversy.[8]

Physician's "Agents," Group Practice, and the Electronic Signature

Attending physicians may wish to delegate access rights to various agents, i.e., to residents, medical students, and to their office personnel. Some of these physicians argue that their agents should have the same security clearance as the attending physician. On occasion, attendings want the agents to have identical identification badges and security codes.

Most probably, doctors who request such privileges are reflecting experiences with procedures under the previous paper-based system of record keeping. By allowing a few trusted workers to sign for them, these doctors avoided paperwork. Undoubtedly, also, they felt that they could oversee the actions of their underlings. As one attending physician insisted at a computer system design committee meeting, "I want my secretary to be able to [electronically] `sign' my charts just as she has always done. If she messes up, I'll fire her." Others in the committee pointed out that the secretary could be granted the same level of permission as the attending physician, but that she would be given a different identification badge and password. Thus, in this scenario, she would have the access level he determined but her actions would be accountable to only her use of the system.

A very similar situation arose in relation to group practice arrangements and the electronic signature. Doctors often form group practice arrangements, treating each others' patients. In such arrangements, for example, all of the cardiologists in a group practice may need to be able to see the records of all of the patients in that practice and would demand reciprocal access rights to all patients within that group practice.

Some group practice physicians, again, perhaps reflecting the earlier paper-based methods, wanted a single identification badge for all members of their group. Providing a set of identical badges for all members of the group would defeat the security system. However, the solution was easily handled by the system designers: the computer was programmed to allow all members of a particular group practice to receive access to the charts of patients being treated by any member of that group.

Access to Data: Doctors and Nurses

It can be argued that because of their generalized knowledge and their value in emergencies, doctors should be granted access to all patients' data. The argument for nurses' total access to data, however, is less compelling. Nevertheless, because of the nurses' power within the hospital, the administration and the computer system designers are reluctant to make the argument for restricting nurses' generalized access. Eventually there may be a notable violation of confidentiality that would have been avoided if nurses' general access to the system were restricted. If such an event occurs, the hospital will again confront the question.

New Systems, New Problems

Issues involving confidentiality of patient records existed with the old paper system. St. George's staff is discovering that the MAGIC System forces them to change many policies and procedures, both formal and informal. Specifically, formal procedures ensuring confidentiality of patient information need to be modified in light of the greater availability of electronic records.

While all computer systems require security arrangements, St. George's programmers and systems analysts find that many of the computer access safeguards used in business settings are inappropriate for hospitals. For example, one computer access issue routinely confronted by hospitals but unlikely in other settings is the need for *immediate* access to *all* parts of a chart at unpredictable times (for example, the need to review recent diagnostic and treatment data on a patient in medical distress and, perhaps, the need to order appropriate tests, medications, and procedures). Because immediate access to such functions is crucial and because care must be provided on a 24 hour basis, those functions must be accessible and manipulable by a wide range of unspecified personnel.

In addressing these issues, the system designers find that they cannot rely on usual business security protocols for access to private data. In hospitals, the usual situation is reversed; the data's "owner," the patient, almost never inspects the data and does not have access to the computer system in which it is stored. Thus, use of a secret code or password known only to the data's owner is meaningless. In fact, almost everyone else in the hospital must have access to the patient's data, but access limited only to what is needed to fulfill preprogrammed functions (e.g., the dietary department needs to know what bed the patient is in and what type of food he or she requires, but has no need to know of the patient's personal history). Moreover, it is the general skills of doctors and nurses and the unforeseeable nature of patient care that increases the difficulty of setting limits on their computer system access.

Heightening the dilemma of access to, versus protection of, extremely private information is the extraordinary cost of *not* allowing access to such information immediately on demand. A patient undergoing cardiac arrest must have his or her records accessible to appropriate hospital personnel. If the computer system only allows the patient's medical record to be seen by a specific list of medical practitioners and they are not immediately available, the patient may be given inadequate or inappropriate emergency care. Thus, unlike financial transactions, the risks entailed in *not* providing immediate access to data are greater than those of allowing inadvertent access.

Making Decisions

Doctors are used to making difficult decisions. St. George's doctors and staff are now grappling with the policy and design issues involving access to the computer system. It has become clear that no simple answer can be found. The original assumption of the software designers, "whoever has the `need' shall be granted access," is proving insufficient amid the large volume and variety of claims of "need." Also, not surprisingly, some of the more powerful stakeholders in the organization perceive and advocate reasons for allocating access that are not universally accepted.

Conflict Among Stakeholders: Endemic But Necessary

St. George's has created several computer policy committees and disciplinary computer system design groups. These groups seek to establish access rules and design changes on the basis of what makes sense for them. Conflict is thus endemic to the process; the concept of "need to know" is defined differently by each profession or department. The process of balancing the needs of the several participants becomes a political process.

Doctors and nurses often have differing perceptions of critical priorities. The legal, accounting, medical records, and information services departments also see the hospital and its information system in differing ways. The hospital's design committees are now focusing on the tradeoffs implicit and explicit in the design decisions. For example, doctors and others in the computer design committees are now directly asking about the tradeoffs between patient data confidentiality and hospital efficiency and about tradeoffs between patient data confidentiality and physician practice efficiencies. The technical computer design questions are assumed to be trivial or surmountable.

Last, it is important to note that many of these questions existed before the computer system. What is new is often the reality that the new computer system raises value issues that were implicit but not previously addressed. That is, because of the systematic and explicit nature of computer system design, the implementation of the computer system often highlights tradeoffs that were hidden, ignored, or avoided with previous methods of operation. The new system, for example, allows many hospital staff to view and modify records. It can be argued, however, that with electronic security precautions the new system actually offers more safeguards than under the previous system. That is, while concern about confidentiality of records existed before the new computer system, installation of the new system forces staff to confront issues that have always been important but were viewed as intractable or were not viewed at all.

Endnotes

1. See Donette Herring (1989) "Bedside Terminal Systems," in *Current Issues in MIS*, Baltimore, MD: KPMG Peat Marwick. In 1988, approximately 135 U.S. hospitals had point-of-care systems and that figure had tripled by 1990. See C.L. Packer (1988, October 20), "Information Management: Nursing input critical to bedside systems" *Hospitals*, p. 90.

2. *Hospital Trends*, American Hospital Association (1992) and Dr. Joel L. Telles, Delaware Valley Hospital Council, personal communication, January 26, 1993.

3. See J. Lubitz and R. Prihoda (1984) "The Use and Cost of Medical Services in the Last Two Years of Life" *Health Care Financing Review*, v.5, pp. 117-131; and J. Newhouse (1993) "An Iconoclastic View of Health Cost Containment" *Health Affairs Supplement*, v.12 pp. 152-171.

4. Herring, 1989, op. cit.

5. Jean Tribulski (1989, December) "Why Aren't More Nurses Using This Valuable Tool?" *RN* pp. 54-58; Mary T. Koska (1989, February 5) "Inside Track: Underautomated medical records clog system" *Hospitals* pp. 36ff.

6. Also, in addition to the free form notes discussed above, the electronic patient chart allows several different formats for task-specific notes. These include: Operative Notes, Progress Notes, and Nursing Care Plans. Each has its own format and system of menu choices.

7. The hospital has established training seminars for clerks and other employees who wish to improve their knowledge of the computer system. It is hoped that the seminars will lead to advancement within the hospital.

8. We note that most hospitals are not *teaching* hospitals and, thus, do not have the same sort of potential for conflict between attendings and residents. Also, there are several different orientations toward the role of attending physician. Some hold that an attending should never place an order. Rather, attending should just give very general guidance as to diagnoses and treatment. Others, however, see attending as more involved in the direct care of the patient.

References

Aitken, Hugh G. J. 1960. *Taylorism at Watertown Arsenal; Scientific Management in Action, 1908-1915*. Cambridge, MA: Harvard University Press.

Attewell, Paul and James Rule. 1984. "Computing and Organizations: What We Know and What We Don't Know." *Communications of the ACM* 27:1184-1192.

Aydin, Carolyn E. 1989. "Occupational Adaptations to Computerized Medical Information Systems." *Journal of Health and Social Behavior* 30:1963-1979.

Badham, Richard and Bernard Schallock. 1991. "Human Factors in CIM Development: A Human Centred View from Europe." *International Journal of Human Factors in Manufacturing*, April, 121-141.

Bansler, Jörgen. 1989. "Systems Development Research in Scandinavia: Three Theoretical Schools." *Scandinavian Journal of Information Systems* 1(August).

Bariff, Martin and Jay Galbraith. 1978. "Intraorganizational Power Considerations for Designing Information Systems." *Accounting Organizations and Society* 3:15-27.

Barley, Stephen R. 1986. "Technology as an Occasion for Structuring: Evidence from Observations of CT Scanners and the Social Order of Radiology Departments." *Administrative Science Quarterly* 31:78-108.

Becker, A., A. Windeler, and Günter Ortmann. 1989. "Computerization and Power: A Micropolitical View." Paper presented at the 9th EGOS-Colloquium. Berlin, 11-14 July.

Bell, Daniel. 1956. *Work and Its Discontents*. Boston: Beacon Press.

_____. 1960. *The End of Ideology: On the Exhaustion of Political Ideas in the Fifties*. Glencoe, IL: Free Press.

Beniger, James R. 1986. *The Control Revolution: Technological and Economic Origins of the Information Society.* Cambridge, MA: Harvard University Press.

Bennett, Robert A. 1988. "Nation's Biggest Banks Had Worst Year in 1987 Since the Depression." *The New York Times.* 16 February, D3.

Berg, Eric N. 1987. "Banks Study Strategies to Replenish Reserves." *The New York Times,* 13 August, D1.

Bijker, Wiebe E., Thomas P. Hughes, and Trevor J. Pinch. 1987. *The Social Construction of Technological Systems: New Directions in the Sociology and History of Technology.* Cambridge, MA: MIT Press.

Bittner, Egon. 1983. "Technique and the Conduct of Life." *Social Problems* 30(3, February):249-261.

Bjørn-Andersen, Niels and Bo Hedberg. 1977. "Designing Information Systems in an Organizational Perspective." *Prescriptive Models of Organizations: Studies in the Management Sciences* 5, edited by P. C. Nystrom and W. H. Starbuck. New York: North-Holland Publishing Company.

Bjørn-Andersen, Niels and Paul Pedersen. 1980. "Computer Facilitated Changes in the Management Power Structure." *Accounting, Organizations, and Society* 5:203-217.

Blackler, Frank and Colin Brown. 1986. "Alternative Models to Guide the Design and Introduction of the New Information Technologies Into Work Organizations." *Journal of Occupational Psychology,* January, 187-313.

Boehm, Barry W. 1981. *Software Engineering Economics.* Englewood Cliffs, NJ: Prentice-Hall.

Boguslaw, Robert. 1965. *The New Utopians, a Study of System Design and Social Change.* Englewood Cliffs, NJ: Prentice-Hall.

Boland, Richard J. Jr. and Wesley F. Day. 1989. "The Experience of System Design: A Hermeneutic of Organizational Action." *Scandinavian Journal of Management* 5(2):87-104.

Bourdieu, Pierre. 1991. *Language and Symbolic Power.* Cambridge, MA: Harvard University Press.

Bowerman, Robert G. and David E. Glover. 1988. *Putting Expert Systems Into Practice.* New York: Van Nostrand Reinhold Company.

Bramel, Dana and Ronald Friend. 1981. "Hawthorne, the Myth of the Docile Worker, and Class Bias in Psychology." *American Psychologist* 36(8, August).

Braverman, Harry. 1974. *Labour and Monopoly Capital*. New York: Monthly Review Press.

Brödner, Peter. 1990. *The Shape of Future Technology-the Anthropocentric Alternative*. London: Springer-Verlag.

_____. 1986. "Skill Based Manufacturing vs. 'unmanned Factory'—which is Superior?" *International Journal of Industrial Ergonomics* 1:145-153.

Brown, Alex and Sons, Inc. 1986. "Computer Services Industry Overview: The Move to Mission Critical Systems." Baltimore. Maryland.

_____. 1986. "Computer Services Industry Overview: The Move to Mission Critical Systems - Up from the Slump." Baltimore, MD.

Brunsson, Nils. 1985. *The Irrational Organization*. New York: John Wiley and Sons.

Burawoy, Michael. 1979. *Manufacturing Consent: Changes in the Labor Process Under Monopoly Capitalism*. Chicago: University of Chicago Press.

Quint, Michael. 1989. "Banking's High-Tech Retail Chase." *The Los Angeles Times* December 31, Section 3, p. 1.

Carey, Alex. 1967. "The Hawthorne Studies: A Radical Criticism." *American Sociological Review* 32:403-416.

Cern, Frank. 1989. "Information Management: Study Finds Bedside Terminals Prove Their Worth." *Hospitals*, 5 February, 72.

Cherns, Albert. 1987. "Principles of Sociotechnical Design Revisited." *Human Relations* 40(3):153-162.

Child, John, Hans-Dieter Ganter and Alfred Kieser. 1987. "Technological Innovation and Organizational Conservatism." *New Technology as Organizational Innovation: The Development and Diffusion of Microelectronics*, edited by Johannes M. Pennings and Arend Buitendam. Cambridge, MA: Ballinger Publishing Company.

Cockerham, Williams C. 1986. *Medical Sociology*. Englewood Cliffs, NJ: Prentice-Hall, Inc.

Coombs, R., D. Knights and H. C. Willmott. 1992. "Culture, Control and Competition; Towards a Conceptual Framework for the Study of Information Technology in Organizations." *Organization Studies* 13(1):51-72.

Corbett, J. Martin, Lauge B. Rasmussen and Felix Rauner. 1991. *Crossing the Border: The Social Engineering Design of Computer Integrated Manufacturing Systems*. London: Springer-Verlag.

Cotton, John L., David A. Vollrath, Mark L. Lengnick-Hall and Kirk L. Froggatt. 1990. "Fact: The Form of Participation Does Matter—a Rebuttal to Leana, Locke, and Schweiger." *Academy of Management Review* 15(1):147-153.

Cotton, John L., David A. Vollrath, Kirk L. Froggatt, Mark L. Lengnick-Hall and Kenneth R. Jennings. 1988. "Employee Participation: Diverse Forms and Different Outcomes." *Academy of Management Review* 13(1):8-22.

Coulter, Jeff. 1979. *The Social Construction of Mind*. London: Macmillan.

_____. 1983. *Rethinking Cognitive Learning*. London: Macmillan.

Cusumano, Michael A. 1991. *Japan's Software Factories: A Challenge to U.S. Management*. New York: Oxford University Press.

Danziger, James N. and Kenneth L. Kraemer. 1986. *People and Computers: The Impacts of Computing on End Users on Organizations*. New York: Columbia University Press.

David, Paul A. 1985. "Clio and the Economics of QWERTY." *The American Economic Review* 75(May):332-337.

Davis, Louis and James Taylor. 1975. "Technology Effects on Job, Work, and Organizational Structure: A Contingency View." *The Quality of Working Life*. New York: Free Press.

Davis, William S. 1983. *Systems Analysis and Design: A Structured Approach*. Reading, MA: Addison-Wesley.

DeLong, David. 1988. "Computers in the Corner Office." *The New York Times*.

DeMarco, Tom. 1978. *Structured Analysis and System Specification*. Englewood Cliffs, NJ: Prentice-Hall.

DeRossi, Claude J. and David L. Hopper. 1984. *Software Interfacing—a User and Supplier Guide*. Englewood Cliffs, NJ: Prentice-Hall.

Dierkes, Meinolf and Ute Hoffman. 1992. *New Technology at the Outset: Social Forces in the Shaping of Technological Innovations*. Frankfurt/New York: Campus Verlag.

Domhoff, G. William. 1990. *The Power Elite and the State How Policy is Made in America*. New York: Aldine De Gruyter.

Dreyfus, Herbert. 1979. *What Computers Can't Do*. New York: Harper and Row.

Dubin, Robert. 1956. "Industrial Workers' Worlds: A Study of the 'Central Life Interests' of Industrial Workers." *Social Problems* 3(January):131-142.

Edwards, Richard C. 1979. *Contested Terrain: The Transformation of the Workplace in the Twentieth Century*. New York: Basic Books.

Ehn, Pelle. 1989. *Work-Oriented Design of Computer Artifacts*. Stockholm: Arbetslivscentrum.

Ellul, Jacques. 1964. *The Technological Society*. New York: Vintage Books.

The Federal Deposit Insurance Corporation. 1991. *1991 Annual Report*. Washington, D.C.

_____. 1990. *1990 Annual Report*. Washington, D.C.

Ferguson, Eugene S. 1979. "The American-ness of American Technology." *Technology and Culture* 20(1):3-24.

Fischer, Frank and Carmen Sirianni. 1984. *Critical Studies in Organization and Bureaucracy*. Philadelphia: Temple University Press.

Flood, Ann B. and W. Richard Scott. 1987. "Professional Power and Professional Effectiveness: The Power of the Surgical Staff and the Quality of Care." *Hospital Structure and Performance*. Baltimore, MD: The Johns Hopkins University Press.

Florman, Samuel C. 1976. *Existential Pleasures of Engineering*. New York: St. Martin's Press.

_____. 1981. *Blaming Technology: The Irrational Search for Scapegoats*. New York: St. Martin's Press.

Fombrun, C. J. 1986. "Structural Dynamics Within and Between Organizations." *Administrative Science Quarterly* 31:403-421.

Form, William. 1983. "Sociological Research and the American Working Class." *The Sociological Quarterly* 24:163-184.

Fox, Alan. 1980. "The Meaning of Work." *The Politics of Work and Occupations*, edited by Geoff Esland and Graeme Salaman. Toronto: University of Toronto Press.

Franke, Richard H. and James D. Kaul. 1978. "The Hawthorne Experiments: First Statistical Interpretation." *American Sociological Review* 43(October).

Franke, Richard H. 1979. "The Hawthorne Experiments: Re-view." *American Sociological Review* 44.

Franz, Charles R. and Daniel Robey. 1984. "An Investigation of User-led System Design: Rational and Political Perspective ." *Communications of the ACM* 27(12, December):1202-1209.

Freeman, Peter. 1985. *Concepts for Understanding Design Methods*. Unpublished paper. University of California, Irvine: Department of Information and Computer Science.

Friedman, Andrew L. 1989. *Computer Systems Development: History, Organization and Implementation*. Toronto: John Wiley & Sons.

Giddens, Anthony. 1984. *The Constitution of Society*. California: University of California Press.

Gillespie, Richard. 1991. *Manufacturing Knowledge: A History of the Hawthorne Experiments*. New York: Cambridge University Press.

Gordon, David, Richard Edwards and Michael Reich. 1982. *Segmented Work, Divided Workers*. New York: Cambridge University Press.

Gorz, Andre. 1980. *Farewell to the Working Class*. Boston: South End Press.

Graham, Margaret and Stephen R. Rosenthal. 1986. "Flexible Manufacturing Systems Require Flexible People." *Human Systems Management*.

Grint, Keith and Steve Woolgar. 1992. "Computers, Guns, and Roses: What's Social About Being Shot?" *Science, Technology, & Human Values* 17(3, Summer):366-380.

Grudin, Jonathan. 1991. "Systematic Sources of Suboptimal Interface Design in Large Product Development Organizations." *Human-Computer Interaction* 6:147-196.

_____. 1991. "Interactive Systems: Bridging the Gaps Between Developers and Users." *Computer*, April, 59-69.

Gruneberg, Michael and Toby Wall. 1984. *Social Psychology and Organizational Behavior*. New York: John Wiley & Sons.

Hall, Richard H. 1987. *Organizations: Structures, Processes, & Outcomes*. Englewood Cliffs, NJ: Prentice-Hall Inc.

Hamilton, Richard F. 1972. *Class and Politics in the United States*. New York: John Wiley.

Hamper, Ben. 1992. *Rivethead: Tales From the Assembly Line*. New York: Warner Books.

Harris, Catherine L. 1985. "Information Power: How Companies Are Using New Technologies to Gain a Competitive Edge." *Business Week*, October, 108-114.

Harrison, Bennett. 1991. "The Failure of Worker Participation." *Technology Review* 94(1, January).

Hart, Ann Weaver. 1990. "Work Redesign: A Review of Literature for Education Reform." *Advances in Research and Theories of School Management and Educational Policy* 1:31-69.

Hauser, John and Don Clausing. 1988. "The House of Quality." *The Harvard Business Review*, May-June, 63-73.

Hedberg, Bo and Enid Mumford. 1975. "The Design of Computer Systems: Man's Vision of Man as an Integral Part of the System Design Process." *Human Choice and Computers*. New York: American Elsevier.

Herring, Donette J. 1989. "Bedside Terminal Systems." *Current Issues in MIS: Health Care Information Systems*. Baltimore, MD: KPMG Peat Marwick.

Hicks, James O. 1976. *Management Information Systems: A User Perspective*. New York: West Publishing Company.

Hirschheim, Rudy A. 1985. "User Experience with Assessment of Participative Systems Design." *MIS Quarterly*, December, 295-303.

Hirschheim, Rudy and Heinz K. Klein. 1989. "Four Paradigms of Information Systems Development." *Communications of the ACM* 32(10, October):1199-1215.

Hirschhorn, Larry. 1984. *Beyond Mechanization: Work and Technology in a Postindustrial Age*. Cambridge, MA: MIT Press.

Hughes, Thomas P. 1987. "The Evolution of Large Technological Systems." In *The Social Construction of Technological Systems*, edited by Wiebe E. Bijker, Thomas P. Hughes and Trevor Pinch. Cambridge, MA: The MIT Press.

"Information Management: More Hospitals Automate Their Pharmacies." 1989. *Hospitals*, 5 October, 77.

Ives, Blake, Margaret H. Olsen and J. Baroudi. 1983. "The Measurement of User Information Satisfaction." *Communications of the ACM* 26:785-793.

Ives, Blake and Gerard Learmonth. 1984. "The Information System as a Competitive Weapon." *Communications of the ACM* 27:1193-1201.

Ives, Blake and Margaret H. Olsen. 1984. "User Involvement and MIS Success: A Review of Research." *Management Science* 5.

Janda, A. 1983. *Human Factors in Computing Systems.* New York: North Holland.

Johnson, Bonnie McDaniel and Ronald E. Rice. 1987. *Managing Organizational Innovation: The Evolution from Word Processing to Office Information Systems.* New York: Columbia University Press.

Jones, Stephen R. G. 1992. "Was There a Hawthorne Effect?" *American Journal of Sociology* 98(3, November):451-468.

Kaiser, K. M. and R. P. Bostrom. 1982. "Personality Characteristics of MIS Project Teams: An Empirical Study and Action-research Design." *MIS Quarterly* 6:43-60.

Keen, Jeffrey S. 1981. *Managing Systems Development.* New York: North Holland.

Kiechel, Walter III. 1992. "When Management Regresses." *Fortune*, 9 March, 157-158.

Kimberly, John R. and Michael J. Evanisko. 1981. "Organizational Innovation: The Influence of Individual, Organizational, and Contextual Factors on Hospital Adoption of Technological and Administrative Innovations." *Academy of Management Journal* 24(4):689-713.

King, William R. and Jamie I. Rodriguez. 1981. "Participative Design of Strategic Decision Support Systems: An Empirical Assessment." *Management Science.*

Kling, Rob. 1980. "Social Analysis of Computing: Theoretical Perspectives in Recent Empirical Research." *Computing Surveys* 12:61-110.

_____. 1984. "Assimilating Social Values in Computer-based Technologies." *Telecommunications Policy.*

_____. 1985. "Computerization as an Ongoing Social and Political Process." *Proceedings of Conference on Development and Use of Computer-based Systems and Tools, Part II.* Aarhus, Denmark.

_____. 1987. "Defining the Boundaries of Computing Across Complex Organizations." *Critical Issues in Information Systems Research*, edited by Richard Boland and Rudy Hirschheim. London: John Wiley.

_____. 1991. "Reply to Woolgar and Grint: A Preview." *Science, Technology, & Human Values* 16(3, Summer):379-381.

_____. 1991. "Behind the Terminal: The Critical Role of Computing Infrastructure in Effective Information Systems Development and Use." In *Systems Analysis and Design*. Edited by William Cotterman and James Senn. London: John Wiley.

_____. 1992. "When Gunfire Shatters Bone: Reducing Sociotechnical Systems to Social Relationships." *Science, Technology, & Human Values* 17(3, Summer):381-385.

_____. 1992. "Audiences, Narratives, and Human Values in Social Studies of Technology." *Science, Technology, & Human Values* 17(3, Summer):349-365.

Kling, Rob and Suzanne Iacono. 1984. "The Control of Information Systems After Implementation." *Communications of the ACM* 27:1218-1226.

_____. 1984. "Computing as an Occasion for Social Control." *Journal of Social Issues* 40:77-96.

Koppel, Ross, Eileen Appelbaum and Peter Albin. 1988. "Implications of Workplace Information Technology: Control, Organization of Work and the Occupational Structure." *Sociology of Work* 4:125-152.

Koska, Mary T. 1989. "Inside Track: Underautomated Medical Records Clog System." *Hospitals*, 5 February, 36ff.

_____. 1990. "Physician Practices Go Under the Microscope." *Hospitals*, 20 February, 32-37.

Kroninger, Stephen. 1992. "Deconstructing the Computer Industry." *Business Week*, November 23, 90-100.

Kumar, Kuldeep and Niels Bjørn-Andersen. 1990. "A Cross-Cultural Comparison of IS Designer Values." *Communications of the ACM* 33(5):528-538.

Leana, Carrie R., Edwin A. Locke and David M. Schweiger. 1990. "Fact and Fiction in Analyzing Research on Participative Decision Making: A Critique of Cotton, Vollrath, Froggatt, Lengnick-Hall, and Jennings." *Academy of Management Review* 15(1):137-146.

Leibenstein, Harvey. 1987. *Inside the Firm: The Inefficiencies of Hierarchy*. Cambridge, MA: Harvard University Press.

Ling, Richard. 1988. "Alternative Valuation of Computer Software: A Case Study Examining the Software Production Process." Unpublished paper. Oslo, Norway: Gruppen for Ressursstudier, Resource Policy Group.

Livesay, Jeff. 1989. "Structuration Theory and the Unacknowledged Conditions of Action." *Theory, Culture & Society* 6:263-92.

Locke, Edwin, David Schweiger and Gary P. Latham. 1979. "Participation in Decision Making: One More Look." *Research in Organizational Behavior*, edited by B. Staw. Greenwich, CT: JAI Press.

Locke, Edwin A. and David M. Schweiger. 1979. *Participation in Decision-Making: One More Look*. Greenwich, CT: JAI Press, Inc.

Locke, Edwin A. 1984. "Job Satisfaction." *Social Psychology and Organizational Behavior*, edited by M. Gruneberg and T. Wall. Chichester: John Wiley & Sons Ltd.

Locke, Edwin A., David M. Schweiger and Gary P. Latham. 1987. "Participation in Decision Making: When Should It Be Used?" *Organizational Behavior and the Practice of Management*. Glenview, IL: Scott, Foresman and Company.

Lowith, Karl. 1964. *From Hegel to Nietzsche: The Revolution in Nineteenth-century Thought*. New York: Holt, Rinehart and Winston.

Lucas, Henry C. Jr. 1985. *The Analysis Design and Implementation of Information Systems*. New York: McGraw Hill.

Lund, Robert T., Albert B. Bishop, Anne E. Newman and Harold Salzman. 1993. *Designed to Work: Production Systems and People*. Englewood Cliffs, NJ: Prentice-Hall.

Magdoff, Harry. 1982. "The Meaning of Work: A Marxist Perspective." *Monthly Review*, October, 1-15.

Magjuka, Richard. 1990. "Participation in Decision Making: An Empirical Analysis." *Advances in Research and Theories of School Management and Educational Policy* 1:237-277.

Mahar, Maggie. 1990. "Shooting the Messenger: The White House Asks Bill Seidman to Please Go Home." *Barron's*, 26 (7 May), 1.

Main, Jermey. 1989. "At Last, Software CEOs Can Use." *Fortune*, March, 77-83.

Majchrzak, Ann and Harold Salzman. 1989. "Introduction to the Special Issue: Social and Organizational Dimensions of Computer-Aided Design." *IEEE Transactions on Engineering Management* 36(3, August):174-179.

March, James G. and Herbert A. Simon. 1958. *Organizations*. Wiley and Sons.

Marcus, Steven. 1966. *The Other Victorians*. New York: Basic Books, Inc.

Marglin, Stephen. 1974. "What Do Bosses Do? The Origins and Function of Hierarchy in Capitalist Production." *Review of Radical Political Economics* 6(Summer):33-60.

Markus, M. Lynne and Jeffery Pfeffer. 1983. "Power and the Design and Implementation of Accounting and Control Systems." *Accounting, Organizations, and Society* 8:205-218.

Markus, M. Lynne. 1984. *Systems in Organizations: Bugs and Features*. Boston: Pitman Publishing Inc.

Marx, Karl. 1977. *Capital*. New York: Random House.

McLaughlin, Mary M. and Martin H. Wolfson. 1988. "The Profitability of Insured Commercial Banks in 1987." *Federal Reserve Bulletin* 74(7):403-413.

Meehan, John. 1992. "America's Bumbling Bankers: Ripe for a New Fiasco." *Business Week*, 2 March, 86-87.

Meiksins, P. F. and J. M. Watson. 1989. "Professional Autonomy and Organization Constraint: The Case of Engineers." *Sociological Quarterly*, December.

Meyer, Marshall W. and Associates. 1978. *Environments and Organizations*. San Francisco: Jossey-Bass Publishers.

Meyer, John W. and Brian Rowan. 1991. "Institutionalized Organizations: Formal Structure as Myth and Ceremony." In *The New Instituionalism in Organizational Analysis*, edited by Walter W. Powell and Paul J. DiMaggio. Chicago: The University of Chicago Press.

Miller, Delbert C. and William H. Form. 1980. *Industrial Sociology: Work in Organizational Life*. New York: Harper & Row Publishers, Inc.

Mirvis, Philip H. and Edward E. III Lawler. 1983. "Systems Are not Solutions: Issues in Creating Information Systems That Account for the Human Organization." *Accounting, Organization, and Society* 8:175-190.

Mumford, Lewis. 1934. *Technics and Civilization*. Harcourt, Brace & World, Inc.

Mumford, Enid. 1981. *Values, Technology and Work*. Boston: Nijhoff Publishers.

_____. 1983a. *Designing Participatively*. England: Manchester Business School.

_____. 1983b. *Designing Human Systems*. England: Manchester Business School.

_____. 1987. "Sociotechnical System Design: Evolving Theory and Practice." *Computers and Democracy—A Scandinavian Challenge*, edited by G. Ehn Bjerknes, P. & Kyng. Aldershot, England: Avebury Press.

Nash, Nathaniel C. 1987. "U.S. Banks' Profit Drop Linked to Brazil Loans." *The New York Times*. 22 May, D5.

_____. 1988. "Banks' Net at Record $5.9 Billion." *The New York Times*. 13 December, D1.

National Center on Education and the Economy. 1990. *America's Choice: High Skills or Low Wages-the Report of the Commission on the Skills of the American Workforce*. Rochester, NY: National Center on Education and the Economy.

Newman, Michael and Faith Noble. 1990. "User Involvement as an Interaction Process: A Case Study." *Information System Research* 1(March):89-113.

Noble, David F. 1977. *America by Design*. New York: Oxford University Press.

_____. 1984. *Forces of Production: A Social History of Industrial Automation*. New York: Oxford University Press.

Offe, Claus. 1985. *Disorganized Capitalism*. Cambridge, MA: MIT Press.

Olerup, Agneta. 1989. "Socio-technical Design of Computer-assisted Work: A Discussion of the ETHICS and Tavistock Approaches." *Scandinavian Journal of Information Systems* 1(August):43-71.

_____. 1993. Personal Communication. University of Lund. March.

Ollman, Bertell. 1976. *Alienation: Marx's Conception of Man in Capitalist Society*. New York: Cambridge University Press.

Orlikowski, Wanda J. 1992. "The Duality of Technology: Rethinking the Concept of Technology in Organizations." *Organization Science* 3(3, August):398-427.

Ortmann, Günter, A. Windeler, A. Becker, H.-J.Schulz. 1990. *Computer und Macht in Organisationen: Mikropolitische Analysen*. Opladen: Westdeutscher Verlag.

Osterman, Paul. 1988. *Employment Futures: Reorganization, Dislocation, and Public Policy*. New York: Oxford University Press.

Packer, C. L. 1988. "Information Management: Nursing Input Critical to Bedside Systems." *Hospitals*, 20 October, 90.

Palmer, Bryan. 1975. "Class, Conception and Conflict: The Thrust for Efficiency, Managerial Views of Labor and the Working Class Rebellion, 1903-22." *Review of Radical Political Economics*.

Pava, Calvin. 1983. *Managing New Office Technology: An Organizational Strategy*. New York: The Free Press.

Perrow, Charles. 1965. "Hospitals: Technology, Structure, and Goals." *Handbook of Organizations*, edited by James G. March. Chicago: Rand McNalley.

_____. 1983. "The Organizational Context of Human Factors Engineering." *Administrative Science Quarterly* 28:521-541

_____. 1984. *Normal Accidents: Living with High-Risk Technologies*. New York: Basic Books, Inc.

_____. 1986. *Complex Organizations: A Critical Essay*. New York: Random House.

Perrucci, Robert and Joel E. Gerstl. 1969. *Profession Without Community: Engineers in American Society*. New York: Random House.

Petroski, Henry. 1982. *To Engineer is Human: The Role of Failure in Successful Design*. New York: St. Martin's Press.

Pfeffer, Jeffrey. 1978. "The Micropolitics of Organizations." *Environments and Organizations*. San Francisco: Jossey-Bass Publishers.

_____. 1981. *Power in Organizations*. Cambridge, MA: Ballinger Publishing Company.

Piaget, Jean. 1967. *The Child's Conception of the World*. Totawa, NJ: Littlefield.

_____. 1970. *Structuralism*. New York: Harper & Row Publishers.

Pine, Art. 1988. "13 More Thrifts Rescued at Cost of $411 Million." *Los Angeles Times*, Part IV. 30 December, 1.

Powell, Walter W. and Paul J. DiMaggio. 1991. *The New Institutionalism in Organizational Analysis*. Chicago: Chicago Press.

Rammert, Werner. 1992. "Research on the Generation and Development of Technology: The State of the Art in Germany." In *New Technology at the Outset*, edited by Meinolf Dierkes and Ute Hoffmann. Frankfurt/New York: Campus Verlag.

Rauner, Felix, Lauge Rasmussen and J. M. Corbett. 1988. "The Social Shaping of Technology and Work: Human Centred CIM Systems." *AI & Society* 2:47-61.

Rauner, Felix and Klaus Ruth. 1990. "Perspectives of Research in `Industrial Culture'." *Ergonomics of Hybrid Automated Systems II*.

Robey, Daniel and Dana Farrow. 1982. "User Involvement in Information System Development: A Conflict Model and Empirical Test." *Management Science* 28(1, January):73-85.

Robey, Daniel and M. Lynne Markus. 1984. "Rituals in Information System Design." *MIS Quarterly*, March, 5-15.

Rockart, John F. and David W. DeLong. 1982. "The CEO Goes On-line." *Harvard Business Review*, January/February, 82-88.

Rockart, John F. and Michael E. Tracy. 1988. *Executive Support Systems: The Emergence of Top Management Computer Use*. Homewood, IL: Dow Jones-Irwin.

Rosenberg, Nathan. 1976. *Perspectives on Technology*. New York: Cambridge University Press.

Rosenthal, Stephen R. and Harold Salzman. 1990. "Hard Choices About Software: The Pitfalls of Procurement." *Sloan Management Review*, Summer.

Rosenthal, Stephen R. 1992. *Effective Product Design and Development*. Homewood, IL: Business One Irwin.

Russell, Raymond. 1988. "Forms and Extent of Employee Participation in the Contemporary United States." *Work and Occupations* 15(4, November):374-395.

Salzman, Harold. 1989. "Computer-aided Design: Limitations in Automating Design and Drafting." *IEEE Transactions on Engineering Management* 36(4).

_____. 1991. "Engineering Perspectives and Technology Design in the United States." *AI & Society*.

_____. 1992. "Skill-based Design: Productivity, Learning, and Organizational Effectiveness." In *Usability: Turning Technologies Into Tools*, edited by Paul S. Adler and Terry A. Winograd. New York: Oxford University Press.

Salzman, Harold and Robert Lund. 1993. "Skill-based Technology Design." unpublished paper.

Sashkin, Marshall. 1984. "Participative Management is an Ethical Imperative." *Organizational Dynamics*, Spring, 5-22.

Schniederman, Ben. 1987. "Designing Computer Systems for People." *Contemporary Psychology* 32:779-780.

Schweiger, David and Carrie Leana. 1986. "Participation in Decision Making." *Generalizing from Laboratory to Field Settings*, edited by Edwin Locke. New York: Lexington Books.

Scott, W. Richard. 1987. *Organizations Rational, Natural, and Open Systems*. Englewood Cliffs, NJ: Prentice-Hall.

_____. 1988. *Technology and Structure: An Organizational Level Perspective*. Paper presented to the Conference on Technology and Organizations, Carnegie-Mellon University.

Segal, Howard P. 1985. *Technological Utopianism in American Culture*. Chicago: The University of Chicago Press.

Sewell, William H. Jr. 1992. "A Theory of Structure: Duality, Agency, and Transformation." *American Journal of Sociology* 98(1, July):1-29.

Skidmore, Dave. 1992. "Bank, S & L Failures Declined in '91, but Analysts Expect a New Upswing." *The Washington Post*. 2 January.

Souder, William E. 1987. "Disharmony Between Research, Development and Marketing." *Industry Marketing Management* 10.

Stinchcombe, Arthur L. 1990. *Information and Organizations*. Berkeley: University of California Press.

Strassman, W. Paul. 1959. "Creative Destruction and Partial Obsolescence in American Economic Development." *The Journal of Economic History* 19(3, September).

Sykes, A. J. M. 1965. "Economic Interest and the Hawthorne Researches." *Human Relations* 18.

Tait, Peter and Iris Vessey. 1988. "The Effect of User Involvement on System Success: A Contingency Approach." *MIS Quarterly*, March, 91-108.

Taylor, Fredrick W.. 1911. *The Principles of Scientific Management*. New York: W. W. Norton.

Texas Center for Production and Quality of Work Life. 1983. *An Assessment of US Work Improvement Case Studies and Lessons: Learnings from Other Organizations Change Efforts*. unpublished paper. University of Texas.

Thomas, Paulette. 1989. "Thrift Bailout, Lacking a Chief and Floundering as Officials Feud, Slows and Grows More Costly." *The Wall Street Journal*, 11 October, A20.

_____. 1989b. "Comments by Bush Suggest Danny Wall Lacks President's Support in S & L Post." *The Wall-Street Journal*. 14 November, A6.

_____. 1990. "Washington's Inept Handling of S & L Bailout Will Mean Even Higher Burden on Taxpayers." *The Wall Street Journal*, 15 February, A16.

Thomas, Robert J. 1993. *What Machines Can't Do: Politics and Technology in the Industrial Enterprise*. Berkeley: University of California Press.

Thuesen, G. J. and W. J. Fabrycky. 1989. *Engineering Economy*. Prentice-Hall.

Tribulski, Jean. 1989. "Why Aren't More Nurses Using This Valuable Tool?" *RN*, December, 54-58.

Trist, Eric L. 1981. "The Evolution of Socio-technical Systems." *Ontario Quality of Working Life Center*.

_____. 1982. "The Sociotechnical Perspective." *Perspectives on Organization Design and Behavior*, edited by A. H. Van de Ven and W. F. Joyce. New York: Wiley.

Trist, Eric and Hugh Murray. 1990. "Historical Overview—the Foundation and Development of the Tavistock Institute." *The Social Engagement of Social Science: A Tavistock Anthology*, edited by Eric Trist and Hugh Murray. Philadelphia: The University of Pennsylvania Press.

Turkle, Sherry. 1984. *The Second Self: Computers and the Human Spirit*. New York: Simon and Schuster.

Turner, Jon A. 1981. "Achieving Consensus on Systems Requirements." *Systems, Objectives, Solutions*.

U.S. Department of Commerce. 1988. *U.S. Industrial Outlook*. Washington D.C.: U.S. Government Printing Office.

_____. 1986. *U.S. Industrial Outlook*. Washington D.C.: U.S. Government Printing Office.

Walton, Richard E. 1985. "From Control to Commitment in the Workplace." *Harvard Business Review*, March-April, 77-84.

Wells, Donald M. 1987. *Empty Promises: Quality of Working Life Program and the Labor Movement*. New York: Monthly Review Press.

Weltz, Friedrich. 1991. "Der Traum Von Der Absoluten Ordnung Und Die Doppelte Wirklichkeit Der Unternehmen" ("The Ideal of Absolute Order and the Dual Reality of the Firm"). Betriebliche Sozialverfassung Und Veraenderungsdruk. Berlin.

Whalley, Peter. 1986. *The Social Production of Technical Work: The Case of British Engineers*. State University of New York Press.

Winner, Langdon. 1977. *Autonomous Technology: Technics-out-of-control as a Theme in Political Thought*. Chicago: The University of Chicago Press.

Winograd, Terry and Fernando Flores. 1986. *Understanding Computers and Cognition: A New Foundation for Design*. Reading, MA: Addison-Wesley Publishing Company, Inc.

Woolgar, Steve. 1991. "The Turn to Technology in Social Studies of Science." *Science, Technology, & Human Values* 16(1, Winter):20-50.

Yang, Catherine and Howard Glechman. 1988. "The S & L Mess—And How to Fix It." *Business Week*, 31 October, 130-140.

Zuboff, Shoshana. 1988. *In the Age of the Smart Machine: The Future of Work and Power*. New York: Basic Books.

Zussman, Robert. 1985. *Mechanics of the Middle Class: Work and Politics Among American Engineers*. Berkeley: University of California Press.

Index

345

DATE DUE